ISBN 978-1-332-17596-3
PIBN 10294060

1 MONTH OF
FREE
READING

at
www.ForgottenBooks.com

By purchasing this book you are eligible for one month membership to ForgottenBooks.com, giving you unlimited access to our entire collection of over 700,000 titles via our web site and mobile apps.

To claim your free month visit:
www.forgottenbooks.com/free294060

THE

PASTORAL CARE.

BY THE LATE
ALEXANDER GERARD, D.D. F.R.S.E.

PROFESSOR OF DIVINITY IN THE UNIVERSITY,
AND KING'S COLLEGE OF 'ABERDEEN;

AND

ONE OF HIS MAJESTY'S CHAPLAINS IN ORDINARY
FOR SCOTLAND.

———————

PUBLISHED BY HIS SON AND SUCCESSOR,

GILBERT GERARD, D.D.

ONE OF HIS MAJESTY'S CHAPLAINS IN ORDINARY
FOR SCOTLAND.

———————

LONDON:

PRINTED FOR T. CADELL JUN. AND W. DAVIES, IN THE
STRAND; AND A. BROWN, AT ABERDEEN.

1799.

ADVERTISEMENT.

THE following Work was part of my late father's Theological Prelections, as Profeſſor of Divinity. I know not whether he ever intended to publiſh it ; but had he lived to prepare it for the preſs, it would have appeared in a much more perfect form than that in which it is now offered to the Public. I found part of it carefully reviſed and corrected, and tranſcribed on a different and more extenſive plan than what is followed in his original notes on the ſubject. This plan I have endeavoured to complete, though conſcious of its being executed in a very inferior manner to what himſelf would have done. It is difficult to enter into another's ideas, ſo as to make them entirely one's own, or to purſue his hints ſo as to preſerve uniformity and conſiſtency. Whatever defects, therefore, there may be in this reſpect,

or

or whatever inaccuracies in point of ftyle, muft be charged folely on the Editor. Such as it is, it is hoped the Work will be ufeful. This was the only view of its Author, who compofed it for the benefit of thofe Candidates for the Miniftry who were under his care; a long fucceffion of whom iffued from his fchool, and can, doubtlefs, bear teftimony to the pleafure and inftruction they derived from this part of his Theological Courfe: and although it is peculiarly adapted to the fituation of Clergymen of the Church of Scotland, yet it may not be unprofitable to thofe alfo of other perfuafions, who will find it throughout breathing a fpirit of rational and elevated piety, and marked with that candour and moderation which diftinguifhed his character.

GIL. GERARD.

King's College,
Aberdeen, Feb. 7, 1799.

CONTENTS.

CHAP. IV.

PART III.

CHAP. I.

CHAP. II.

THE

PART III.

The Requisites for performing the Duties of the Pastoral Office - - - 404

CHAP. I.

CHAP. II.

THE

PASTORAL CARE.

INTRODUCTION.

IN every pursuit, it is of great importance, first of all, to fix a proper end: for the nature of the end·determines the ·means which are suitable, and the course which we must take, in order to attain it; ·and, if we fix a wrong end, it cannot fail to mislead us into an improper track. The end of every part of education, and every kind of study, ought to be, to fit men either for the general duties of life incumbent upon all, or for some of those particular employments which, for the common convenience, are distributed to different men. Whatever contributes to neither of these purposes, is unprofitable or perverted: nothing can be of real value, but so far as it promotes one or the other of them.

Every

Every employment requires fome education or preparation for it: and this muft always be adapted to the nature of that employment. It muft always include two things :—inftructions concerning the principles and functions of the art;—and exercifes fit for begetting a habit of acting according to thefe principles, and executing thefe functions. In a mechanical art, for example, a perfon muft firft learn the nature of the feveral materials and in-ftruments belonging to it, and the manner of ufing them ; and next he muft be accuftomed to ufe them, till he gradually acquire dexterity. Both thefe are neceffary: without knowlege, practice would be undirected, lame, and blunder-ing ; and without exercife, the greateft knowlege could not prevent our being awkward, and at a lofs in attempting to perform.

Different employments require different methods of education. Inftructions and exercifes neceffary in an apprenticefhip for one art, would be ufelefs, or even abfurd, in an apprenticefhip for another. The peculiar education proper for any art, can be afcertained only by attention to the nature of that art. Its nature ought to be conftantly kept in view, that the proper ftndies and exercifes may be felected, and conducted in fuch a manner as to become moft effectually fubfervient to it. This is in fome degree requifite even in the mechanical employments: but it is more indifpenfably neceffary in thofe profeffions which hold of the fciences.

In

In the former, a great deal may be learned merely by habit, and performed mechanically, by thofe who are almoft totally ignorant of the principles from which the practice is derived. The philofo-pher explains thefe principles—the ingenious artift reduces them to practice; but the ordinary me-chanic acquires the practice without underftanding the principles on which he works. The mecha-nical powers, with their feveral combinations, are every day employed by perfons who know nothing of the theory of them. Yet even in thefe arts, knowlege of the principles gives a great advan-tage for practice: it diftinguifhes the inventor, the improver, the workman of ingenuity and tafte, from the mere artificer. But in fcientifical pro-feffions, no part of the practice is wholly mecha-nical; no ftep can be taken but in confequence of knowlege of the principles: and the practice will always be more or lefs proper in proportion to the accuracy of that knowlege. A phyfician, for in-ftance, cannot practife his art without underftand-ing medicine; wherever his knowlege fails, his practice muft be deficient; and without a previous idea of what the bufinefs of a phyfician is, he could not with any degree of fuccefs prepare himfelf for it.

The paftoral office is of this kind. It cannot be properly exercifed by a perfon who knows not the feveral duties belonging to it, who is not acquaint-

ed

ed. with the principles and fentiments requifite in difcharging them, and who has not learned the proper manner of teaching and treating mankind, fo as to accomplifh the end of his office. The nature of the paftoral office is therefore a fubject very neceffary to be examined in the courfe of your theological ftudies. The right difcharge of its functions is the very end to which all your private ftudies, all the inftructions delivered from this place, and all the exercifes prefcribed to you, ought to be fubordinate. So far only as they qualify you for that, they are ufeful, or at leaft peculiar to you as ftudents of theology. A juft conception of the paftoral office will enable you to perceive, what ftudies are neceffary to prepare you for it, and to diftinguifh in what degree they are neceffary, that your attention to them may be in proportion to their utility. It will enable you to difcern, how every part of ftudy is applicable to the execution of that office, and to learn the proper ufe of the feveral parts of fcience, while you are acquiring the knowlege of their principles. In whatever period of your theological ftudies you happen now to be, the paftoral office may very profitably engage your attention. If you are but beginning them, it will fix a proper aim at your firft fetting out. If you are nearly finifhing them, it is high time to think ferioufly of the office which you may be foon called to undertake. At every ftep, a juft idea of it will afford a light by which

you

you may review your paſt, and direct your future ſtudies.

Every perſon who conſiders the preſent ſtate of things, muſt be ſenſible that there is great need to inſiſt on the real nature of the paſtoral office. In all ages the beſt men have complained, that the generality entered on it too forwardly, and with- out ſufficient preparation. At preſent, many ſeem to think ſcarcely any preparation neceſſary. They beſtow very few years upon it : and they muſt be conſcious, how ſmall a part even of theſe they em- ploy for the very purpoſe of qualifying themſelves for it. While a long apprenticeſhip is required for every ordinary trade, while intenſe ſtudy and ap- plication are acknowleged to be neceſſary for every other learned or liberal profeſſion, little ſtudy or application is imagined to be needful for the buſi- neſs of a clergyman. This cannot fail to render many unfit for performing it with ſatisfaction to themſelves, or with honour in the eyes of the world : and it plainly tends to bring the office into diſcredit, and to make men think that any perſon is ſufficiently qualified for being entruſted with it. An effectual check to this evil, by public authority, would be highly deſirable : but, I fear, it can ſcarcely be expected. It is for this reaſon the more neceſſary to endeavour to impreſs you with a ſenſe of the genuine nature of the paſtoral office, for which you are candidates. This will aſſiſt you in your preparation for it : and this will leave it on

every

every one's own confcience to determine, how far he is really fit to enter on it.

This fubject may be reduced to three general heads;—the importance of the paftoral office,—the duties belonging to it,—and the requifites for performing them.

THE

PASTOR AL CARE.

PART I.

The Importance of the Pastoral Office.

THE importance of the pastoral office may be confidered as arifing from two circum- ftances :—its dignity, and its difficulty ; which it will be proper to examine feparately.

CHAP. I.

The Dignity of the Pastoral Office.

IN examining the dignity of the paftoral office, we fhall point out—the real nature of its dig- nity ; and the fentiments fuitable to it, which it requires, both in thofe who hold that office, and in others.

SECT.

The true Nature of the Dignity of the Pastoral Office.

IT is on many accounts neceſſary and proper to aſcertain the true nature and grounds of that dig‑ nity which belongs to the paſtoral office. By ſome, its dignity has been, not deſcribed and delineated, but diſplayed in all the pomp of eloquence, and exaggerated by an accumulation of the boldeſt figures [a]. A florid imagination prompted them to repreſent it in this manner: the taſte and bias of the times bore it, or even invited it. The prin‑ ciples of the preſent age would give no indulgence to declamation of that kind. It is indeed improper in itſelf. Magnificent figures, if they be not ſtrictly juſt, convey no preciſe ideas: they may amaze, but they infuſe no permanent ſentiments: they may produce an unmeaning emotion for a moment, but they form no determinate and durable temper. To raiſe the dignity of the paſtoral office above the naked truth, by vague images and indefinite am‑ plifications, is not uſeleſs only; I am afraid, it is hurtful alſo. Did it really obtain credit, it would lead every modeſt, ſerious, conſcientious perſon to conſider that office as too ſublime for any mortal man, and too pure for any imperfect creature to venture on; as not deſirable, but tremendous; and

[a] Gregor. Nazianz. Apologet. Chryſoſtom. de Sacerdot.

and by all means to be avoided. They who have delighted in giving such representations of it, have likewise thought themselves obliged to affect declining it, to flee into desarts, and to seem to be dragged thence by violence to the acceptance of it. They shewed, however, that their fancy had a greater share in these representations than their judgment, and that they did not fully give credit to them: for without attempting to confute them, they afterwards suffered themselves to be invested with that very office. None who sincerely regarded it in that point of view, could think of undertaking it, except they were so worthless as to have no conscience, no sense of obligation, no concern to fulfil their duty [b]. They who ventured to occupy it, would be elated with pride and arrogance: others would either pay them excessive and perverted veneration, or ridicule the extravagance of their claims. What has real dignity and importance, stands not in need of exaggeration: and it must suffer by it. A simple exposition of its intrinsic moment, is sufficient for procuring it that kind and degree of honour which it merits, and will most effectually procure it.

It has been common to represent the pastoral office as holy, as placing those who hold it in a peculiar relation to God. There is a foundation both

---

[b] Stillingfleet, Ecclesiastical Cases, Part I. charge ii p. 116, &c.

both in fcripture and in reafon, for the reprefentation, provided it be properly underftood.   Under
the Old Teftament, not only Aaron and his fons,
but the priefts alfo, and the Levites, were declared
to be " holy unto their God," and to be " fancti-
" fied," and " confecrated to ftand before the Lord,
" and to minifter to him^c." Solemn rites, very
circumftantially defined, were exprefsly appointed
by God himfelf, for their feparation to their offices.
The gofpel not being, like the law, a difpenfation
of ceremonies, God has not, with equal precifion,
fixed rites for the feparation of perfons to the
Chriftian miniftry : nor do the writers of the New
Teftament apply to this office all the fame terms
which are ufed concerning the ancient priefthood ;
and which had, perhaps, a reference to the manner of feparation for it.   But Chriftian minifters
are fpoken of in terms which plainly imply, that
their office places them in a peculiar relation to God.
It is, I doubt not, partly with a refpect to their
infpiration and their immediate commiffion from
Chrift, that the Apoftles are called " ambaffadors
" for" him^d : but uninfpired teachers are called by
a name nearly equivalent, " angels^e," or meffen-
gers.   The infpired apoftles were in a peculiar
fenfe, " ftewards of the myfteries of God^f," which
were

---

^c Exod. xxviii. 1. 3, 4. 36. 41. Lev. xxi. 6, 7, 8. Num. iii.
12, 13. 41.
^d 2 Cor. v. 20.   ^e Rev. ii. 1.   ^f 1 Cor. iv. 1.

were revealed to them: but every Chriftian paftor is likewife a " fteward of God [g]," in a place of truft and authority in his family, appointed to difpenfe inftruction to others. The teachers of the gofpel are all, in a fenfe in which other Chriftians are not, the fervants and minifters of God; peculiarly appropriated to him, and fet apart for prefenting the devotions of others to him, and publifhing his will to them.

It cannot, however, be denied, that the idea of the fanctity of the paftoral office has been often mifunderftood and abufed. Confufed and improper notions of it have been propagated, and perverted to the bafeft purpofes of fuperftition. That idea has been fo much overftretched and diftorted, as to be made to imply an exemption from the authority and jurifdiction of magiftrates, from fubjection to all human laws, and from the common obligations of men in fociety; a power of giving, in a greater or a lefs extent, according to the different degrees of the clerical character, a virtue and efficacy, a kind of magical charm, to the ordinances of religion; a privilege of obtaining a higher meafure of the favour of God, than other men, or of obtaining it on different and eafier terms; a fort of intereft with God, to engage him in all their views, to render every caufe of theirs his caufe, to make it impious to oppofe them,

[g] Tit. i. 7.

them, or to punifh their crimes, and to draw down his judgments on all whom they reckon their enemies. Such unholy claims cannot poffibly be founded on the holinefs of the miniftry : they are the offspring of ignorance and arrogance; they are by turns the nurfes and the nurfelings of fuperftition. The Chriftian miniftry is truly an holy office : but it is fo, only in this fenfe, that it is occupied about holy things, that its object is religion. They who exercife this office, are holy only in this fenfe, that they " minifter about holy " things," and that they are ftrictly obliged to real holinefs, to moral goodnefs, without which their character muft be repugnant to the fubject of their profeffion. The confideration, therefore, of the nature of the paftoral office, will lead us to the very fame view of its dignity, to which we fhould be led by a juft conception of its fanctity : and it will render the exhibition of it more diftinct and precife, and lefs liable to mifconftruction or abufe, as well as more agreeable to the ftile of the New Teftament. Following this track, we fhall afcertain the real dignity of the paftoral office, by the confideration of its acknowleged end, and of its natural functions.

In every cafe, the dignity of an occupation depends, in a great degree, upon its end. From this fource, the Chriftian miniftry, of all occupations, derives the greateft dignity. The gofpel of Chrift, which it is the bufinefs of that office to

preach,

preach, " is the power of God unto falvation [h]."
All the kinds of teachers in the Chriftian church,
are given for this purpofe, " for the perfecting of
" the faints, for the edifying of the body of
" Chrift [i], that, warning every man, and teaching
" every man, in all wifdom, they may prefent
" every man perfect in Chrift Jefus [k]." The
confequence of the right difcharge of this office
will be, that they fhall " both fave themfelves,
" and them that hear them [l]". It is its direct
aim, to carry forward, in a certain degree, that
difpenfation of grace, which has, through all ages,
been the grand and favourite object of God's providence in this lower world; in promoting which
all the hofts of angels are employed; in the execution of which the Son of God was incarnate
and crucified, and the Holy Spirit given; and
which terminates in conferring eternal life on as
many as comply with it. While thus employed,
minifters are not only " fellow-fervants" of the
angels [m], but alfo " workers together with God,
" befeeching men, as though God did befeech
" men by them; praying them in Chrift's ftead,
" that they be reconciled to God, and that they
" receive not the grace of God in vain [n]." The
paftoral office is concerned, not about the fortunes
of men, not about their lives, but about what is
infinitely nobler, about their fouls: it is concerned
about

---

[h] Rom. i. 16.　　[i] Eph. iv. 12.　　[k] Col. i. 28.
[l] 1. Tim. iv. 16.　[m] Rev. xxii. 9.　[n] 2 Cor. v. 20. vi. 1.

about the interefts, not of time, but of eternity. In a far fublimer fenfe than that in which the ancient painter gloried, the Chriftian minifter works for immortality. If the lawyer fucceed not in his caufe, his client may be reduced to poverty; if the fkill of the phyfician prove ineffectual, his patient will die: but, in whatever cafe the end of the paftoral office is defeated, everlafting deftruction is the confequence. Such being the end of that office, to fuppofe any infenfible of its importance, would be to fuppofe them befotted by the vanities of time, and blind to the interefts of eternity. And does this end reflect no dignity on the office which is adapted to it? Can it but be an honourable employment, to promote fo great a defign?

The paftoral office derives dignity and importance from the nature of its functions, as well as from the fublimity of its end. For our perceiving this, it will not be neceffary to enter into a minute detail of thefe functions; they will be explained afterwards. At prefent it will be fufficient to obferve in general, that they confift in "teaching[o]" pure religion, "inftructing[p]" men in the nature of it, "convincing[q]" men of its principles and obligations, "exhorting[r]" men to the belief and practice of it, "reproving and rebuking[s]" every fin,

[o] 1 Tim. iv. 11. vi. 2. 2 Tim. ii. 2. Eph. iv. 11. Rom. xii. 7.
[p] 2 Tim. ii. 15.
[q] Acts, xviii. 23. Tit. i. 9.
[r] 1 Tim. vi. 2. Tit. i. 9. ii. 15.
[s] 2 Tim. iv. 2.

fin, " warning[t] " men of the temptations to which
they are expofed, and of the danger of yielding to
them; in " watching[v] " for men, and " over-
" feeing[u] " them for thefe purpofes, taking every
proper opportunity, in public and in private, of
promoting them; in " being enfamples to the
" flock[w], in all things fhewing themfelves pat-
" terns of good works[x];" in endeavouring without intermiffion to qualify themfelves more and
more for all this, and then exerting themfelves
indefatigably in it; in a word, in ufing every
means that can be ufed by one man for infufing
knowlege and goodnefs into other men. That
thefe functions confer dignity on the office to
which they belong, will be evident, whether we
confider them in themfelves in relation to their
end, or in refpect of their neceffity and ufefulnefs
to the people.

Some exercifes are in their nature low and
mean; to be engaged in them, finks a perfon in
the eyes of others. The gofpel engages its minifters in no exercifes of this kind. It lays them
under peculiar obligations to practife and improve
in all piety and virtue; if they fulfil the obligations, they acquire that righteoufnefs which renders

---

[t] Acts, xx. 31. Col. i. 28. 1 Theff. v. 14.
[v] 2 Tim iv. 5. Heb. xiii. 17.
[u] Acts, xx. 28. Phil. i. 1. 1 Tim. iii. 1, 2. Tit. i. 7.
[w] 1 Pet. v. 3.   [x] Tit. ii. 7.

ders a man "more excellent than his neighbour[y]."
It engages them in the fearch of truth, and in
communicating knowlege : and if it be any part of
the dignity of man, that he is a reafonable crea‑
ture, it. muft be honourable to be employed in
fearching after truth, and diffufing it among men.
To difcover truth in that extent which belongs to
the paftoral office, requires, befides a confiderable
compafs of previous knowlege, the exertion both
of the acutenefs of the philofopher, and of the
judgment of the critic.   In communicating it fuc‑
cefsfully to others, the talents of the orator. muft
be, in fome degree, employed. Each of thefe
characters has always been acknowleged refpect‑
able : to deny, therefore, that the paftoral office,
which requires the union of . them all, is refpect‑
able, would be to judge of this one cafe, in con‑
tradiction to the natural fentiments of all mankind
in every other cafe.   To promote any kind of
ufeful knowlege, has fome merit ; the name of a
teacher gives a perfon fome elevation, in that one
refpect at leaft, in comparifon of thofe who are
taught by him : and the elevation bears always a
proportion to the fubject which a perfon is qualified
to teach, and engaged in teaching.   It is the very
office of minifters of the gofpel, to teach others :
and the fubject of their teaching is the fublimeft,
the moft important, --the moft interefting : it is
honourable to be occupied in teaching it ; it is
very

very honourable to be fit to teach it. It is the
very bufinefs of minifters, to inculcate the nobleft
truths, thofe which regard God and divine things;
to recommend univerfal goodnefs, the glory of
human nature; to form the fouls of men to that
divine temper which will fit them for the everlafting fociety of God; to " feed" and " overfee"
with care, that church on which the Lord fet fo
high a value, as to " purchafe it with his own
" blood ^{z}." The office of a teacher implies authority, the kind and degree of authority which
fuits its nature. The teachers of Chriftianity have
authority in the church; they " are over you,"
fays the apoftle, they " have the rule over you in
" the Lord ^{a}." Their authority is of the kind
which is congruous to their work: they neither
are " Lords over God's heritage ^{b}," nor " have
" dominion over men's faith ^{c}." They often
have claimed temporal power, political authority,
and civil dignities: but the claim is ufurpation;
thefe are the pre-eminences of the kingdoms of
this world, but their office is folely in the kingdom
of Chrift, which " is not of this world ^{d}:" thefe
have a relation to the fecular affairs of men, but
this office only to their fpiritual concerns. Even
in their fpiritual concerns, the authority of minifters

^{z} Acts, xx. 28. ^{a} 1 Theff. v. 12. Heb. xiii. 17.
^{b} 1 Pet. v. 3. ^{c} 2 Cor. i. 24. ^{d} John, xviii. 36.

nifters is very far from being abfolute or unlimited.
It includes no power over the confciences of men;
no right to impofe upon them, any principles of
belief, or rules of conduct, but thofe which the
fcripture has impofed; no right to obtrude upon
them our explications of fcripture or deductions
from it.   The claim or exercife of fuch rights, is
not the government of Chrift, but the tyranny of
Antichrift: both to the people and to minifters,
the fcripture is the only ftandard of religion: minifters have authority to teach only what it
teaches; and by it, and by it alone, it is the
right of the people, and their duty alfo, to examine what is taught.   Even thofe doctrines and
thofe precepts which are clearly contained in fcripture, the paftoral office gives no authority to enforce by methods of violence: thefe are the inftruments of political authority, the authority of paftors is purely fpiritual.   Religious belief and practice are of no value if they be not voluntary, if
they proceed not from conviction and confcience.
Whenever civil penalties are applied to force them,
they are mifapplied.   This is, impotently to attempt promoting the kingdom of Chrift, by an
unnatural alliance with the kingdoms of the world.
Perfecution never can be but improper; but in a
minifter of the gofpel it is moft improper.   When
irreligion, vice, or fuperftition, fo directly affect
the proper interefts of fociety, as to render it moft
juft to check them by laws, as civil crimes, the
enacting

enacting and executing thefe laws, is the province of the rulers of the ftate, not of the rulers of the church. Their authority is only a right to teach the truths which the fcriptures teach, to inculcate the duties which they require, to rebuke and cen-fure the fins which they forbid, and to be liftened to while they do fo : and they are entitled to fup-port this authority by no other engines, but the power of perfuafion and the influence of exemplary virtue. It is the dignity which refults from this kind of authority, and it alone, that belongs to the paftoral office.

The functions of the paftoral office, thus worthy in themfelves, will appear ftill more worthy and important, when they are confidered in relation to their end. It is fo fublime, that it reflects ho-nour and importance on whatever has any, even the remoteft, connexion with it; but the clofer the connexion of any functions is with it, and the ftronger their tendency to promote it, the greater in proportion will be their moment. Exercifes mean in themfelves, ceafe to be mean when they are undertaken for fome great or good end : then men will glory in them, who in any other fitua-tion would have blufhed to have been found em-ployed in them. The functions of the paftoral office are the natural, the direct, and proper means of promoting the moft important of all ends : this is fufficient to ennoble fuch of them as are meaneft in appearance. Paftors are " watch-

" men^e:" but it is for " the foul^f," the immortal part, that they watch. They are " fol-
" diers^g:" but it is in " the good fight of faith^h."
They are " labourers," but it is " together with
" God," and in " his vineyard, his hufbandry,
" his harveftⁱ." They are " builders;" but it is
of the " temple of God^k." Such metaphors,
though fome of them fhould be fuppofed to be
taken from mean employments, rife in their fignification, when they are applied to the exercifes of
an office which has eternity for its aim; as an
infignificant piece of canvas comes to be of great
price when it is made the ground of a capital picture. They are intended only to exprefs the difficulties and the labours of that profeffion. Thefe
leffen not its dignity: they add to it. Some of
the moft eminent offices are very laborious; but
their toils are honourable. Whenever they are of
great utility, and extenfive confequence, it is noble
to encounter them, it is worthy to be indefatigable
in undergoing them, it is glorious to vanquifh
them.

Finally, the paftoral office is important, and
ought to be reckoned honourable by the people,
becaufe to them it is needful. The end of all its
functions is their falvation; and in proportion to

its

---

^e Jer. vi. 17. Ezek. iii. 17. xxxiii. 7.   ^f Heb. xiii. 17.
^g 2 Tim. ii. 3, 4. Phil. ii. 25.   ^h 1 Tim. vi. 12.
ⁱ Mat. ix. 37, 38. 1 Cor. iii. 6.—9.   ^k Ver. 9, 10. 12. 16.

its neceſſity for this end, it is intereſting to them. It is ſolely for the ſake of the people, that God has appointed paſtors in his church; and to the people all their funƈtions have an immediate relation. It belongs indeed to every individual, to " work out " his own ſalvation [1]:" without his own care, as well as the grace of God, all the labours of the miniſter cannot enlighten his underſtanding, ſanctify his heart, or ſave his ſoul. Yet the labours of the miniſter are ſtriƈtly neceſſary to the people. With abhorrence we diſclaim the falſe pretenſion, that religious knowlege is, or ought to be confined to the clergy: God has eſtabliſhed no ſuch baſe or ſlaviſh dependence of reaſon and conſcience upon fallible men. The people, as well as their paſtors, have acceſs to the ſcriptures; it is equally their right and their duty to " ſearch" and " know " them [m]:" and they " are able to make them " wiſe unto ſalvation [n]." But the bulk of mankind are, and will always neceſſarily be, much occupied about worldly affairs; and, thus occupied, will want the inclination, the leiſure, the opportunities, the capacity, the education, or the means, requiſite for collecting religious knowlege, and fixing good impreſſions on their hearts. The weak, the ignorant, the thoughtleſs, the diſſipated, the buſy, the corrupted, have abſolute need of one to

inſtruƈt

---

[1] Phil. ii. 12.   [m] John, v. 39.   [n] 2 Tim. iii. 15.

inſtruct them, to direct them, to remind them of ſpiritual things, to excite them to their duty. Without this, very many will infallibly neglect it, and loſe their ſouls by the neglect. It is no exag-geration to ſay, that the future happineſs or miſery of at leaſt ſome of the people, depends on the proper or the improper conduct of their teachers. We juſtly complain that the paſtoral office, even when its functions are performed with the greateſt ſkill and care, produces not ſo great or happy effects as it ſeems to be fit for producing : but were that office to ceaſe, the ignorance and wicked-neſs of the world would ſoon demonſtrate, that it does produce very great and very happy effects. It cannot be a mean employment, which is both ſo neceſſary and ſo profitable to mankind. The care of immortal ſouls is the moſt important of all truſts : the training of them for heaven is the moſt excellent of all occupations[o].

Thus I have evinced the importance of the paſtoral office, by ſhewing its dignity and excel-lence. Avoiding all vague panegyric, declining indefinite declamation concerning its ſanctity, I have ſatisfied myſelf with coolly aſcertaining the real kind and degree of dignity, which it evidently derives from the ſublimity of its end, and the worthy and intereſting nature of its functions.

---

[o] Burnet's Paſtoral Care, chap. i. Scougal's Synod Serm.

SECT.

SECT. II.

Of a juſt Senſe of the Dignity of the Paſtoral Office.

SUCH as we have deſcribed being the dignity of the paſtoral office, let us next inquire, what ſentiments its dignity ought to impreſs, both on thoſe who occupy it, and on thoſe who aſpire to it. It certainly becomes them to cultivate and preſerve a ſenſe of its importance, and likewiſe to render that ſenſe juſt and properly directed. It is neceſſary to do both; a failure in either will be productive of pernicious conſequences.

The want of all ſenſe of its dignity, will lead men to conſider it in the low and paltry light of only a trade or living. This would demonſtrate a very abject ſpirit, and it would render it every day more abject. Conſidered in that light, it muſt appear one of the meaneſt of all employments; for there are few whoſe profits are not more conſiderable. Men would, however, enter on it with merely intereſted views. They would long for it, as a proviſion. They would not be much concerned either to qualify themſelves for its duties, or to exert themſelves in performing them. They would be ſatisfied with receiving the profits, though they were negligent or little capable of doing the work. In the language of ſcrip ure, emphatically expreſſive of the haſeneſs of this mercenary ſpirit, they would " feed

" them-

" themfelves," and " not feed the flock [p]," but
leave it to be " ftolen, killed, and deftroyed [q]."
It is your fetting out with a high fenfe of the dignity and importance of your profeffion, and your
conftantly maintaining that fenfe, that will beft
preferve you from thinking or acting beneath it,
and will form you to fuch elevation of views, fuch
exertion, and fuch dignity of conduct, as become it.

Your fenfe of its dignity muft not only be high,
but likewife juft.   As the nature of its dignity may
be mifconceived, fo the fenfe of its dignity may
be perverted: and every perverfion of it will produce correfpondent ill effects on the temper and
the conduct.

A general and indefinite conception of the paftoral office, as merely an honourable employment,
efpecially if it were at the fame time exaggerated
and extravagant, would excite an unhallowed ambition and impatience for it as a pre-eminence, till
it were obtained; and would afterwards elate the
heart with arrogance, pride, and infolence. Thefe
paffions are naturally enough produced by the honours which confift only in diftinguifhed rank and
titles, and which are founded wholly in imagination: but by the dignity of the Chriftian miniftry,
they

---

[p] Ezek. xxxiv. 2, &c.   [q] John, x. 10.

they cannot be produced, except it be totally mifunderftood; for its dignity refults folely from the
real utility of its functions.   Thefe are paffions the
moft unbecoming in the fervants of the humble
Jefus, fit only to render themfelves odious, and
to pervert the whole fpirit and tenor of their miniftrations.   Therefore, the apoftle directs, that a
bifhop be not an uninftructed, inconfiderate " no-
" vice, left being lifted up with pride, he fall
" into the condemnation of the accufer[r]."

A vague and ill-digefted opinion of the fanctity
of the paftoral office, would beget the moft prefumptuous kind of pride: it would give it the
blackeft of all its forms: it would forge a claim to
fuperftitious refpect and blind veneration from the
people.   This is the temper which Chrift reproves
fo feverely in the Pharifees, who " loved the up-
" permoft rooms at feafts, and the chief feats in
" the fynagogues, and greetings in the market-
" places, and to be called of men, Rabbi, Rab-
" bi[s]."   But the teachers of his religion he commands, " Be not ye called Rabbi, neither be ye
" called Mafters[t]:" exact not the admiration of
the multitude, as if you were, in confequence of
your holding an holy office, holier than they,
higher in God's favour, or poffeffed of any myf-
terious power in matters of religion.   An ill-
defined

---

[r] 1 Tim. iii. 6.   [s] Mat. xxiii. 6, 7.   [t] Ver. 8. 10.

defined fenfe of the fanctity of the paftoral office .
would lead us, it has led the priefts of another
church, to a demand of privileges moft foreign to
its real fanctity, and a licence in practices moft
repugnant to every conception of holinefs. It is
undoubtedly proper that we be fenfible of its
being an holy office : but our fenfe of this muft be
formed and defined by a diftinct conception of the
real nature of its holinefs. It is not a notion that
the mere occupation of it can render us holy; but
a fettled perfuafion that it will lay us under the
ftricteft obligation to labour to become holy, and
ftill more holy. It is a fixed perfuafion, that unhallowed hands and an unfanctified heart are unfit
to be employed in its holy functions. It is a lively
fenfe, that all impurity is more incongruous to the
fubject of the Chriftian miniftry, than the moft
vulgar manners, the moft fordid fpirit, and the
coarfeft fentiments, would be to the higheft rank.
It is a conviction that that office gives thofe who
exercife it, great advantages for becoming holy;
united with a conviction that, except they be careful to improve them, they will not make them
holy, but will on the contrary confirm and harden
them in wickednefs ; and that the ftrength of their
obligations, and the greatnefs of their advantages,
will render the guilt of neglecting holinefs heinous,
and its punifhment fevere. In a word, a fenfe
that the paftoral office will place you in a near and
peculiar relation to God, fhould make you to look
upon yourfelves as bound to approach as near to

him

him as you can, in your temper, by ſtrict purity,
exalted virtue, and fervent piety. ;

A juſt ſenſe of the dignity of the paſtoral office
muſt be formed and directed by a preciſe idea of
the nature and grounds of that dignity, and be
rendered perfectly correſpondent to it. It is a
ſenſe, that the duties of that office are of the moſt
excellent nature, and of the moſt ſacred obligation, and that it is of infinite moment that they be
diſcharged aright. Such a ſenſe of its dignity,
however high it be, will produce none of thoſe
evil paſſions which ſpring ſo naturally from a
vague or perverted conception of it. It can give
no encouragement to falſe ambition, pride, or
haughtineſs: it will be the moſt powerful antidote
againſt them. It will lead you often to compare
the " treaſure" of the goſpel, with the " earthen
" veſſels," in which " we have" it ᵘ; the weight
of the functions, with your unworthineſs and the
ſlenderneſs of your abilities; the eternal conſequences which are ſuſpended on your performance
of them, with the weakneſs of the means which
you can uſe. The compariſon forced the great
apoſtle of the gentiles to exclaim, " And who is
" ſufficient for theſe things ᵛ ?" The compariſon,
ſeriouſly made, will lead you to undertake this
office with diffidence, to be converſant in it with
awe,

ᵘ 2 Cor. iv. 7.   ᵛ Chap. ii. 16.

awe, and in all its duties to " ferve the Lord with
" all humility of mind ʷ." Such a fenfe of the
dignity of your profeffion, carefully formed, fteadily maintained, ftudioufly cherifhed, and inva-
riably acted upon, will have the happieft influence
on your views, on your exertions, and on your
whole character: and that the more effectually,
the higher it is raifed.

A well-formed fenfe of the importance of your
profeffion will refine and elevate your views and
aims in choofing, in undertaking, and in executing
it. It neceffarily includes an impreffion of the importance of the end of your profeffion. To promote that end, will be your principal view in entering upon it, and your leading aim in exercifing
it. You will think of entering on it, with a confiderable degree of deliberation; and when you
determine to undertake it, it will be with a fincere
and fupreme defire, and an ardent concern, to
contribute all you can to the improvement and the
falvation of the fouls of men. Liable as all men
are to indifpofition, depreffion, and diftraction of
thought, it will require pains to keep fo fublime
an end conftantly in view, and to act with a fteady
regard to it. A lively fenfe of its moment is the
only means of furmounting the difficulty. This
will lead you to think explicitly of it very frequently;

ʷ Acts, xx. 19.

ly; and it will enable you to have an habitual eye
to it, even when you do not actually think of it.
It will be in perpetual readinefs to occur to you,
and that with fuch force as to determine you to
contrive how every miniftration may be performed
in the way fitteft to promote it.   Attention to fo
fublime an end will prevent your ever fubordi-
nating any of the paftoral functions to bye-ends,
to worldly intereft, or to the gratification of a favourite paffion.   It will prevent your directing any
of your performances merely to the difplay of your
own talents, to courting the favour of the great,
or to fcrambling for popularity among the multitude.   It will excite you to exert your powers,
only that you may do the greater good; to
" pleafe" others only for their " edification ˣ,"
only when it is right to pleafe them, and would be
wrong not to pleafe them.   Concern to accomplifh
the end of your profeffion, is too noble a principle
to admit any partnerfhip with mean defigns.   It
implies love to God, affection to Chrift, the higheft
fpecies of benevolence, benevolence to the fouls of
men, zeal for the advancement of religion, a conviction of the incomparable importance of eternity,
all united together, deriving power from, and im-
parting it to, one another.   Thefe will be in fome
degree the principles and views of every ingenuous
candidate; whoever is wholly deftitute of them,
muft be unworthy to bear the facred character:
                                                thefe

ˣ Rom. xv. 2.

thefe will be the principles and views of all who are duly affected with the importance of the office, and the great fprings and regulators of all their exertions in their profeffion.

A fenfe of the importance of the paftoral office, enlightened by a diftinct apprehenfion of the nature of that importance, will add fpirit to all your endeavours, both in preparing yourfelves for it, and in executing it. Not dreaming that it has fuch fanctity as can of itfelf · confer virtue on the ordinances which it is employed in difpenfing, you cannot expect that they will have virtue and efficacy, if you be incapable of difpenfing them aright, or if you be not careful to do fo. Important functions fhould not be performed negligently, and cannot be performed without the proper abilities. Senfible of the importance of yours, if you have any regard to duty or propriety, you will decline no application that is neceffary to accomplifh you for them, however laborious it may be, or whatever length of time it may require. Till you be confcious that you are fufficiently accomplifhed for them, you will by no means think of undertaking them. Without diligent application, no man can excel, or even make a tolerable figure in the very meaneft profeffion: and can a man be fit for fo excellent an occupation, without being indefatigable in acquiring the knowlege and habits requifite for exercifing it? The teacher of all truth and goodnefs, cannot be formed in a day.

6   The

The importance of his office demands that he be
affiduous in rendering himfelf fitter for it every
day, and ready to undergo any labour that can be
conducive to his difcharging it in the beft manner.
It may be eafy to go through all the duties of that
office, fo as not to incur the imputation of omitting
them, without entering into the true fpirit of any
one of them : but to be fatisfied with this, is inconfiftent with your either valuing or loving your
profeffion.   The fenfe that its duties are in their
very nature worthy and honourable employments,
will not only prompt you to bring to them the requifite accomplifhments, but alfo fupport and enliven you in the performance of them.   Mean exercifes a man enters on with reluctance, and performs with regret and languor : he is afhamed of
them, and by fhame his efforts are repreffed, and
his induftry enervated.   But you need not be
afhamed of the gofpel of Chrift, or of the office
of preaching it : you may glory in preaching it,
and with confcious elevation ftretch all your faculties in preaching it.   The fenfe that all the paftoral
functions are directly fubfervient to the greateft of
all ends, the purity, perfection, and happinefs of
immortal beings, will determine you to adapt all
your ftudies and exercifes to that end; to avoid
barren fpeculations, frivolous controverfies, fubtle
and unedifying queftions ; not to feek after what
may pleafe the imagination, gratify the curiofity,
or humour the. prejudices of the people : but to
inculcate only the fimple doctrine of the gofpel,
which

which tends wholly to fanctification, and to fet
every part of it in thofe points of view, in which
it has the ftrongeft tendency to affect the heart, improve the temper, influence the practice, and thus
fit men for eternal life. From a lively impreffion
of the connexion of your functions with this end,
and of their neceffity to the people, what ardor,
zeal, alacrity, and diligence in performing them,
muft arife? It will make you cheerfully continue
and increafe your labours, and never give them
over, till you have accomplifhed their end, at leaft
till you have freed yourfelves from blame, though
they fhould fail of actually reaching it.

A lively fenfe of the genuine importance of the
paftoral office will have a great influence on the
whole of your character. It will powerfully infti-
gate you to all goodnefs. It implies a fenfe of the
importance of eternal falvation, which is the end
of all the functions of that office. And with this
in your view, can you be but concerned for your
own falvation, and careful to fecure it? Can you
indulge yourfelves in fin, which muft forfeit it, or
neglect that holinefs without which it cannot be
obtained? Salvation is the moft commanding object that you can hold forth to others, for coun-
teracting the temptations of the world, for baffling
the power of fin, for furmounting the difficulties
of religion, for encouraging them to climb the
heights of virtue: and if you yourfelves have a
conftant fenfe of it, it is impoffible that it fhould
have

have no influence on your own temper and conduct. It will be your very bufinefs, to teach men,
in all poffible ways, " the doctrine which is ac-
" cording to godlinefs ʸ:" can you, teach it without ftudying it? and can ¡you make it the bufinefs
of your lives to ftudy it, without feeling any thing
of its power in forming yourfelves to godlinefs?
It is doubtlefs poffible to go through the functions
of the paftoral office, without their having any
effect on your own fouls: but it is not poffible to
perform them with due attention to their nature,
or a real confcioufnefs of their tendency, without
their having a great effect. They are the means
which infinite wifdom has ordained for reforming
and fanctifying the world: and can you uprightly
employ yourfelves in applying them to this purpofe, and yet yourfelves remain totally unreformed
and unfanctified? A fenfe of the juft importance
of the paftoral office, impreffed on the heart, will
form you, not only to goodnefs, but to dignity
of character and demeanour. A ftation of dignity
requires dignity of character: and it is the trueft
dignity of character, that the ftation of minifters
requires. This is widely different from that ftate-
linefs and haughtinefs which highly mifbecome
them, but which fome have affected in its ftead:
it is perfectly confiftent with the lowlieft humility;

nay,

ʸ 1 Tim. vi. 3.

D

nay, in the exertions of genuine humility, it is often moft confpicuous. It exalts the foul, but elates it not; it produces condefcenfion, not af-fuming; affability, not diftance: it difgufts not the moft jealous fpectator; it forces approbation, and commands efteem. The apoftle certainly had it in his eye, when he directed, not to the people, but to the minifter, the exhortation, " Let no " man defpife thee[z]." It is nothing elfe but eminence of virtue. It is founded on a ftrong perception of the excellence of virtue and the bafe-nefs of vice, and on a permanent fenfe of the vanity of prefent outward things, and the un-fpeakable moment of things fpiritual and eternal. It fhews itfelf in a fuperiority to all the allurements of fenfe and intereft, whenever they are incon-fiftent with ftrict virtue; in liberty from the do-minion of vice, which is the loweft degradation of a reafonable foul; in the poffeffion and vigorous exercife of a high degree of piety, benevolence, and every worthy affection; in difdaining to fpeak or do any thing which betrays mean fentiments, little views, or wrong paffions; in being above blufhing to perform offices feemingly the loweft, whenever they are ufeful to the body or the foul of any man, or conducive to the interefts of reli-gion. This is true dignity of character: and this is the dignity, and the only dignity, to which

your

---

[z] Tit. ii. 15. 1 Tim. iv. 12.

your profeſſion can naturally prompt you to aſpire.
A proper conception of the end of that profeſſion
will kindle your ambition for it; acquaintance
with the ſubjeƈt of your profeſſion, will form you
to it; aſſiduity in the duties of your profeſſion,
will draw it out into conſtant exertion, and by
conſtant exertion will confirm and perfeƈt it. But
the foundation both of goodneſs and of dignity of
charaƈter muſt be laid early. A perſon under the
full power of thoſe ſentiments which flow from a
ſenſe of the excellence of the paſtoral office, will,
from the firſt moment that he thinks of chooſing
it, ſtudy to aƈt in every reſpeƈt ſuitably to its true
genius. He will ſtudy to preſerve that manner
from the very firſt, which would be graceful and
becoming if he were already inveſted with the
ſacred charaƈter of a miniſter of religion, in his
aƈtions, in his words, in his whole behaviour.
Whatever would be declared by the general ſenſe
of mankind indecent in a clergyman, can never
be altogether decent in a perſon who intends to be
a clergyman. Any behaviour unſuitable to the
charaƈter which you hope ſoon to bear, can proceed only, either from blameable thoughtleſſneſs,
from a turn of mind ill correſponding to it, or
from a deſire not to have it known that you are
deſigned for that profeſſion. All theſe are incon-
ſiſtent with a due ſenſe of its dignity and importance; which will produce in you a conſtant ſoli-
citude to ſpeak and aƈt worthy of it; and will

effeƈtually

effectually .prevent your running into any fpecies
of conduct which can imply, that you are afhamed
of it, or that you do not reckon it your greateft
honour to be preparing for it, or engaged in it.

SECT. III.

Of the Efteem due to the Paftoral Office.

IT is incumbent, not only on thofe who occupy
or afpire to the paftoral office, but likewife on all
others, to have a juft fenfe of its dignity and importance. Becaufe it is both excellent 'in itfelf,
and highly beneficial to the people, they are
obliged to efteem it, and to think highly of it.
We are affected towards all offices, according to
our opinion of their nature: we look with contempt on thofe which we reckon mean; we refpect thofe which we reckon honourable or important: we feel thefe fentiments though we ourfelves have no connexion with fuch offices. If the
moment of the paftoral office be meafured by the
rank which it gives in the prefent world, or the
emoluments which it yields, men can have but a
low opinion of it. But thefe are not the ftandards
by which its dignity fhould be eftimated. Its bufinefs is to teach religion; its end is to promote
the eternal happinefs of mankind: its intrinfic
dignity is in proportion to thefe purpofes; and in
proportion to men's fenfe of the excellence of
thefe,

thefe, their efteem of it will always be. If thefe appear to men, as they really are, infinitely nobler and more momentous than all earthly riches and honours, they cannot entertain a low idea of the paftoral office. This would be to think meanly of the gofpel, which is the fubject of it, and to fet little value on eternal happinefs, which is its aim. This is inconfiftent with men's being Chriftians. It demonftrates a bafe perverfion and depravation of fentiment. It would be inexcufable, though the paftoral office had no immediate relation to themfelves. But when it has the neareft relation to themfelves; when it is for teaching them the gofpel, and promoting their falvation, that this office is inftituted; when, confidering their want of leifure and opportunities, they could fcarce at all obtain thefe purpofes without it; when they are fo deeply interefted in it, and that for pur-pofes of fuch unfpeakable confequence to their fouls; not to hold it in high efteem, fhows not merely infenfibility to its nature, but alfo indif-ference about their own moft valuable interefts; thofe eternal interefts, indifference about which is a complication of the groffeft folly and the bafeft degeneracy of foul. Such extravagant or miftaken notions of the dignity or the fanctity of the paftoral office, as were formerly mentioned, would produce a blind and fuperftitious veneration of it, as per-nicious in its confequences as the want of all re-fpect for it. It is only a value for it, founded on a diftinct conception of its real utility, and cor-

refpondent

respondent to it, that either is due, or can be profitable.

The importance of the pastoral office demands likewise from the people, respect for those who bear it. These two sentiments, a value for the office, and esteem of those who exercise it worthily, are inseparable, and must in every man be in exact proportion to one another: they who are sensible of the importance of the work, and of its utility to them, will " for the work's fake esteem " them very highly in love," who labour in it[a]. In whatever belongs to their office, they are superior to the people and have an authority over them; this implies a right to correspondent respect and deference, the refusal of which is a failure in duty. Whenever ministers are exercising their office, they are doing something for the instruction, the sanctification, or the salvation of the people: and by being employed for purposes so beneficial to them, they cannot but be entitled to their affection and gratitude. To refuse these attachments, is to declare that they reckon these no services. Love and esteem will add force to one another, and will lead them to treat ministers both with respect and kindness, and to do them all the good offices in their power, with an acknowleged sense that they are due to them. An implicit dependence

---

[a] 1 Theff. v. 13.

pendence on the opinions and fentiments of minifters, a fuperftitious dread of punifhing their
crimes, or of vindicating the rights of other men
againft them, a filly admiration of them, as if they
were beings of an higher order or endued with
fupernatural powers, are no parts of the deference
that is due to them; they will be paid only hy the
ignorant or the deluded, and accepted only by the
weak or the defigning; they are warranted by
nothing in the real nature of the paftoral office:
but it does demand that rational efteem and love
for thofe who difcharge it uprightly, which is
proportioned to its moment, and congruous to its
functions.

A perfon may, doubtlefs, by behaving un-
worthily in his office, forfeit the efteem to which
it would have otherwife entitled him. In this
cafe, the very importance of the office which he
holds, will render him the more contemptible, or
the more deteftable. But a real value for the
paftoral office will give fome check to the feverity
of men's cenfures, and will often even prevent
them. It is plain that they who have leaft refpect
to the office, are generally the moft forward to
find fault with individuals belonging to it, and the
readieft to pronounce that they have forfeited their
title to efteem. And by the manner of expreffing
their contempt or indignation againft individuals,
they betray the principles by which they are actuated: they exprefs it with pleafure or exultation,

with

with flight or acrimony againft the office itfelf, or
fometimes even with a fort of triumph over religion.
Indeed, perfons of very oppofite pretenfions fometimes fhew the fame propenfity to undervalue or to
cenfure individuals of the clergy. It is often-ob-
fervable in thofe who profefs a high fenfe of the
importance and fanctity of the office, and great
zeal for the interefts of religion. Their idea of
the office is fo overftrained as to make them exact
from thofe that hold it more than is reafonable,
and expect more than is practicable: or their zeal
for religion is of a falfe and fiery kind, embittering
their fpirits, and rankling them into malevolence:
or their religion itfelf is of a fpurious kind, difpofing them to confider indifferent things as wrong,
and trivial things as momentous: or their pretences to religion are hypocritical, and overdone
in order to conceal the impofition. A real and
juft fenfe of the importance of the paftoral office,
will extinguifh the propenfity to feek for faults in
minifters; and, when faults are confpicuous, will
mix the cenfure of them with regret, concern, and
tendernefs. It is not every failing, or every imperfection in virtue, that can forfeit any part of the
efteem due to a minifter on account of his office:
for fallibility and imperfection are the characterif-
tics of human nature in this mortal ftate. If it
could, God would never have commanded to
efteem them. Men's confcioufnefs of their own
faults fhould lead them to expect fome in minifters, difpofe them to bear with them, and not
eafily

eafily to contract prejudices againft them. They are men like other men; they live in the world, befet with the like temptations; it is not reafonable to expect from mortals the innocence or the perfection of angels [b].

A juft and well-regulated efteem of the paftoral office, and of thofe who occupy it, will render men well affected to all their miniftrations in it. In whatever degree that office is important, in the very fame degree it is of confequence for men to attend upon the functions of it. If it be defigned for promoting their moft important interefts, and if they think highly of it on this account, they muft attend upon its functions; for without this it can be of no advantage to them. An opinion that the paftoral functions operate as it were magically, merely by being performed and attended upon, produces, in thofe who entertain it, a high value for them, and a fcrupulous punctuality in attending on them: but as it fprings from a wrong principle, it muft likewife have a wrong direction. If a rational perfuafion of their real utility produce not as great an efteem of them, and affiduity in them, it muft be owing to its being too weak, or too little reflected upon. But the degree of regard to them, which fprings from fuch a perfuafion, whatever it is, will at leaft be properly directed.

---

[b] Stillingfleet, Ecclefiaft. Cafes, vol. i. p. 105.

rected. It will not be merely formal; it will be beſtowed with a ſingle view to apply them all to themſelves, and with care to render them profit-able for their inſtruction and improvement. Every inſtance of diſregard to the functions of miniſters betrays a defect in men's value for their office; and every failure in improving by their functions, ſhews ſome perverſion in the manner of conceiving the importance of their office.

SECT. IV.

Of the Contempt of the Clergy.

THOUGH the paſtoral office be in its very nature worthy and important, and entitle thoſe who oc-cupy it to honour and eſteem, it is too plain that it is neverthelefs very generally undervalued, and they who hold it, ſpoken of with contempt or ran-cour. This ſpirit ſhews itſelf in different ways.

Sometimes it breaks out directly againſt the paſ-toral office itſelf. This office is thought and ſpoken of with diſreſpect. It is accounted mean, and de-ferving of very little honour. In eſtabliſhments where it leads to riches or political pre-eminence, it is reproached as proſtituted to worldly views; and in others where it can ſcarcely raiſe the occu-piers of it above poverty, it is deſpiſed as on that account low and unreputable. By ſome it is ridi-culed,

culed, as excluding thofe who hold it from that external polifh, eafinefs of manner, and graceful-nefs of deportment, which are found in fome other orders of men. It is fometimes even held up to the deteftation of mankind, as tending to corrupt the moral character of thofe who are in-vefted with it. By artfully confounding its na-tural and primary tendency, with the abufes of it after this tendency has been refifted and defeated; by exaggerating thefe abufes, and the ill effects re-fulting from them; and by overlooking every cir-cumftance in the office, which can counterbalance them; it has been mifreprefented as having a fixed and unalterable tendency to promote in minifters the grofs vices of hypocrify, fuperftition, ambition, vanity, party-fpirit, rancour, and revenge [c].

The fame fpirit leads men to feek out the faults of individuals of the clergy, to exaggerate and fet them in the moft invidious lights, and to publifh them with a malicious eagernefs and exultation. Imaginary faults are converted into real vices; fmall failings are exalted into atrocious crimes; and great blemifhes are condemned with the moft fpiteful bitternefs, and without making the leaft allowance for the weaknefs of human nature, or the temptations of the world. They often are not fatisfied with bitternefs againft the individuals who

are

[c] Hume's Effay on National Characters. Gerard, vol. ii. Serm. 2. Carlyle's Synod Serm.

are guilty.: they impute them to the whole order; they take every occafion of ridiculing and reproaching all who belong to it. It cannot be denied that there is a real propenfity in human nature, to afcribe the character of fome individuals with whom we are beft acquainted, to the whole fociety of which they are members. This is a fpecies of inference which it is impoffible wholly to avoid; for it is derived from that mental principle which difpofes us to form general rules of judging, and from which many of our moft important intellectual operations proceed. But whenever we form a general rule haftily, without having experience in a fufficient number of inftances; whenever we apply the conclufion to individuals diffimilar to thofe of whom we had experience, in the circumftances on which the conclufion was originally founded, however like they may be in other circumftances; whenever we do not exercife judgment in allowing the neceffary exceptions; that principle leads us into mere prejudices, inftead of juft conclufions. From whatever caufe the unfairnefs proceeds, it is certain that our general rules concerning characters, are much oftener founded on the faults than on the virtues of men, that we are readier to defcribe a fociety or nation, by the blemifhes than by the excellences of fuch individuals belonging to it as we are acquainted with. It is obvious too, that men impute the faults of individual clergymen to the whole order, more generally, more confidently, and with lefs

care

care to make exceptions, than in the cafe of any other profeſſion [d].

But the ſpirit of difaffection reſts not even here. The faults of the clergy are charged on religion itſelf: the contempt of their office grows into contempt of religion. If men be diſſatiſfied with a particular lawyer or phyſician, they commonly content themſelves at the utmoſt with blaming all who are of the profeſſion; they ſeldom go ſo far as, on account of the faults of the practitioners, to call in queſtion the virtues of medicines, or the utility of curing difeaſes, to revile the laws of the land, or the inſtitution of civil government. But, not ſatisfied with defpiſing or reproaching the whole clerical order for the vices of a few individuals, they would make the religion which they teach anſwerable for them, and expreſs ſuſpicions concerning the truth, the excellence, the importance, or the practicability of the goſpel. There may be circumſtances which give a ſpecioufneſs to this partiality, and betray men thoughtleſsly into it: but ſtill it is an unreaſonable partiality, and ſeems to proceed in a great meaſure from this, that the depravity of men makes them more eager to find out ſomething to the difcredit of religion, than to that of the ſubject of any other profeſſion.
When

---

[d] Stillingfl. Ecclef. Caſ. vol. i. p. 176. Secker's 1ſt Charge, Oxf. Gerard, vol. ii. Serm. 2.

When men's contempt of the clergy proceeds
not fo far as to the contempt of all religion, yet
it often fhews itfelf in a contempt of their miniftrations, and indifference for attendance on them.
Thefe two things, contempt of their perfons and
neglect of their miniftrations, are nearly connected:
the tranfition is eafy from the one to the other.
Both imply an infenfibility to the importance of
the end and functions of the office. When men
are in any way prejudiced againft the perfon, they
cannot have a great refpect to his labours, nor the
expectation of much advantage from them.

Contempt of the paftoral office is very common
in all thefe forms. Whence can fentiments proceed fo repugnant to thofe that are naturally due
to its excellence and importance? They proceed,
in different cafes, from different caufes.

Infidelity is one very natural caufe of fentiments
either of contempt or of rancour againft the paftoral office and thofe who exercife it. Atheifts,
who regard all religion as weaknefs and fuperftition, and infidels, who look on revelation as an
impofture, a falfe and pernicious fuperaddition to
natural religion, cannot have a great efteem for the
office of the teachers of religion. They muft of
courfe either defpife them as weakly credulous, or
diflike them as deceivers, carrying on a difhoneft
craft, impofing upon men doctrines which themfelves believe not, and rules of conduct which
                                        themfelves

themfelves know to be of no obligation. Thefe are the only fentiments which they can confiftently entertain. But in them alone they can appear confiftent or reafonable. In all who profefs to believe the gofpel, to regard it as a divine reve-lation of true religion, of a ftupendous difpenfa-tion carried on by God, from the foundation of the world, for the falvation of mankind, and exe-cuted by the moft wonderful means; it never can be-reafonable to flight the office of teaching reli-gion, of propagating the principles and inculcating the practice of Chriftianity, or to undervalue thofe who are employed in it. To defpife the order in general, is to defpife the work, and to defpife the gofpel which they themfelves believe; for the gof-pel is both the fource and the fubject of the em-ployment of that order. This is abfurdity and in-confiftence in the extreme: but it is very far from being uncommon [e].

In fuch, the contempt of the clergy fometimes arifes from the contagion of the fpirit of infidelity. The prevalence of infidelity often corrupts the fen-timents and practice of thofe whofe faith it cannot abfolutely fubvert. Men adopt the maxims of in-fidels without perceiving their confequences; they catch fomething of their fpirit, while they reject their principles. While fpeculative tenets often have

[e] Gerard, vol. ii. Serm. 2.

have not a great or conſtant influence on the beha⸗
viour, ſympathy is ſo ſtrong in human nature, that
it leads us to enter readily into the ſentiments and
opinions of others, and to receive them by a kind
of infection, without conſidering how far they are
conſiſtent with our own real belief. By this means,
the contempt and ridicule which infidels are na⸗
turally led by their tenets to pour out upon the
miniſters of religion, diffuſes itſelf and ſpreads the
ſame ſpirit among thoſe who, by their own princi⸗
ples, ought to honour them[f].

Attachment to vicious habits and practices, not⸗
withſtanding a belief of the Chriſtian religion, is
another very natural cauſe of diſreſpect or averſ⸗
ſion to the Chriſtian miniſtry. It is not ſurpriſing
that they who are addicted to wickedneſs, ſhould
diſlike thoſe who endeavour to check wickedneſs ;
or that they who hate to be reformed, ſhould hate
thoſe whoſe very buſineſs it is to labour to reform
them. Corruption of manners is often both a
cauſe and an effect of the contempt of the mini⸗
ſters of religion. Men's acknowlegement of the
religion which they teach, cannot be expected to
prevent their contempt, any more than it has pre⸗
vented their own depravity ; for it is not more
contradictory to the former than to the latter.
Perſons of abandoned morals cannot ſet a proper
value

---

[f] Gerard, vol. ii. Serm. 2.

value on the perfons or the office of minifters, except. they conceived a virtue in their functions, to fecure their falvation without their being obliged to relinquifh their vices; and this miftaken conception has fometimes led men of fuch morals to an extravagant adulation or admiration of the clergy, and a fuperftitious dependence on their functions; as dangerous to themfelves, and as difgufting to them, as the moft open contempt or difrefpect.

Even too low a fenfe of the excellence and moment of religion, though not accompanied by grofs immorality, will fink men's efteem of the paftoral office. As long as men are fo inattentive to the importance of eternity, as to be drawn off from a due regard to it by every prevailing paffion or prefent intereft, it is impoffible that they can have a juft fenfe of the importance of an office, which is dignified chiefly by its being calculated for training men up for eternity. Accuftomed to eftimate every thing according to its value in this world, they will refpect the paftoral office only in proportion to the degree of rank, or weight, or influence, which it gives the poffeffor in civil fociety; and confequently their refpect will be both too low, and of a kind that is improper and incongruous to the real nature of the office.

Differences

Differences of opinion in matters of religion sometimes contribute very powerfully to some sort of contempt of the clergy. The adherents to one sect, bigotedly attached to its peculiarities, and violently set against all who differ from them, direct their spite principally against the ministers of other sects; reproach them as irreligious or enthusiasts, as loose or over-rigid, as fools or hypocrites, according as circumstances give the easiest handle for one charge or another. Such abuses have been reciprocally heaped by different parties and different churches on the teachers of each other. Every difference in the situation of these teachers has been turned by the rest into a reproach against them: their faults have been searched out, discovered with joy, exaggerated without mercy, and turned into reasons for contempt or aversion towards all the teachers of the same persuasion. The dissentions of those who ought to have considered themselves as brethren, have been greedily laid hold of by the enemies of religion, received with an eager faith, retorted upon them all, and improved into a confession, that the ministers of any denomination cannot be entitled to much esteem. Some sects of Christians, being misled by some of their peculiar principles to disclaim the ministry as a separate office or profession, have, in consequence of this, professedly despised all who have devoted themselves to the exercise of it; and in their ridicule or invective against them, have

sometimes

fometimes equalled, or even furpaffed, the open enemies of all religion [z]. On the other hand, the raifing the meafures of the paftoral duty too high, though owing to an exalted idea of the importance of the office, tends directly to produce contempt or difaffection towards thofe who occupy it. Fofter-ing in men an expectation of more from minifters, than is in their power to do, they will never think that they have done enough, and will be diffatisfied with them after they have done all they can.

When thefe or other caufes have in any degree introduced a contempt of our order, it can fcarcely fail to fpread. The giddy and inconfider-ate will run into it by imitation, without examin-ation of its juftice, without reflection on its tendency, without any fettled ill defign. The gay and fprightly will choofe it as an eafy way of difplaying their wit and humour. The bearifh will lay hold of it, as offering a defirable opportunity of venting their rudenefs without giving general offence. Some will affect it as a mark of politenefs, of freedom of fentiment, of fuperiority to vulgar prejudices, of exemption from fuperftition : and fome, by depreciating the clergy, and difregarding their functions, hope to exalt themfelves as above the need of any inftruction or direction from them.
When

---

[z] Barclay's Apology. Letters on Theron and Afpafia.

When the fpirit of contempt of minifters, and of their office, has become prevalent, no fituation, no behaviour can procure them that honour and refpect to which it entitles them. If by the eftablifhment of religion to which they belong, honours and riches be annexed to their office, they are reproached as proud, ambitious, and covetous. If their provifion be fcanty, they are defpifed for their poverty, and charged with meannefs of fpirit, and ungenteelnefs of appearance. If they are ferious and grave, it is conftrued into grimace, hypocrify, or morofenefs. If they are cheerful and lively, it is mifreprefented as unbecoming levity, or even an indication of their having no fenfe of religion. The caufes of all this lie not in themfelves; elfe, by removing them, they might avoid it: but they lie in the giddinefs, the vices, or the prejudices of others, which they have it not in their power to correct, and which thefe unfavourable fentiments of them, in a great meafure, cut them off from opportunity of endeavouring to correct. Thefe caufes too are fo various and even oppofite in different men, that if they efcape contempt from one quarter, they may lay their account with cenfure from another, and perhaps the more for the very means by which they have contrived to make that efcape. All that they have in their power is, to prepare themfelves for bearing it, and to behave with propriety under it.

In

In this fituation of things, it is highly neceffary that, to a fenfe of the dignity and importance of the paftoral office, you fhould unite a fenfe of the contempt to which it is in fact expofed: and it is no lefs neceffary to give the fenfe of this contempt a right direction and a proper regulation. If you be not careful to direct and regulate it, it will have a very bad effect on your temper and behaviour. Catching by fympathy the fentiments of thofe who entertain, and are forward to exprefs, contempt for your profeffion, you may contract a difpofition to defpife it yourfelves, and be led to fpeak or act as if you were afhamed of it. Amidft a torrent of ridicule or abufe poured out againft it, the firft motions of this difpofition may, from the influence which the fentiments of others involuntarily have upon us, be nearly unavoidable. But you fhould attentively obferve every tendency to it, as it begins to rife, and immediately check it. The feeming to diffemble your profeffion, the imitation of the manners of the laity, the attempting to throw off the clergyman, the fpeaking or acting in any manner unfuitably to it, the appearing not to have an habitual impreffion of its bufinefs and its defign; by fuggefting that yourfelves look upon it as defpicable or unreputable, will, by their fympathy with your fentiments, increafe their contempt of it, and direct their contempt particularly againft you. Whatever can infufe a fufpicion that you do not love it for its own fake, and for the fake of its employments, will lead them to confider

you

you in the pitiful light of exercifing it only as a trade for a livelihood.

To fpeak with feeming pleafure of the gaieties, amufements, and diffipations of fafhionable life, to enter into them as far as you think decency can at all permit you, or occafionally to go a little farther than is confiftent with the common maxims of decorum, may procure you, fome external careffes, or even fome inward liking from fuch as delight in them ; but it will fink you even in their efteem, and make others defpife you as totally unfit for the profeffion which you have chofen. Were you to affect difclaiming your profeffion, by appearing to think favourably of any vice, or flightly of any thing which truly belongs to religion, it might prevent the wicked, the irreligious, and the unbelieving, from hating you, for the fame reafon that they revile your office : but it would raife their indignation againft you, and their contempt of you, as low, deceitful wretches, who live by religion, and yet betray it. Let never your confcioufnefs of the undeferved contempt with which your profeffion is commonly treated, induce you to fpeak a word, or do an action, which can be confidered as infinuating that you have a mean opinion of it, or little value for it. This would increafe their contempt of you, and render you deferving of it. This additional contempt you have great reafon to be folicitous to avoid ; and you will moft fuccefsfully avoid it by making the worthy clergy-

man

man always confpicuous in your demeanour. But that contempt which is directed primarily againft your profeffion, and only rebounds on you as belonging to it, when you recollect the caufes from which it proceeds, you certainly cannot be folicitous to avoid ; for if it were poffible, it could be avoided only by your being affimilated to the infidel, the profane, the vicious, and the world-ling[h].

Inftead of vainly endeavouring to avoid it by improper means, turn it to your advantage. If properly confidered, it may be rendered productive of very beneficial effects on your temper and behaviour. A juft and well-formed fenfe of the contempt with which you and your office are liable to be treated, will teach you not to expect all that honour which the importance of the facred functions might claim ; and by preventing the expectation of it, will prevent the pain and mortification of difappointment, when you mifs it. It will forbid your laying claim to exceffive refpect or authority, by making you certain that it would be refufed, perhaps with redoubled flight and ridicule. You fhould never indeed allow, or feem to allow, that your profeffion is trivial or defpicable ; for this would

---

[h] Stillingfleet, Eccl. Cafes, vol. i. p. 176. Secker's 1ft Charge, Cant. and 1ft Charge, Oxf. Warburton; Doct. of Grace, part iii. c. 1. p. 202, 203.

would be to betray its rights : and it is doubtlefs
proper at fome times explicitly to vindicate it, and
avow its dignity. This is permitted to perfons of
all other profeffions. The meaneft artificer is not
blamed for fpeaking of the real degree of utility
which his trade poffeffes : a magiftrate or judge
may, without incurring cenfure, claim and enforce
the honour that is due to his office. It is only
when men would give dignity to mean employments, or challenge, to fuch as are honourable, a
refpect in its nature unfuitable, or in its meafure
extravagant, that they meet with either ridicule or
difapprobation. It cannot therefore be reafonable
to infift, that minifters alone fhould leave mankind
to throw undeferved contempt, not only upon
themfelves, but upon their office alfo, without
daring to tell them that they are in the wrong. It
is even lefs reafonable to expect it from them than
from-men of any other profeffion : it is directly
their bufinefs to point out the various duties of
men ; and it cannot be incumbent on them, or
even allowable in them, to pafs by thofe duties of
which the paftoral office is the object. Regard to
the gofpel forbids it ; it would be to fuffer, without
reproof, an office to be vilified, which has its
foundation in the gofpel. Regard to men's own
fouls forbids it ; it would be to fuffer an office,
which was intended for their edification, to become
of no advantage to them, by their learning to
defpife it. The moft important interefts of men,
their fpiritual improvement and their everlafting
happinefs,

happiness, may be very much affected by the sentiments which they entertain of their Christian teachers. Yet it is certain, however unreasonable, that such a vindication of our profession as would be readily allowed to others, would by many be censured as priestly pride and assuming haughtiness. On this account, even when it becomes most necessary, it must be undertaken with great caution and prudence. You must not claim any honour, either improper and undue in its kind, or extravagant in its degree; nor even any honour that can, with plausibility, be suspected of being such. You must express your demands with great care and precision, avoiding every term that is pompous or indefinite. You must rather keep considerably below what truth and justice evidently warrant. And with all this reserve, you must show no anxiety to enter upon the subject, but touch it very sparingly, and only when a proper occasion invites it. You will most effectually gain respect by not being over-eager to claim it. A proper sense of the contempt with which the pastoral office is too commonly treated, will likewise check the pride and vanity which the consideration of its importance might excite in light and inconsiderate persons, who do not sufficiently reflect on the true nature of that importance. Serving as a counterbalance to these, it will have a direct and powerful tendency to form you to a temper of humility. It will accustom you neither to court nor to set a high value on the opinions and applauses of men; not to act

with

with a view to them, but from a regard to what is
right in itfelf, to the approbation of your own
minds, and the unerring judgment of God. By
conftantly laying your account with it, that you
fhall incur part of the contempt which is fo liberally
caft on your profeffion, you will be prepared for
bearing unjuft reproach and obloquy without being
provoked or exafperated, and to fubmit to it with
patience and meeknefs. It will give you ample
fcope for exercifing thefe virtues, and rendering
them more and more habitual. Haughtinefs or
refentment would be fo far from fcreening you
from the contempt of thofe who are difpofed to beftow it, that they would only fuperadd their hatred.
By receiving it with dignity tempered by mildnefs,
you will moft effectually convert it into refpect [1].

Contempt is neceffarily difagreeable. However
much you are prepared for bearing it properly
when you meet it, it muft be natural for you to
wifh to avoid it ; and therefore a due fenfe of the
prevailing contempt of the clergy cannot but excite
you to ufe every proper means of avoiding it, or
at leaft of mitigating it as much as poffible. It
will excite you to avoid all fuch faults and failings
in your character and behaviour, as are the natural
objects of contempt; for by indulging thefe, you
muft increafe the contempt of the whole order, and
together

---

[1] Secker, Ch. 1, Oxf. Ch. 2, 3. Cant. Stillingfleet, Eccl.
Cafes, vol. i. p. 179.

together with it incur likewife perfonal contempt
drawn upon you juftly by yourfelves. It will excite
you to acquire and to endeavour to excel in thofe
qualifications which are acknowleged to be refpectable : for thefe will procure you a degree of perfonal
refpect and honour, which may, in men's behaviour
to you, in a great meafure, counterbalance their
difpofition to defpife or revile your profeffion.
From your education, and from the very nature of
your profeffion, a competent degree of knowlege
is juftly expected : if you have it not, you will foon
be detected by the difcerning, and thought deficient even by the ignorant : grofs ignorance expofes any perfon to contempt, and it muft expofe
you to double contempt, for in you it will
appear highly fhameful. Knowlege is univerfally
accounted eftimable and ornaméntal : and ufeful
knowlege cannot fail to do you credit in the eyes
of men. A defire therefore not to ftand low in
their opinion, will be a fpur to you in acquiring
fuch a degree of it as may adorn your profeffion.
The acquifition of knowlege neceffarily fuppofes
application and ftudy : a life in a confiderable
degree ftudious, befits your character and bufinefs,
and is neceffary for preferving you from the degrading fufpicion of mif-fpending your time in idlenefs or trifles. Imprudence of every kind neceffarily leads to follies, which muft fink you in the
eftimation of mankind, and render you fometimes
ridiculous, and fometimes defpicable : your averfion to thefe humiliating fituations cannot fail to

prompt

prompt you to that prudence, circumfpection, and wifdom of behaviour, which will place you out of the reach of them. Whatever is looked upon as mean, inevitably provokes contempt. So much regard has been paid to this, that bodily defects and remarkable meanneffes of appearance have been deemed fufficient to exclude men from the priefthood in fome religions: and they certainly have fo great an influence on the fentiments of mankind, that they who have the misfortune to lie under them, will need, and fhould employ, the greater pains to acquire fuch refpectable qualities, confpicuous accomplifhments, and fhining virtues, as may overcome that influence, and force mankind to forget their exterior defects. But whatever betrays a littlenefs of mind, narrow and contracted fentiments, or low and grovelling views, is much more juftly defpicable, and will more certainly and generally be defpifed. A regard to reputation fhould therefore difpofe you to avoid even vulgarity and rufticity of manners, and not to reckon the common rules of good breeding below your attention; but much more to keep at a great diftance from all mean practices, felfifh defigns, and attachment to trivial points of intereft; and to difplay a fuperiority even to confiderable worldly objects, and fuch difintereftednefs as may convince men that you prefer doing your duty, and faving their fouls, to any profit of your own. Not only fuch vices as are reckoned degrading to the character of every man, will fubject you to

infallible

infallible contempt, but every vice whatever; and by no means can you fo effectually guard againft the contempt which you muft naturally wifh to avoid, as by fhowing yourfelves to be free from every vice, and poffeffed of every virtue. In particular, that wifh will prove a ftrong prefervative againft all faultinefs in your own profeffion; for negligence in its proper duties is one of the moft obvious grounds of contempt, and will fooneft bring it upon you; or if the irreligious and the wicked fhould feem to be the better pleafed with you, the lefs you do in your own bufinefs, yet even they will inwardly both difapprove and defpife you, and you muft lofe the good opinion of all who have the trueft value for your office, and the warmeft love to virtue and religion, and whofe good opinion alone can be really honourable to you. That wifh will be the ftrongeft incentive to confcientious diligence in the peculiar duties of your profeffion; for fuch diligence will force men to fee that you are ufeful, and fet you out of the reach of at leaft many of the reproaches which they delight in cafting upon the order [k].

I have now endeavoured to reprefent, in a proper light, the importance of the paftoral office as refulting from its dignity; and to point out the fentiments and temper with which that importance requires

---

[k] Stillingfleet, Eccl. Cafes, p. 178. Secker, Ch. 1. Oxf. Ch. 1, 2. Cant.

requires that you enter on it, and which will pre-
difpofe you to its feveral duties. Its importance
ought to produce efteem of it in the people; but
as it is neverthelefs very generally treated with
contempt, I have. inquired into the caufes of this
contempt, and fhewn how you fhould be affected
by it, and to what purpofes you fhould improve it.
I neither defigned nor pretend to have exhaufted
the fubject, but only to have given fuch hints as
may prompt you to think of it, and purfue it for
yourfelves. It will be of great advantage that you
think of it often, and ferioufly. It fuggefts many
exercifes on which you may very properly put
yourfelves. You may confider what are the means
by which you may beft excite in yourfelves a due
fenfe of the excellence of your profeffion. You
may contrive beforehand, how you could, in different fuppofed fituations, act up to it, and fupport your character with propriety. You may
reflect on the feveral expreffions of flight or
reproach which you have obferved or known to
be caft upon the clergy; and you may examine in
what manner you ought to behave if you met with
them, and by what means you might moft effectually efcape or confute them. By frequent meditation on fuch topics, or even by putting your
thoughts in writing, you will render the proper
fentiments familiar to you, and will enter on your
office deeply poffeffed with them. Your temper will
be both congenial to your employment, and adapted
to your fituation. For this purpofe all the fenti-

ments

ments which I have mentioned muſt be cheriſhed in conjunction : the expectation of contempt muſt not ſuppreſs the ſenſe of the dignity of your pro‐ feſſion, elſe it would either depreſs or miſlead you : it muſt only be united to it, that this ſenſe may not elate you, and that you may be diſpoſed to reſt contented with the degree of reſpect which you can obtain by the virtues proper to your profeſſion, and not court a ſpurious reſpect for qualities foreign to your character, or perhaps miſbecoming it.

CHAP. II.

The Difficulties of the Pastoral Office.

THE pastoral office is rendered important, not only by the dignity of its functions, but also by their difficulty. As it is of great moment that they be performed well, it is likewise no easy matter to perform them well. To be acquainted with its difficulties, is necessary for your knowing how to combat and surmount them; and it will confirm those sentiments which ought to be entertained by all who enter on that office, and which, if they be heartily entertained, will have an extensive influence on the right discharge of all its functions.

SECT. I.

The Nature of its Difficulties.

THAT the difficulties of the pastoral office are very great, is evident from the very names by which the scripture describes those who exercise it. It is remarkable that there is scarcely one of these that does not imply either skill, or labour, or both; not even those which are most expressive of their dignity. They are called " rulers," and said to
" have

" have, rule" over Chriftians; Every office of
government is attended with no inconfiderable
difficulty : but their's is a government of souls,
the hardeft of all arts; it is the government of
men, not in refpect of external behaviour and
overt acts, but likewife of the habits and difpofitions of their hearts ; and that too carried on, not
by violent or coercive methods, by which temporal rulers may force obedience to the civil laws,
but folely by the gentler methods of perfuafion,
which men, if they be determined on it, may more
eafily refift. They are called the "ambaffadors"
of God, by a metaphorical application of the name
of an employment, very honourable indeed as
implying an important truft ; but which cannot be
executed without great abilities, or without the
faithful and indefatigable application of thofe
abilities to promote the end of the embaffy, to
prevent whatever can obftruct it, to contrive every
method of forwarding it, and to maintain the
dignity and the rights of the prince whofe commiffion they bear. They are termed " the ftewards
" of God ;" which implies their being employed in
the difficult tafk of caring for all the members of
that great family of which Chrift is the head, of
difpenfing to them their fpiritual food, and directing their practice in their feveral provinces. By a
name of the like import, they are called " bifhops,"
overfeers, or infpectors ; to intimate the obligation
which they are under, to take heed to the conduct
and the fpiritual interefts of thofe who are com-

F   mitted

mitted to their charge. They are called " paſtors,"
or " ſhepherds;" by the name of an employment
very reſpectable in the ſimple and earlier ages; but
which expoſed thoſe who exerciſed it to great toils
and hardſhips, ſome of which Jacob deſcribes from
his own experience, when he ſays; " In the day
" the drought conſumed me, and the froſt by
" night, and my ſleep departed from mine eyes."
Our Saviour, in deſcribing himſelf under this character, repreſents the occupation as both difficult
and dangerous : " I am the good ſhepherd : the
" good ſhepherd giveth his life for the ſheep. But
" he that is an hireling, and not the ſhepherd, ſeeth
" the wolf coming, and leaveth the ſheep; and
" fleeth; and the wolf catcheth them, and ſcattereth
" the ſheep. But I am the good ſhepherd, and
" know my ſheep, and am known of them, and I
" lay down my life for the ſheep." The epithet
is often in ſcripture applied to God, and is meant
to intimate his tendereſt care of his church, in
reſpect of which he repreſents himſelf as " feeding
" his flock like a ſhepherd, gathering the lambs
" with his arm, and carrying them in his boſom,
" and gently leading thoſe that are with young."
Such being the ideas connected with the name in
holy writ, it is plainly given to the miniſters of
religion, on purpoſe to intimate the aſſiduity and
tenderneſs of that care which they are required to
take, of thoſe who are entruſted to them by Chriſt
Jeſus, " the great ſhepherd of the ſheep ;" in
feeding or teaching them, in looking after and
defending

defending them, in guarding them from every sin and error, in applying remedies to all their spiritual diseases, and in encountering every danger in discharging these several duties towards them. The teachers of religion are denominated the " ministers or servants of God ;" implying that they must labour in serving him in that work which, by his authority and under his direction, they are employed to carry forward in his church. They are particularly called " labourers" in his husbandry and his vineyard ; and this designation, borrowed from those who earn their bread by their daily labour, and must exert themselves diligently and constantly, evidently implies, that the teachers of religion must make it their daily employment, their occupation for life, to promote the instruction and improvement of Christians; that their work is hard and laborious; that it must be applied to with diligence and perseverance ; that it will return upon them every day ; and that it can never be intermitted or given over as long as they live. They are called " watchmen," by a metaphor taken from those who were placed on high towers, to attend day and night, and to be always ready to give the alarm on every appearance of danger ; and therefore plainly intimating, that ministers ought to be alert in observing whatever can hurt the souls of men, and give them warning of it ; and that for this purpose incessant vigilance and earnest circumspection are absolutely necessary. They are called " soldiers," expressly to declare

that

that their employment calls them to " endure
" hardnefs," to encounter difficulties, fatigues,
and dangers. Minifters are defcribed in fcripture
by fo many epithets implying various kinds of
exertion, on purpofe to imprefs them with a deep
fenfe that their bufinefs is difficult and laborious,
and demands vigorous application and unwearied
diligence. In like manner, the exertion incumbent upon them is defcribed in terms expreffive
of its intenfenefs and conftancy. They are exhorted to " wait on," to " ftudy," to " take heed
to," to " give attendance to," to " give them-
" felves continually to," to " be inftant in," to
" labour in," the feveral duties of their office.
Injunctions in fuch terms would be fuperfluous, if
there were not great difficulty in performing thefe
duties aright. But being the words of the Holy
Spirit, they cannot be fuperfluous ; and they are
no ftronger than the nature of the fubject demands [1].

The end and defign of the paftoral office is fo
purely-fpiritual, and fo fublime, that it cannot be
eafy for a perfon clothed with a mortal body, and
furrounded with worldly objects, to keep it conftantly in view, and to act with a fteady regard to
it. The purpofe of its inftitution is defcribed by
the apoftle in this manner : " He gave fome, apof-
                                        " tles ;

---

[1] Stillingfleet, Eccl. Cafes, vol. i. p. 179. Burnet, Paft.
Care, c. 1.

" tles ; and fome, prophets ; and fome, evangelifts ;
" and fome, paftors and teachers ; for the perfect-
" ing of the faints, for the work of the miniftry,
" for the edifying of the body of Chrift : till we
" all come in the unity of the faith, and of the
" knowlege of the Son of God, unto a perfect
" man, unto the meafure of the ftature of the ful-
" nefs of Chrift ᵐ." It is the bufinefs of a minifter
to enlighten the understandings of men with all
religious knowlege, and to bring them to good
practice. It is not enough that he perfuade them
to external blamelefnefs, or to abftinence from
grofs vices ; though often this is found to be
difficult enough, and even impracticable. But
his aim muft be to prevail upon them to forfake
every vice, to extirpate all bad habits ; to form
them to inward purity, to unfeigned humility, to
calm refignation, to the ardent love of God, to
that univerfal charity which will make them regard
the interefts of others as their own ; to infpire
them with the love of virtue, to exalt them to the
divine image, to raife them above the world, to
fpiritualize their temper to fuch a degree, that
they may be fit for afcending to " Mount Zion,
" and to the city of the living God, the heavenly
" Jerufalem, and to an innumerable company of
" holy angels, to the general affembly of the firft-
" born,

ᵐ Ephef. iv. 11, 12, 13.

F 3

" born, and to God all-pure, the judge of all,
" and to the fpirits of juft men made perfect, and
" to Jefus Chrift the righteous, the mediator of the
" new covenant[n]." No miniftration of the facred
office can be performed aright, except it be performed with a refpect to thefe important ends.
But men muft, without the greateft care, frequently
lofe fight of them. At one time they will be
ready to go through what they muft do, without
confidering whether it be or be not well calculated
for anfwering thefe purpofes. At other times a
regard to their own intereft or reputation will mix
with and fophifticate their aims. Even when they
keep them moft directly in their eye, they will
find it very difficult to difcover how every part of
their bufinefs may be performed in the manner
fitteft for promoting them, to force themfelves to
perform it in that manner, and to continue and
increafe their labour till they have done all in their
power to accomplifh them. Were it incumbent
on a minifter actually to attain thefe ends, his
work would be, not merely difficult, but altogether
impracticable : but it is incumbent on him, both
fincerely to aim at them, and to omit nothing
that he can do in order to attain them. To fatisfy
himfelf of this, he muft be confcious that he has
uniformly employed his utmoft abilities and induftry in the duties of his office. How difficult it
is

---

[n] Heb. xii. 22, 23, 24.

is to promote thefe ends, with any tolerable fuccefs, in a parifh, a man may perceive by only reflecting how difficult it is to accomplifh them in himfelf, or by making trial of forming any one to whom he has the neareft and moft conftant accefs, to fuch a temper and behaviour as he would wifh him to acquire.

The functions of the paftoral office, appointed for promoting thefe ends, are in their very nature attended with confiderable difficulty. It may be' eafy to go over them, and difpatch them in fome way or other : but it is a very different matter to execute them conftantly in the moft ufeful and improving manner. It is not difficult to difcourfe fluently enough on different fubjects of religion, or to teach people to repeat explications of them by rote : but it is both difficult and irkfome to fay the' fame things over and over, to fet them in one light after another, to contrive a variety of illuftrations, till the dulleft can really underftand them. With proper preparation and moderate care, a man may compofe a very correct difcourfe : but it is not fo eafy to preach properly and ufefully. To exprefs the truths and duties of religion, fo plainly as to be underftood by the meaneft without difgufting the moft knowing ; to reprefent what they know already and hear often, fo as to engage their attention and make an impreffion upon them ; to fix the meafures of duty, fo as neither to alarm the fcrupulous, nor give undue licence to the lax ; to

awaken

awaken the hardened finner, without difturbing the
timorous with undeferved terrors ; to exprefs every
fentiment in the way fitteft :to give a ftrong conception of divine truth; and to touch the heart ;
to admit no fentiment but what has a real tendency
to make men wifer and better; to reject every
thought foreign to this purpofe, however fit it
might be for pleafing or gaining applaufe ; to preferve all thefe views, and to be under the influence
of them, all the time a perfon is compofing and
delivering a difcourfe ; cannot but be arduous :
yet it is neceffary to preaching well. It is ftill
more difficult to find out the different tempers of
all the variety of perfons with whom a minifter is
concerned ; to difcover the beft ways of applying
to each ; to acquire the extent of knowlege requifite for thefe different applications; to keep it fo
diftinctly in view, as to be able to recollect and
make ufe of it as occafion requires ; and after the
neceffary knowlege is obtained, it is ftill difficult
to learn the addrefs which muft be employed in
applying to men in the feveral ways proper for
a clergyman, and to conduct his applications
with that prudence which will render them moft
effectual.

· The work of a minifter appears, from this reprefentation of it, to be abundantly difficult, though
all things fhould confpire in the moft friendly
manner with his endeavours to promote and execute it. But the difficulty is immenfely increafed
by

by the great and numerous obſtructions which are oppoſed to his endeavours. They ariſe both from himſelf, and from the people. Many obſtructions muſt ariſe from the unavoidable infirmities and imperfections of a man's own nature. It is not eaſy to throw off the indiſpoſition, which indolence will at times produce, to his employing all the time and pains neceſſary for the right diſcharge of all his duties; to overcome the falſe tenderneſs which makes it painful to declare diſagreeable truths; or the reluctance which modeſty muſt feel againſt reproving one's ſeniors or ſuperiors with becoming freedom; to attain the reſolution which will enable him to incur whatever inconveniences may ariſe from his admoniſhing thoſe on whom his intereſt depends; or to encounter the ridicule, contempt, and obloquy, to which he will be expoſed by fairly condemning prevailing errors, faſhionable evils, and polite or popular vices. Obſtructions at leaſt equal to theſe ariſe from the ſtupidity, the prejudices, and the vices of other men. In order to perform the buſineſs of his calling, a miniſter muſt infuſe knowlege into thoſe who are ſo dull as to be ſcarcely capable of diſtinct thought. He muſt teach thoſe who have very little leiſure, and very little inclination, perhaps even an averſion, to learn. He muſt diſcover the inward vices and depravities of thoſe who do all they can to conceal them from him. He muſt treat with ſkill the diſeaſes of the ſoul, which are more latent and ſtubborn than many of thoſe
bodily

bodily diftempers which phyficians find it very hard to cure. He muft make men willing to correct faults which they fondly hug ; and to conquer habits which they have ftrengthened by thoufands of acts repeated almoft every day. · He muft give them in an hour good impreffions, which may have ftrength enough to continue and influence them for many days, in oppofition to all the objects which tend moft ftrongly to obliterate them. He muft bring them to a temper and conduct directly oppofite to that which is powerfully recommended to them by the example of the generality of thofe with whom they converfe. He muft perfuade them to that from which all their corrupt paffions draw them off. He muft perfuade the ambitious to flight power and honours, and to afpire only to the heavenly kingdom ; the covetous, to value no riches in comparifon with the invifible treafures which are above ; the fenfualift, to facrifice the pleafures for which he has always had a relifh, for the fake of more refined pleafures, which he is incapable of tafting till he be purified from the love of external gratifications. He muft bring faith and hope to prevail over fenfe ; and withdraw all the affections of human nature from thofe objects which folicit them moft directly, and gratify them moft immediately, to objects remote or future. He muft " wreftle, not againft flefh and blood only, " but againft principalities, againft powers, againft " the rulers of the darknefs of this world, againft " fpiritual wickednefs in high places ;" and in

order

order to be fuccefsful in his occupation, he muft wreftle fo as to baffle all their power, and difappoint all their artifices. It is only fo far as a minifter furmounts thefe obftacles, and, notwithftanding them, accomplifhes the reformation and improvement of mankind, that he attains the end and defign of his vocation. Not actually to do fo in any inftance, would be to be abfolutely ufelefs in his ftation: and fo far as he fails by negligence in any part of his duty, he is anfwerable for the failure. But in order to effect all this in a few inftances, in order to perform what is proper for effecting it, in fuch a degree as not to be really blameable for negligence, very great pains and labour muft neceffarily be beftowed.

I would not willingly exaggerate the difficulties of the paftoral office: exaggeration could only produce defpondence, and, by reprefenting them as infurmountable, might reprefs every endeavour to furmount them, and occafion an entire neglect of every duty. But it is equally dangerous to extenuate them; it would be to deceive you; and by thinking that you have little to do, you would be tempted to do almoft nothing, and incur all the ill confequences of incapacity or idlenefs. The difficulties which I have defcribed are all real; they are either exprefsly pointed out in fcripture, or they grow out of the very nature of the functions and defign of the paftoral office: and therefore you ought not to diffemble them from yourfelves.

If

If they require a great degree of exertion, and fuggeſt a high ſtandard of duty, by having it in your eye you will at leaſt approach nearer to it, than otherwiſe you would have even thought of attempting. In what manner the view of them ought to affect and influence you, and what obligations you lie under to do your utmoſt that you may ſurmount them, I ſhall next explain.

SECT. II.

Of the Obligations reſpecting the Difficulties of the Paſtoral Office.

IT is not perhaps altogether uncommon for men to chooſe the profeſſion of a clergyman as one of the eaſieſt ways of gaining their bread. This view is not more ſordid than it is erroneous. If this profeſſion exempt men from the labours of the body, it ſubjects them to great labours of the mind: if it impoſe not the drudgeries which require only muſcular ſtrength or animal agility, it requires exertions which will at leaſt as much fatigue and exhauſt even the body. Its difficulties are evidently ſuch, as ought to deter every man from undertaking it, who is not determined to devote himſelf to its duties, to make it really his buſineſs to labour in it with aſſiduity. To think or to ſay, "Put me into one of the prieſts' offices, "that I may eat a piece of bread," betrays a total

9. ignorance

ignorance and infenfibility of the arduous nature of thefe offices.

If you imagine that the occupation which you have chofen is attended with little difficulty, the certain confequence is, that you will be at little pains to qualify yourfelves for it; for you will think a little pains fufficient. But by being previoufly well aware of its feveral difficulties, by often thinking of them, by cultivating an habitual fenfe of them, you will never want a fpur to diligence in your preparation for them. You will think no preparation too much; you will be difpofed to exceed if poffible, rather than run the rifk of falling fhort of what is neceffary. You will never reckon yourfelves perfectly prepared, but will continue through your whole lives to become fitter for ftruggling againft them. A difficult work requires both fkill and diligence, in order to its being well executed: the foundations of both muft be laid in your preparation for entering on the paftoral office. It is not enough that you acquire all the knowlege, a right application of which would contribute to your right difcharge of its functions: it is proper likewife that you learn in fome meafure to apply it to that purpofe. You may in various ways have opportunities of performing functions in, fome degree fimilar to this office; to pupils, for inftance, and younger friends; and the inuring of yourfelves to thefe, and ftudying to perform them in the moft ufeful manner, will train you for the right execution

tion of like functions in a more extensive sphere. You may likewise suppose to yourselves particular situations of difficulty, which may possibly hereafter occur to you in the business of a minister; or you may observe or get information of such as have occurred to others : and you may consider deliberately how you could most successfully exert yourselves in that situation; and what you determine concerning it at one time, you may examine at another time, and alter, correct, or improve it as you find reason. It will likewise be extremely useful, if you have opportunity, to accompany some minister who performs them well, in the several duties of his parish, to observe his manner, and even to attempt the performance of them in his presence, and by his direction, and to receive and profit by his remarks on your performance. I said that the foundations of diligence, as well as of skill, must be laid during your preparation for the pastoral office : they can be laid only by your accustoming yourselves to diligence in whatever you are employed, whether your private studies, any branch of teaching, or any other business; and particularly by accustoming yourselves readily to obey every call to good offices or active exertion, without suffering indolence, recluseness, or the love of study, to withhold you from them.

A sense of the difficulties of the pastoral office will be a strong incentive to diligence, not only in preparing yourselves for it, but also in performing its duties when you shall be called to it. Under a

lively

lively fenfe of the arduous nature of his work, a minifter will ftudy, by all the methods of inftruc-tion, exhortation, admonition, reproof, terror, confolation, perfuafion, in public and in private, in their health and their ficknefs, amidft the diffipation of profperity and the depreffion of adverfity, to enlighten the ignorant with religious knowlege, to form the young to impreffions of truth and goodnefs, to fix the unthinking, to awaken the fecure, to reclaim the wicked, to refolve the doubting, to confirm the wavering, to ftrengthen the weak, to perfect the faints. To this he will devote his time, his ftrength, and all his talents. He confiders it as what properly belongs to him; and though he cannot be every hour employed in it, yet all other purfuits, even fuch as would moft laudably gratify his curiofity or his tafte, and fuch as are moft indifpenfably neceffary for his temporal concerns, he will reckon only avocations in com-parifon, fubordinate to this, and cheerfully poftpone, when he has an urgent call to any part of this.

Under a ferious view of the difficulties of the paftoral care, the fouls of men would fink, if they were not confcious that it is the work of God, and that God himfelf is engaged in it. This reflection fupports them under all their exertions, by the hope of his affiftance, and by the affurance, that if they be not blameably deficient, he will render their exertions fuccefsful, as far as the views and plan of his providence permit. It will likewife make every recollection of difficulty in their work,

an

an irrefiftiblemotive toearneft prayer for his aid,both
in qualifying them for it, and in performing it, and
for fuccefs in all their miniftrations. A fpirit of
devotion is abfolutely neceffary in all of your profeffion, and will be the natural confequence of a
juft fenfe of its difficulty, together with a due confcioufnefs of your own weaknefs.

It is needlefs to enlarge on thefe topics. The
fentiments and difpofitions which I have mentioned
flow neceffarily from a view of the nature of the
paftoral office, and are by it rendered indifpenfably
obligatory. But a new and ftrong obligation to
them arifes from confidering farther, that a failure
in thefe, and the improper or imperfect execution
of that office, which will be occafioned by it, are
highly criminal, are productive of the moft pernicious confequences, and will render fuch as are
chargeable with them obnoxious to the fevereft
punifhment. There are two diftinct claffes of
duties incumbent on all perfons who occupy a
public ftation; the one, of thofe duties which
belong to them in common with others, as men
and Chriftians; the other, of fuch as are peculiar
to that public ftation in which they are placed.
The latter are no lefs neceffary than the former to
complete goodnefs of character; and the neglect
of them is no lefs blameable, no lefs hurtful to
fociety, no lefs feverely punifhable. It is not
enough that a judge be blamelefs in his private life;
it is equally neceffary that he execute juftice in his
public

public capacity, and promote the interefts of fociety by his authority and influence; and if he grofsly neglect the opportunities of doing fo, or wilfully pervert juftice, he is as highly blameable as if he had been guilty of fimilar omiffions or injuries in private life, as much hurts fociety, and can as little expect to efcape punifhment from God. In like manner, though a minifter fhould be unblameable and virtuous in common life, though he fhould be chargeable with nothing that would have been faulty if he had been only a private Chriftian; yet if he have no activity in the bufinefs of his office, no zeal for attaining its end; if he fpend that time in indolence, in amufement, in worldly bufinefs, or even in learned ftudy, which ought to have been employed in preparing him for inftructing his people to more advantage, or in doing good offices among them; he is highly faulty and vicious. In his ftation he cannot be a good man, without being a good minifter. The criminal omiffion or the carelefs performance of the duties of his public ftation, will be at leaft as hurtful to the great interefts of men, as pofitive acts of vice in his private life. If by his negligence he fuffer men to lofe the impreffions of religion, or if by his unfkilful and improper methods of inftructing them, he fow the feeds of folly, bigotry, fuperftition, or enthufiafm, the ill effects may continue through many generations. He cannot be free from the blood of thefe generations, nor innocent from thefe mifchiefs, whofe incapacity or negligence gave occafion to

G   them.

them. So far as thefe were criminal, they muft expofe him to fevere punifhment under the government of a righteous God[o]. Negligence in the paftoral office reflects more difhonour upon God, than negligence in any other profeffion, becaufe this profeffion, more immediately than any other, regards God and religion. It is likewife productive of worfe confequences : the improper exercife of other profeffions may produce particular inconveniences, or promote fome vices ; but the improper exercife of this tends directly to promote all vice, to obftruct all goodnefs, to bring religion into difcredit, and to ruin, not the greateft temporal interefts of mankind, but their eternal falvation. Self-love, benevolence, confcience, every principle of human nature that can have any influence on conduct, muft urge a clergyman, with their greateft force, to avoid all negligence and impropriety in the functions of his office. A crime attended with fo mifchievous confequences, and committed in oppofition to fo ftrong obligations, muft imply heinous guilt, and infer a dreadful punifhment. The fcripture warns us of its demerit and its punifhment. God declares to Ezekiel, that if he neglected to warn the wicked " man " from his way," when God commanded him to give warning, " the fame wicked man fhould die in " his iniquity, but his blood would God require at " his

_____

[o] Leechman, Syn. Serm.

"his hand[p];" and that "the ſhepherds who fed "not the flock," but by their neglect ſuffered them to be ſcattered and loſt, he would "require "his flock at their hand[q]." The firſt of theſe declarations has a peculiar reſpect to the prophet's immediate commiſſion from God to reprove particular perſons, for their ſins, in his name; but certainly implies, that teachers who have a general commiſſion to warn men of all ſin, are really chargeable with their guilt, if they neglect to warn them when they are bound to warn them. For this is expreſſed in the ſecond, which is profeſſedly directed to the ordinary religious inſtructors of the Iſraelites[r]. In the New Teſtament it is threatened, that the unfaithful and unwiſe ſteward, who neglects or abuſes his truſt, ſhall be "cut in ſun-"der, and have his portion with the unbe-"lievers[s]:" they who preach the goſpel are "charged before God, and the Lord Jeſus Chriſt, "who ſhall judge the quick and the dead at his "appearing[t]," to the greateſt diligence in the ſeveral parts of their duty; and it is plainly intimated, that in order to their being "pure from "the blood of all men," they muſt be able to "take them to record, that they ceaſed not to "warn every man, that they kept back nothing "that

[p] Ezek. iii. 18. xxxiii. 8. [q] Chap. xxxiv. 2—10.

[r] Stillingfleet, Eccl. Caſes, vol. i. p. 109, &c. Burnet, Paſt. Care, c. 2.

[s] Luke, xii. 46. [t] 2 Tim. iv. 1, 2.

" that was profitable unto them, but have fhowed
" them, and taught them publicly, and from houfe
" to houfe, that they have not fhunned to declare
" unto them all the counfel of God[u]," and that
they have declared it in the beft manner that their
utmoft care could enable them to do it[v].

On the other hand, to execute an office of fo
great importance with fidelity and diligence, to
promote the improvement and perfection of the
nobleft creature in this lower world, to endeavour
to fave the fouls of men by giving them leffons of
knowlege and virtue, to co-operate with God in
fpreading happinefs ; is praife-worthy and glorious,
and will be crowned with a reward proportioned
to the dignity and difficulty of the work. They
who labour carefully in it " fhall at leaft deliver
" their own fouls, though the wicked to whom
" they give warning, turn not from his wicked-
" nefs, but die in his iniquity[w]." They fhall,
we are affured, " fave their own fouls[x] ;" and
" when the chief fhepherd fhall appear, they fhall
" receive a crown of glory that fadeth not away[y]."
Probably too, they fhall fave many of thofe that
" hear them[z]," and fhall thence, both by the
joyful reflections of their own minds, and by the
remuneration of the God whom they ferved,

derive

---

[u] Acts xx. 19, 26, 27, 31. [v] Burnet, Paft. Care, c. 3.
[w] Ezek. iii. 19. xxxiii. 9. [x] 1 Tim. iv. 16.
[y] 1 Pet. v. 4. [z] 1 Tim. iv. 16.

derive a very great acceffion to their happinefs : for " they that turn many to righteoufnefs, fhall fhine " as the brighnefs of the firmament, and as the " ftars for ever and ever ²."

Thus all that application, diligence, and care, which the difficulty of the paftoral office requires, and therefore renders incumbent on thofe who occupy it, is farther enforced upon them by the moft interefting motives, by alarming apprehen-fions of dreadful punifhment in cafe of failure, and encouraging profpects of a great reward in cafe of fincere and faithful exertion. A conftant refpect to thefe muft be maintained ; and if it be, will pre-vent their ever finking under the labours of their calling. It fhould likewife be fteadily maintained by you, through the whole courfe of your prepa-ration for that calling ; for I doubt not that every faulty negligence in your preparation expofes you to fome degree of the fame danger, and that every confcientious exertion in your preparation will entitle you to fome degree of the fame reward ; even though you fhould never have an opportunity of actually exercifing it.

ª Dan. xii. 3. Leechman, Syn. Serm.

3

Of the true Spirit of the Pastoral Office.

WE have considered separately, the dignity and the difficulty of the pastoral office, and pointed out the sentiments which arise from, and are suitable to each. But it is necessary that we accustom ourselves always to view them in conjunction. If we look for no difficulty, the meeting with the smallest will disconcert and dishearten us: and we will not be at much pains to conquer great difficulties, if we do not think it of some importance to conquer them. By being viewed in conjunction, they will suggest and imprefs upon us some sentiments of very great moment, additional to those which we have hitherto mentioned. All that I mean by this may be expressed in this single article, that they will infuse into us the genuine spirit of our profession. This spirit is the immediate result of a high sense of the importance of the pastoral office in its full extent, as including both excellence and difficulty; rather, perhaps, it is that sense raised to perfection, and exerting itself with vigour in all its proper energies.

Every profession has its proper spirit. All eminent artists have been fired with the spirit of their art, and could not have become eminent without it. You too must be possessed, deeply possessed,
with

with the fpirit of your profeffion; otherwife you can never be eminent in it, nor even execute its functions tolerably. The fpirit of any profeffion is, an eager and inextinguifhable defire to fucceed in it, and a certain ardour of foul, a boldnefs and enthufiafm in the exercifes of it. The fpirit of your profeffion is, a love to its duties, a zeal to perform them in the beft manner, a warm ambition to accomplifh its end: it is the active operation of love to God, to Chrift, to the fouls of men, to truth, to goodnefs, to religion, raifed to an exalted pitch, and directed to the one point of animating you, firft in qualifying yourfelves for the facred office, and next in devoting yourfelves to the performance of the whole bufinefs belonging to it.

Nothing of the leaft confideration can be executed well by a perfon who does not enter into the fpirit of it. If you be deftitute of the fpirit of your profeffion, you will be languid in every thing relating to it. While you exert yourfelves as often as you are engaged in a favourite ftudy, in amufement, or in bufinefs, all exertion will forfake you as foon as you turn to your proper occupations. It will be a force upon you to turn to them. You will be anxious to run over them as foon and as eafily as poffible. You will content yourfelves with executing them in the moft fuperficial manner: and even this will be an unpleafant drudgery. You will be glad when you have got through it: but ere long it muft return again; and this thought will

damp

damp your joy. The perpetual recurrence of employments for which you have no relifh, and which are for that reafon irkfome, will eat out the comfort of your lives. You will live out of your element, and therefore with conftant diffatisfaction and uneafinefs to yourfelves. Whenever you muft do what belongs to your profeffion, it will be with reluctance, and with regret, for being obliged to interrupt fomething that is more agreeable to you. With all the pain which it gives you, it will be but ill done. You will exert yourfelves feebly, where the greateft vigour is abfolutely neceffary; and be cold and unconcerned, where you fhould be fired with ardour and zeal.

On the contrary, your being animated with the fpirit of your profeffion will make you enter with alacrity into whatever belongs to it. It is he only who poffeffes the fpirit of his art, that will ever attempt any thing great and excellent in it; and to fuch attempts he will never want a powerful impulfe. If you have the true fpirit of your art, all the difficulties which lie in the way of your becoming fit to exercife it, and of your exercifing it with fuccefs, will be fo far from difcouraging or dejecting you, that they will embolden and elevate you. It is a remarkable property of human nature, that, when a man is heartily engaged in a defign, and refolved and fit to profecute it, any difficulty or oppofition in the profecution, inftead of finking him into defpondence, raifes his ambition,

excites

excites his courage, draws forth his ftrength, and adds force to all his motions: and the greater the difficulty is, provided it appear not to be abfolutely infurmountable, the more it invigorates and infpirits the foul; the bolder and more eager it renders a perfon to encounter it, and the more ftrenuoufly he will exert himfelf in order to furmount it. As the virtue of the loadftone would have remained unknown, if iron had never been applied to it, fo the powers of the human mind could never have fully fhewn themfelves, if circumftances had not occurred which required the utmoft ftretch of them. Abilities which have accomplifhed wonders, would have lain for ever latent, but for opportunities which called them forth, but for difficulties which a more languid exertion of them could not have furmounted. An aptitude and pronenefs to be in this manner invigorated and exalted by the peculiar difficulties and labours of any profeffion, is always an effential part of the true fpirit of that profeffion. The true fpirit of your profeffion cannot fail to produce it in the higheft degree. To encounter formidable difficulties for a trifling end, would be a romantic folly: but to find difficulty in the purfuit of an end which we juftly reckon glorious, and on which our heart is intent, will only animate us to uncommon activity. To find ourfelves engaged in an enterprife worthy of our utmoft exertion, and which indifpenfably requires it, cannot but give a greatnefs to the foul, raife it to an heroic elevation, and enable us to act with a

degree

degree of force and vigour of which we fhould never have fufpected ourfelves capable, if we had not been thus roufed to employ it. If your temper be harmonifed with your profeffion, if your heart be wholly engaged in it, the fenfe of the greatnefs of your work will kindle your zeal to do it into a flame; I might almoft fay, will quicken it into a living principle, pervading all your miniftrations, rendering you indefatigable in them, and leading you to perform them well.

By being poffeffed of the true fpirit of your profeffion, you will not only be rendered diligent in whatever belongs to it, but you will likewife take pleafure in it. It is in exertion and activity that men find their higheft enjoyment. There is not a more unhappy or irkfome ftate, than to have nothing to do. Even difficulty is neceffary to our enjoyment. When every thing goes on with perfect eafe, when we meet with nothing that requires the exertion of our powers, the mind is not fufficiently engaged or employed, it finks into an uneafy ftate of languor; it needs fomething to awaken it, before it can enjoy itfelf or any thing elfe. Its life and its enjoyment grow with the obftructions which it is called upon to combat. In confequence of this ftructure of our nature, when men are engaged in a profeffion altogether fuitable to their genius and inclination, the more conftantly they are employed in it, the happier they are. The mechanic has his chief fatisfaction in working

in

In his calling however laborious, and could not live without it; and if he have any ingenuity, a work of some difficulty, out of the ordinary round of his operations, raises him to a state of higher satisfaction. The merchant finds his pleasure in a run of business, and could not bear to be idle. The man who is turned for study, wishes to be employed in it, delights in such researches as require thought and reflection, regrets the interruptions which he meets with, and suffers uneasiness in them. In a word, every man who loves his occupation, willingly and cheerfully labours in it, from morning to evening, day after day. If you therefore sufficiently love your profession, and bring yourselves to the temper which suits it, you will find your natural satisfaction in being wholly taken up with what belongs to it, as your real and proper business. The greatest exertion in its duties will be your delight. Far from appearing weary of them when you are performing them, and longing till they be over, you will joy in them even when you are most fatigued. You will prefer them to every other manner of employing yourselves. A long intermission of them would give you pain. When you are called off by them, from amusements the most agreeable, or from studies the most favourite, you will cheerfully embrace the call as giving you an opportunity of applying yourselves to offices still dearer to you. Its greatest toils, by drawing out your hearty efforts to sustain them, will render your satisfaction more sublime.

If

If the genuine spirit of the pastoral office be not fully conceived by the description which I have given of it, you will perhaps complete your idea by attending to the accounts which the apostle Paul, in various parts of his writings, gives of his own exertions, in all which he was actuated by a large portion of that spirit. Exalted and impelled by it, he " hungered, and thirsted, and was naked, " and was buffeted, and laboured, working with " his own hands [b]: suffering all things, left he " should hinder the gospel of Christ; becoming " all things to all men, for the gospel's sake, that " he might by all means save some [c]; enduring all " things for the elects' sake, that they might " obtain salvation [d]." He would very gladly have spent and been " spent for them [e];" for he accounted them his " hope, and joy, and crown " of rejoicing, in the presence of our Lord Jesus " Christ at his coming [f]." He foreknew that " bonds and afflictions awaited him; but none of " those things," says he, " move me; neither count " I my life dear unto myself, so that I might finish " my course with joy, and the ministry which I " have received of the Lord Jesus, to testify the " gospel of the grace of God [g]: yea, if I be " offered upon the sacrifice and service of your " faith, I joy and rejoice with you all [h]."

The

---

[b] 1 Cor. iv. 11, 12.   [c] Chap. ix. 12, 22.   [d] 2 Tim. ii. 10.
[e] 2 Cor. xii. 15.   [f] 1 Theff. ii. 19.   [g] Acts, xx. 23, 24.
[h] Phil. ii. 17.

The spirit of your profession is a sublime, a celestial spirit. It is of great importance to yourselves, that you be deeply tinctured with it; even in respect of the comfort and joy of your present life, it is of very great importance to you. If any be conscious of no spark of this spirit within himself, and be not resolved to cherish it, he ought by all means to relinquish every thought of undertaking an office in which, without it, he can be neither useful nor happy. A minister of religion, who dislikes the business of his calling, who has not even an ardent love to it, must lead a very unpleasant life. He saunters away life in listlessness; he turns to his proper functions with reluctance; he toils through them with distaste; he performs them ill; and is dissatisfied with himself; and from this dissatisfaction, again performs them worse, and is more uneasy in his own feelings and reflections. The consciousness of performing functions so very important, in a wrong or negligent manner, cannot but be galling. Nothing less than the most stupid thoughtlessness, or the most impenetrable obduracy, can prevent its exciting the most uneasy sentiments and the most alarming apprehensions. But if you have the noble spirit of your profession, you will take it for granted from the very beginning, that the duties of your office will give you constant employment; you will dedicate yourselves wholly to them; you will maintain a constant solicitude to perform

perform them in the beft manner ; you will roufe yourfelves to the exertion neceffary for doing fo ; you will have high enjoyment in it ; and the con- fcioufnefs of it will fill you with inward fatisfaction and cheerful hope [1].

---

[1] Burnet, Paft. Care, chap. 7.

A JUST eftimate of the dignity and difficulty of the paftoral office, accompanied by the fentiments and temper naturally refulting from it, cannot fail to produce, in all who have made choice of it, a folicitude to inquire, what are the particular duties belonging to that office, by means of which its difficulties may be combated, and its momentous end attained. The explication of thefe duties will both confirm the general idea which I have exhibited of its importance, and difcover what its importance requires from thofe who occupy it.

In general, it is the duty of a minifter to promote the falvation of Chriftians, by inftructing them in the principles and precepts of Chriftianity, and leading them to the faith and obedience of them. Whatever is conducive to this purpofe, belongs to the bufinefs of a minifter: and it is plainly a purpofe which there cannot be the flighteft probability of anfwering without diligently ufing a variety of means. A minifter bears an immediate relation to the parifh in which he is fixed; to it his labours fhould be particularly and

15   principally

principally devoted; and in this capacity many duties of different kinds are incumbent on him. He likewife bears a relation to the church in general; and from it arife other duties, in fome degree different from thofe which are parochial.   To affift you in underftanding the paftoral duties, I fhall confider them under four heads, to which they may be all reduced :—private duties, refpecting individuals ;—private duties, refpecting leffer focieties ;—public duties, refpecting a whole parifh; —and ecclefiaftical duties, refpecting the church in general.

CHAP. I.

Private Duties respecting Individuals.

IT seems to be an opinion too prevalent, that the only essential duty of a minister is preaching and dispensing the sacraments, and that after performing these, and answering a few occasional calls in his parish, he needs do nothing more. It is not reckoned necessary for him to converse with all his parishioners, or to converse with them in another manner than any other person would do. The method of education for the ministry, it must be acknowleged, has some tendency to lead men into this mistake ; for it is directed to their preparation for scarcely any other part of the pastoral functions. To fit them for the more private labours in a parish, no means are ordinarily used. Yet a very little reflection will convince you, that there are many private duties essential to the pastoral office. Merely to appear in public at certain stated times, to deliver a set discourse, to put up prayers, and to preside in the ritual parts of religion, cannot possibly either be adequate to the difficulties of that office, and the importance of its end, or come up to the lowest sense of many of the expressions which the scripture uses in describing it. He who does no more than this, cannot

H be

be faid to " take heed to the flock over which he is
" overfeer [k]," fcarcely at all to " take the over-
" fight of it [l]." He cannot be faid to " watch in
" all things [m]," attentive in obferving every thing
that can obftruct the improvement and falvation of
his people, and in readinefs to remove it before its
ill effects have come to any confiderable height. He
cannot be faid to " watch for their fouls as one
" that muft give account [n]." He cannot be faid
to " be inftant in feafon and out of feafon [o];"
that is, uninterruptedly and at all times, feizing
every favourable opportunity of doing fome good,
and even attempting to improve fuch occafions as
feem to be lefs promifing. Yet all thefe are terms
employed by the infpired writers in defcribing the
office and duties of a paftor.

His public duties are doubtlefs of very great
importance and utility: but his private duties are
of no lefs, perhaps of greater. Many of the
people are fo ignorant, and have fo little leifure
and fo few advantages for acquiring knowlege, that
it is almoft only by private and occafional converfation with them, or inftructions to them, that they
can be prepared for underftanding fermons, or
deriving benefit from them : and it is by the fame
means that they can be directed to make a particular

---

[k] Acts, xx. 28.   [l] 1 Pet. v. 2.   [m] 2 Tim. iv. 5.
[n] Heb. xiii. 17.   [o] 2 Tim. iv. 2.

cular improvement of the general inftructions which are given in public. Nothing, therefore, can contribute more to the fuccefs of your public miniftrations, than private addreffes, prudently and familiarly pointed to the fame end. It is obvious that the teachers of fome fects acquire and maintain a furprifing influence over their adherents, by a frequent religious intercourfe with them in private. It is perhaps the greater on account of the fuperftition or the enthufiafm which is blended with their intercourfe. But certainly a rational and fober religious intercourfe, cultivated, with equal affiduity, by a minifter with his people, would give him an influence with them, if not fo abfolute, yet very confiderable, and much more useful. The better he is known to them, the greater influence he will have upon them; and the more perfectly he knows them, the more he will be qualified for employing it to good purpofes.

The private duties of the paftoral office are likewife more difficult than the public. In order to render them effectual, he muft be able to difcern the different capacities and tempers of the perfons with whom he converfes, to diftinguifh the moft fuccefsful manner of applying to each; and muft acquire a readinefs in adapting himfelf to particular emergencies, which occur fuddenly, and which give little time for recollection, and none for preparation. In preaching, great affiftance may be had both from the rules of compofition, and

H 2

from

from models of fermons : but in his private duties, a minister can have much lefs affistance. He is almost entirely left to learn the proper manner of performing them, from his own reflection and prudence ; and to correct the mistakes into which he has fallen at first, by flow degrees, from his own growing experience [p].

The private duties of the pastoral office will therefore deferve your most careful study. Such of them as most strictly regard individuals, I shall give you fome affistance in studying, by considering them under the following heads :—Example ;—Instruction ;—Exhortation ;—Counselling ;—Vifiting the afflicted ;—Reproving ;—Convincing ;— Reconciling differences ;—and Care of the poor.

SECT. I.

Of Example.

I BEGIN with a duty in fome refpects unlike to all others belonging to the pastoral office, and fingular in its kind, but of the greatest importance ; and for both thefe reafons, fit to introduce the catalogue ; good example. The fcripture expressly enjoins this as one of the duties of the office.

[p] Burnet, Past. Care, c. 8. Secker, Charge 1. Oxf. Charge 2, Cant. Wilfon, vol. i. p. 218.

office. Paul commands Timothy to be "an example to the believers, in word, in conversation, in charity, in ſpirit, in faith, in purity[q];" and Titus, to "ſhow himſelf in all things a pattern of good works[r];" and Peter requires, as indiſpenſably incumbent on all elders, to be "enſamples to the flock[s]." It cannot require many words to evince, that, though all Chriſtians are under a real obligation to give a good example, yet miniſters are under peculiar obligations to it, as ſpecially their duty.

They are under peculiar obligations to it, becauſe their office gives them peculiar advantages for becoming exemplarily good. A great part of the vices of other men ariſes from the temptations to which they are expoſed in the courſe of their ordinary buſineſs. Each of them has a temporal vocation, the direct end of which does not coincide with that of their ſpiritual calling, and which ſometimes therefore leads them off from the duties of it. But miniſters have no temporal vocation; their particular as well as their eneral calling is of a ſpiritual nature. Their occupation is to teach religion, to enforce a lively ſenſe of it, to inculcate the practice of all virtue. Every attempt of this kind is an act of virtue, which tends directly to their

[q] 1 Tim. iv. 12. [r] Tit. ii. 7. [s] 1 Pet. v. 3.

their own improvement. They cannot go about
their functions, without having religious and moral
confiderations, precepts, motives, fentiments, examples, or rules of virtue, often prefented to their
thoughts, and impreffed upon them, fometimes
with the moft interefting and affecting circumftances. Having fo many and great advantages
arifing from the very nature of their profeffion,
they are doubtlefs, in the fight of God, under a
ftrict obligation to exemplary goodnefs[t].

It is the very end and defign of their office to
recommend goodnefs to the love and practice of
men. A fhining example of all real goodnefs is
the moft effectual means of reaching this end. It
is needlefs to enlarge here upon its power: its
influence, both in directing and in exciting, is univerfally acknowleged. Minifters are therefore no
lefs indifpenfably obliged to give a good example,
than to aim at the defign of their calling[u].

Such example is, further, abfolutely neceffary
for rendering all the other means that can be ufed,
effectual for anfwering their purpofe. Without
being himfelf virtuous, a minifter cannot ufe any
of thefe means with fpirit. If he be irreligious or
vicious, he cannot heartily or even fincerely oppofe
irreligion and vice: he can fcarcely have the
effrontery

---

[t] Gerard, vol. ii. Serm. 2. Burnet, Paft. Care, c. 8,
[u] Campbell's Syn. Serm.

effrontery to attempt it. If he could put on this effrontery, and become even fo much a mafter of hypocrify as to feem to be in earneft, it would have no effect. If his private conduct be not un-blameable, his doctrine cannot be regarded. If the people fee him immerfed in the world all the week, he can fcarcely expect to perfuade them to renounce the love of it, by all that he can fay on the Lord's day. Warnings againft fin, or reproofs of other men's faults, come with a very ill grace, and can have very little weight, from the perfon whom his hearers know to be himfelf addicted to the fame or to any other vice. They will forwardly conclude, that he himfelf believes not what he fays, becaufe his life is nowife fuitable to it. They will hear him without attention, with indiffer-ence, with prejudice, and defpife all his exhort-ations as mere form, as unfelt declamation. The vicious will take encouragement from his practice, in every thing that is faulty in their own. The beft men will hear him with diftafte and even with horror, condemning himfelf in what they know that he allows and does. But when a minifter is himfelf uniformly pious and virtuous, he will be able to deliver whatever regards the faith or prac-tice of men with force and energy. It proceeds from his own heart; and it will be evident that his heart is in it. He will deliver it with boldnefs and freedom, unreftrained by any apprehenfion that the hearers may retort upon him, " Thou which " teacheft another, teacheft thou not thyfelf?"

When

When in his life he gives an example of all the
chriftian virtues which he recommends, it will add
weight to all his exhortations to them. Senfible
from their effects on his own conduct, that he
firmly believes the truths of religion, men will
liften to his reprefentations of them with attention,
with docility, and with an opinion of their importance. From his lively faith in divine truth, they
will catch, by fympathy, a like faith in it; from his
vigorous perception of it, a like perception; and
from his love of virtue, fome degree of affection
to it. Convinced that he is fincere in all he fays,
and that he earneftly defires their good, they will
receive it with a favourable ear, and be prepared
to allow his arguments, his directions, his admonitions, their full influence upon them [v].

Bad example in a minifter not only renders his
own inftructions ineffectual, but tends likewife to
weaken the force of all religion. Concluding naturally enough from his conduct, that he does not
truly believe religion, and prone to juftify themfelves in their vices, the irreligious will allow themfelves to argue, that he whofe bufinefs it is to examine and to teach it, could not fail to be convinced
of its truth and to act accordingly, if it were really
true and practicable: and the weak and thoughtlefs
will fuffer themfelves to be affected by this fort of
                                    arguing;

---

[v] Burnet, Paft. Care. Stillingfleet, Eccl. Cafes, p. 65.
Secker, Ch. 1. Oxf. Ch. 2. Cant.

arguing; and ·contract, if not a difbelief of religion, at leaft a total indifference and inattention to
it, almoft equally fatal to their fouls. On the
contrary, when a minifter exercifes exemplary
virtue, his conduct cannot but, by the fame way
of thinking, appear to the generality a ftrong confirmation of the truth and importance of religion,
Obferving that fuch as have had beft accefs and
been at greateft pains to examine it, inftead of difcovering any fallacy in its evidences, believe it fo
firmly as to yield themfelves up wholly to its influence, they are more fettled in their conviction that
it is perfectly well founded, and ought to regulate
their conduct. Perceiving what effects it actually
produces in thefe inftances, they are fatisfied that
it ought to produce them, and that it is their own
fault if it produce them not in themfelves, and
become better difpofed to comply with its obligations. Becaufe a good example in minifters thus
coincides perfectly in its tendency with the very
purpofe of their office, it is plainly and indifpenfably
their duty to teach by example.

This duty implies, at the very loweft, careful
abftinence, and entire freedom from all real and
acknowleged vice. Without this a minifter would
give an ill example. Some vices are fo pofitive in
their nature, and fhew themfelves in fuch obvious or
determinate acts, that they cannot fail to be obferved by men, as intemperance, lewdnefs, lying,
injuftice, fwearing, expreffions of impiety. Thefe
will

will always appear fcandalous in a minifter, and cannot but be generally taken notice of. It is not enough that he does not live in thefe vices; it is his duty to keep at a great diftance from all appear-ance of them. If he be not even noted for tem-perance, moderation, truth, juftice, and decency, his behaviour, inftead of being exemplary, will be offenfive; inftead of improving, corruptive. Some omiffions of duty likewife are fo palpable, that the obfervation of them in a minifter muft give great fcandal, and tend to weaken men's fenfe of the general obligations of religion; as the omiffion of acts of devotion, or performing them with manifeft reluctance and indifpofition when occafion plainly requires them. A minifter who allows himfelf in them muft do hurt by his example; his character will be odious, and all his labours ufelefs. Other vices, the indications of which are more indefinite and equivocal, or which may, by fome artful colouring, be paffed on the undifcerning for virtues, will not be fo generally obferved, but whenever they are detected, will be as much detefted, and will as much enervate the influence of his miniftry, who is found to be addicted to them [w].

But we muft not ftop here: we muft remark farther, that in order to render his conduct exem-plary, a minifter muft abftain from or be very

cautious

---

[w] Burnet, Paft. Care. Secker, Ch. 1. Oxf. Ch. 2. Cant. Campbell's Syn. Serm. Gerard, vol. ii. Serm. 2.

cautious in ufing many things which are, confidered simply in themfelves, in a great meafure, indifferent. Of this kind are fuch overflowings of good humour as approach very near to levity. Exceffive mirth will feem to indicate that the important views and affecting fentiments which his functions tend to bring frequently into his mind, and to render habitual to him, have taken little hold of him, and are forgotten and difregarded by him. Cheerful he ought to be; but his cheerfulnefs fhould be confiftent with ferioufnefs, recollection, and felf-poffeffion. Of the fame kind are fuch amufements and public diverfions as, though perhaps innocent, are, from an opinion of their indicating levity and diffipation, from a mifconception of them as having fome immoral tendency, or fuppofe from mere prejudice, generally pronounced to be unbecoming the character of a clergyman. From his allowing himfelf in fuch gaieties, men will confider him as mif-fpending the time which his profeffion calls upon him to apply to much better purpofes; they will fufpect him to be tainted with an immoderate love of pleafure; and feeing him go confiderable lengths in gratifying it, they will think themfelves autho-rifed to go greater lengths, till they be loft in thoughtleffnefs, and divefted of all attention to their moft valuable interefts both in this world and in the next. With refpect to all things of this kind, it is by no means a fufficient excufe for a clergyman's indulging himfelf in them, that it is only an example of real virtue that he is obliged

to

to give, and that there is no virtue in abftinence from things indifferent; or that, being convinced of their innocence, he is at liberty to act according to his own conviction, rather than according to the groundlefs notions of other men. For no man lives merely to himfelf: every man is obliged to care, not only for his own things, but alfo in fome degree for the things of others; and ought in every part of his conduct to have fome thought of how it will affect them: and a minifter has a pecu-liar connection with mankind, which demands from him great confideration of the influence which every part of his conduct may reafonably be expected to have upon their minds. It is cer-tain that levity, diffipation, and the love of plea-fure, are unbecoming the character of a minifter: it is equally certain that very many will look on his indulging himfelf in the things which have been mentioned, as an unqueftionable mark of thefe faulty difpofitions; and therefore cannot fail to be difgufted with the indulgence, as giving an example of real vice. When he knows this, he cannot be innocent in taking it; he fails in giving a pattern in a very eafy and neceffary inftance of felf-denial, which is a real virtue. I will venture to fay far-ther, that indulgences of this kind, though not implying any faulty levity in others, really proceed, in a clergyman, from a levity that is blameable, and a fondnefs for pleafure which is criminal; and that, if he honeftly examine his own heart, he will find thefe to be the actual principles of his conduct.

For

For no other principle could make the gratification arifing from thefe to appear of fuch value in his eyes, that for the fake of it he will offend multi-tudes, and very much leffen his own ufefulnefs. Accordingly, it will be found that thofe clergymen who betray the ftrongeft inclination to difregard the common notions of decency in articles of this kind, are not generally, if ever, the moft blamelefs in other parts of their behaviour, the moft eminent for piety and virtue, the moft diligent in the duties of their office, or the more zealous for its end; but that on the contrary they fhew in other matters fome fault either of the heart or of the head. It is fometimes pled, that a minifter's abftinence from fuch innocent and indifferent things will lead the weak to think that he himfelf condemns them, and will fofter their fuperftition, confirm them in their narrow prejudices, and encourage their cenforious humour. But there is no folidity in the plea. For, in the firft place, to defpife their weaknefs, and violently to combat their prejudices, is not a probable way of curing them : it tends more to confirm them, than even compliance with them ; efpecially if he who acts in contempt or defiance of them in fuch particulars, feem likewife exception-able in other refpects. Befides, a minifter may abftain from what would offend, and yet let the people know that he does fo only from a tendernefs to their weaknefs, and that he himfelf is fully con-vinced of the lawfulnefs of the things from which he abftains. When it is plain that fuch a decla-

ration

ration is not neceffary for a vindication of himfelf,
it will be the better received, and the fitteft for
removing their groundlefs prejudices.   It is certain
that amufements which have at one time been reckoned unreputable in a clergyman, have by a
general change of manners ceafed to be thought fo
at another.   But fuch a change of manners muft
be left to come on gradually and of its own accord;
it cannot be forced in an inftant even by the authority of laws; the man who attempts it by the
obftinacy of his private practice, is fure to hurt
himfelf.   In fuch inftances refpecting the clergy,
they who are readieft to attempt it, the younger
and thofe of the leaft eftablifhed and perhaps not
the moft unexceptionable reputation, are the fureft
to hurt themfelves by it, and the moft unlikely to
produce any favourable alteration in the fentiments
of mankind.   But if the attempt fhould fucceed,
what mighty advantage is gained?   A little more
liberty to himfelf in fuch trifles as no wife man
can reckon of the leaft importance to his happinefs;
and no good paftor can think worth his running
the rifk of lofing, for their fake, the fmalleft
grain of his ufefulnefs.   Perhaps too fome encouragement will be given to others, in that attachment to amufement, frivolity, or fhew, which is
already too prevalent, and of the moft pernicious
influence : a confequence to which every fentiment
and view becoming a clergyman, fhould conftrain him
from contributing.   There is no doubt confiderable
delicacy, in many cafes, in determining how a man
                                                    had

had beft act, with refpect to giving offence by things indifferent or of little moment. The beft general rule that can be laid down is, that a minifter ought never to do or even feem to approve any thing that is unlawful, in order to avoid difpleafing others; but that he ought willingly to abftain from many things which are lawful or which would be agreeable to him, rather than give offence to any. Such decency is truly neceffary for his teaching and edifying by example.

But it is not enough that he give no bad example: it is likewife neceffary that he be a pattern of good works to the people. In order to this it is firft of all neceffary that he really be a good man. Infincere appearances of goodnefs, however artfully affected, will always be unnatural. However ftudioufly they be kept up, the mafk will fall off at fome time or another; the detected hypocrite will be defpifed or detefted by all men: and though he fhould never be detected by men, he is abominable in the fight of God. A temper of Chriftian virtue confifts of many parts; a minifter muft cultivate them all: were it poffible that he could poffefs fome virtues without the reft, they could neither atone for his defects in the judgment of God, nor prevent fcandal from them in the judgment of the world. Virtue really prevailing in the heart will naturally lead to good practice; and that it may be exemplary, the proper exertions of it muft not be fuppreffed or diffembled. Vir-

tuous,

tuous difpofitions which are fincere, often fail of
recommending themfelves to imitation, by being
imperfectly exerted. It is only by being exerted
that they can be perceived by others; and till they
perceive them, they cannot copy after them. It
is of the moft diligent practice of virtue and of the
ftricteft regard to religion, that minifters are bound
to be patterns. But to neglect or to difguife the
exercife of any virtue, when there is a proper opportunity for it, is to neglect the virtue in that
inftance, and often implies even a pofitive tranf-
greffion of the obligations which it lays them
under. They ought, in every fituation, boldly to
avow and profecute the conduct which religion
requires from them., At the fame time, they muft
carefully avoid oftentation in the exertion of their
virtues. This could not fail to difguft, and would
very probably raife a fufpicion of hypocrify. They
muft leave their light to fhine before men by its
own fplendour, without either ftudying to obfcure
it, or endeavouring to render it glaring. It is by
poffeffing virtue in fincerity and in ftrength, that
they will beft preferve this happy medium. To
render their virtue exemplary, it is likewife neceffary that their manner of practifing it be fuch as
will render it attractive. For this purpofe they
muft keep at a diftance from forbidding aufterity,
and ftudy to fhew its native lovelinefs by accompanying it with cheerfulnefs, courtefy, and condefcenfion. They muft preferve the feveral virtues
from thofe exceffes or adulterations which would
　　　　　　　　　　　　　　　　　fully

fully their beauty. Their piety muſt be alike
remote from ſuperſtition and from enthuſiaſm;
their integrity, though inflexible, muſt be free
from ſeverity; their humility, from meanneſs;
their gravity, from moroſeneſs; their cheerfulneſs,
from levity; their zeal, from bitterneſs. By acting
in this manner, miniſters will exhibit an inſinu-
ating example of every good quality that can
adorn the ſoul, and will in ſome meaſure gain both
the love and the imitation of their people.

SECT. II.

Of Private Inſtruction.

BECAUSE knowlege is the only foundation of
religious and virtuous practice, and muſt be conveyed to men before they can be excited to a
becoming conduct, it is the primary duty of the
paſtoral office to inſtruct men in the doctrines and
duties of religion. Paſtors are therefore called
" teachers[x];" and their whole office is often
deſcribed by " teaching." Chriſt's charge to his
diſciples, after his reſurrection, was, " Teach all
" nations; teach them to obſerve all things what-
" ſoever I have commanded you[y]." In conſequence of this charge, his apoſtles " went forth,
" and

---

[x] Eph. iv. 11.   [y] Mat. xxviii. 19, 20.

" and preached every where[z]," and " ceafed not
", to teach and preach Jefus Chrift[a]." The fame
practice they exprefsly require from all minifters of
the gofpel. " A bifhop," fays Paul, " muft be
" apt to teach[b] :". " thefe things command. and
" teach[c] :" " thefe things teach. and exhort[d]."
By the practice of the apoftles themfelves, whom we
fhould regard as our examples, it is clearly afcertained, that thefe and the many, fimilar precepts
require not only public preaching, but alfo private
inftruction. The apoftles at Jerufalem, not only
" daily in the temple," but likewife " in every
" houfe, ceafed not to teach[e] :" and Paul appeals
to the Ephefians, that, during the three years he
had lived among them, not only publicly, but alfo
" from houfe to houfe, he had taught them, and
" fhewed them, and kept back nothing that was
" profitable, and had not ceafed to warn every
" man night and day with tears[f]."

As thefe obfervations evidently fhew that private
inftruction is a duty of the paftoral office, fo the
flighteft attention to its nature and its confequences
is fufficient to prove that it is a very important duty.
Whoever makes the trial will foon difcover that
there is, in the bulk of every parifh, ignorance and
inattention enough to render it neceffary. Public
· difcourfes

---

[z] Mark, xvi. 20.   [a] Acts, v. 42.   [b] 1 Tim. iii. 2.
[f] 1 Tim. iv. 11.   [d] 1 Tim. vi. 2.   [e] Acts, v. 42.
[f] Acts, xx. 20. 31.

difcourfes delivered in a promifcuous audience are
almoft unavoidably too uniform and general to fuit
the various capacities and fituations of all the
hearers. In difcourfes ftudied by a man of liberal
education, there can fcarcely fail to be a degree
of compofition, requifite likewife, it may be,
for preventing difguft in the more knowing,
which muft render a great part of every fermon
of little ufe to the ignorant, who bear no inçon-
fiderable proportion in all ordinary congregations. Amends can be made only by a minifter's
entering frequently into private converfation,
on religious fubjects, with fome or other of his
people.

He may in fome meafure, with little trouble to
himfelf, contribute to the inftruction of all who
can read, by recommending proper books to them.
Only fuch books as are cheap, and written in the
plaineft manner, can anfwer the purpofe. The
greateft part of thofe that fall under this defcription are very exceptionable, not only being in a
ftyle indecently mean, but abounding in flighty,
improper, or enthufiaftic fentiments. It is to be
regretted that fuch are moft generally current
among the lower ranks, and moft acceptable to
them. It were much to be wifhed that there were
a variety of others at leaft equally plain, intelligible, and familiar, but fober and wholly practical.
No compofitions could be more really or exten-
fively ufeful. Were there, however, the greateft

abundance

abundance of such, it could not supersede the obligation which lies on ministers to give their own private instructions to their people: but the paucity of them must strengthen the obligation.

There is no doctrine or duty of religion, which a minister may not find proper occasions of explaining or enforcing in private, or with individuals of his parish separately. He may give them instruction concerning many things which they know not, and directions for particulars in their conduct, which could scarcely be introduced into a public discourse: he may express and illustrate them in a more familiar manner, and set them in a greater variety of lights, than would be allowable in preaching, 'till he find that the person with whom he converses, comprehends them perfectly: he may descend to minuter instances of behaviour, and to advices concerning more trivial actions, than would be consistent with the dignity of the pulpit. In private teaching, a minister has so great advantage for adapting himself to the various capacities and turns of the different persons to whom he addresses himself, that the lower sort will reap more benefit from half an hour of such conversation prudently conducted, than from the sermons of a whole year[g].

Whatever

---

[g] Wilson, vol. i. p. 215, 218, 279.

Whatever is of greateſt importance in religion, ought to be moſt frequently introduced, and moſt, ſtudiouſly inſiſted on, by a miniſter, in his private inſtructions to his people. For this reaſon, what is practical will claim his chief attention: 'He will ſoon diſcover that, when ſome of the common people affect more knowlege than their neighbours, it is generally of a very falſe and perverted kind. They conſider knowlege as beſt diſplayed in deciding queſtions of curioſity and difficulty: and by reading and venting abſurdities on ſuch points, they ſeem to themſelves and to others of their own rank, to be very learned, and, as they term it, great ſcholars. It is not uncommon to meet with perſons in a country pariſh inquiſitive about ſuch queſtions as theſe: At what ſeaſon of the year the world was created? How long the ſtate of innocence continued? Of what ſpecies was the fruit of the forbidden tree? Whether original or actual ſin was firſt? What was the mark ſet upon Cain? &c. And in compariſon with ſuch trifling, uſeleſs, or abſurd queſtions, they deſpiſe the plain doctrines and duties of religion, as things ſo eaſy, that acquaintance with them requires no ingenuity, and confers little merit. The prevalence of this diſpoſition renders it neceſſary for a miniſter to take every opportunity, in private as well as in public, to draw them off from frivolous and unprofitable ſubtleties and ſpeculations, and to inculcate on them, that the only valuable knowlege is that which tends to influence the practice. The ſort of

people

people of whom we are fpeaking, are always conceited, and will be abundantly forward to obtrude
their vain queftions on their minifter. Some of
thefe are perfectly unintelligible, and more of them
wholly indeterminable. In this cafe, the beft way
is, to interrogate thofe who pretend to be acquainted with them, to lead them on by pofing
them, till they involve themfelves in contradiction
and nonfenfe, that thus they may be brought to
convince themfelves of their abfurdity. When the
queftions about which they dote are intelligible,
and perhaps curious in themfelves, but, like all
abftrufe difquifitions, have no connection with
practice, it will be prudent for a minifter, not altogether to decline anfwering them; for the con-
ceitednefs of the propofers would impute this to his
ignorance. Let him enter upon the fubject; fuggeft the arguments on both fides, if it be a matter
of uncertainty, or the proofs of it, if it be only
abftrufe. After having thus fhewn them that he
underftands it better than themfelves, he may with
fafety, and probably not without fuccefs, reprefent
fuch inquiries as of no moment, and inculcate
upon them, that true knowlege is only what tends
to make men better, and that religion confifts in
the goodnefs which naturally proceeds from fuch
knowlege, not in the mere knowlege feparated
from that effect. In both thefe cafes, fuch conduct is conformable to that of Chrift, the great
pattern of Chriftian minifters. Sometimes he puz-
zled thofe who attacked him, by putting appofite
queftions,

queſtions, or making unanſwerable remarks. "Whether is it eaſier to ſay, Thy ſins be forgiven "thee? or to ſay, Ariſe and walk[h]?" "If "Satan caſt out Satan, how ſhall then his king- "dom ſtand? And if I by Beelzebub caſt out "devils, by whom do your children caſt them "out[i]?" "He that is without ſin among you, "let him firſt caſt a ſtone at her[k]." "The bap- "tiſm of John, whence was it? from Heaven, or "of men[l]?" "Render unto Ceſar the things "which are Ceſar's, and unto God the things "that are God's[m]." "If David call him Lord, "how is he his ſon[n]?" On almoſt all the occa- ſions to which theſe retorts belong, and indeed on every occaſion, and whatever was the ſubject intro- duced, he was careful to turn his diſcourſe to matters of practice. Not content with pointing out the abſurdity of aſcribing his miracles to Beel- zebub, he ſubjoins an alarming warning of their danger, and important maxims and directions for their conduct, particularly as reſpecting their words and converſation[o]. Having confounded them by his queſtion concerning John's baptiſm, he ſubjoined two moſt inſtructive parables, and applied them forcibly to their practice[p]. By the very deciſion which he gave in the queſtion concern-

ing

---

[h] Mat. ix. 5.   [i] Mat. xii. 26, 27.   [k] John, viii. 7.
[l] Mat. xxi. 25.   [m] Mat. xxii. 21.   [n] Mat. xxii. 45.
[o] Mat. xii. 31, &c.   [p] Mat. xxi. 28, &c.

ing the paying of tribute, he inculcated fubmiſſion to civil government. The queſtion concerning the greateſt of the commandments, as diſputed among the rabbis, was frivolous, regarding only the preference of one ceremony to another: when it was captiouſly propoſed to Jeſus, he ſeized the opportunity of fixing their attention on the love of God and of mankind, in preference to all ceremonies[q]. A diſciple aſked him, " Are there few " that be ſaved?" a queſtion often moved by mere curioſity, and that not of the moſt liberal or benevolent kind: inſtead of gratifying curioſity, his anſwer only points out the difficulties of religion, and urges all preſent to that diligence in combating them, without which they themſelves could not be ſaved: " Strive to enter in at the ſtrait gate[r]." When Peter aſked Jeſus concerning John, " And " what ſhall this man do?" he both checked his uſeleſs curioſity, and pointed out his own buſineſs: " What is that to thee? Follow thou me[s]." In like manner, when his diſciples aſked him, " Wilt " thou at this time reſtore the kingdom to Iſrael?" he firſt intimated his diſapprobation of their putting the queſtion; " It is not for you to know the " times or the ſeaſons:" and next made it a handle for giving them very important information, that they ſhould " receive power" by " the Holy " Ghoſt coming upon" them, and for turning

their

---

[q] Mat. xxii. 37.　　[r] Luke, xiii. 24.　　[s] John, xxi. 22.

their attention to their peculiar duty, which was,
to " be witneffes unto him" every where [r]. But
the inftances of Chrift's purfuing this conduct,
are innumerable. His uniform practice fhews that
one of the principal fubjects of private inftruction,
indeed of all inftruction, ought to be, to inculcate
upon men that all true religion is practical; and
that the inftruction fhould always ultimately aim
at practice, and tend to inftill fuch fentiments as
are fit to influence practice.

All private inftructions are in a great meafure
occafional: and it will add to their weight, that
they fpring naturally from the occafion, and that
they be fuitable to it. Chrift has given Chriftian
teachers an example of addrefs, both in feizing
every proper occafion, and in adapting their inftructions to it. The inftances juft now produced
might alone prove this: and there are many other
inftances. From the common occurrences and incidental converfations which he met with, he took
an opportunity of propofing his divine inftructions
to fuch as happened to be prefent. Some perfons
talked " of the Galileans whofe blood Pilate had
" mingled with their facrifices;" it would feem as
a piece of ordinary news: he ufed it as a natural
occafion, both for difcouraging the fpirit of rafh
and prefumptuous judgment, and for afferting the
neceffity

---

[r] Acts, i. 6, &c.

neceffity of repentance and enforcing the exercife
of it[u]. Indeed, almoft all his inftructions were
drawn from the objects that furrounded him, or
the fituations and events which occurred, at the
time. With regard to many of them, this is
evident from the relations of the evangelifts ; with
regard to others, it may be deduced from a comparifon of circumftances ; and it holds fo generally, that fome writers have reckoned attention
to the occafion of his difcourfes, as indicated by
the fubject or the turn of them, fufficient for ad-
jufting, in many cafes, the time and order of them,
and of the actions connected with them[v]. His
divine knowlege qualified him for doing this with
perfect eafe and propriety. Infpiration fitted his
apoftles for copying this manner of teaching ; and
they copied it fo much that, not only fuch of their
difcourfes as are recorded, but their writings alfo,
grow out of particular occafions. To uninfpired
teachers, it cannot fail to be attended with confiderable difficulty ; and they muft be liable to go
fometimes wrong in the execution of it. This
fhould only lead them to employ the greater pains
and ftudy in preparing themfelves for it. It cannot extinguifh their obligation to attempt it. It is
the moft eafy, natural, and ftriking mode of inftruction that can be imagined ; and the only

proper

---

[u] Luke, xiii. 1, &c.
[v] Law's Theory, p. 302—315. Lamy Harmon. paffim.
Cleri a Harm. Jortin's Difcourfes, p. 201, &c.

proper mode of private inftruction. By means of it, every thing is improved into an ufeful moral; it touches the more by its congruity to the prefent fituation and circumftances of the hearer; and it will be more eafily retained and more affectingly recollected, by the commoneft objects and events, as having been originally connected with it, becoming ever after monitors and remembrancers of it[w].

It is not, however, alike eafy to introduce occafional inftructions, to all forts of people. Were a minifter to attempt fuggefting them to moft people of rank and fafhion, on as flender an occafion as would procure them attention from the well-difpofed, and at leaft a hearing from the common people in general, or to purfue them with as much freedom, he would run a great rifk of being defpifed as a perfon totally ignorant of good breeding, ridiculed as a pedant, and perhaps, in exemplification of their boafted politenefs, abufed as impertinent and pragmatical. It is only for the fake of doing good, that religious inftructions fhould be occafionally fuggefted : when it is certain that they can do no good, or moft probable that they will do harm, a minifter can be under no obligation to throw them away. But it is only where the cafe
is

---

[w] Law's Theory, p. 302—315.

is very plain, that he can be excufed from every
effay : opportunities, which feem to be very unfavourable, may, by the prudent improvement of
them, turn out to real advantage. It would be
pernicious, rather than beneficial, to be conftantly
obtruding religious fentiments, grave reflections,
and maxims of morality, on the converfation of
the higher ranks. A minifter fhould be careful
not to attempt it in fuch a way as will prevent
thofe good effects, for the fake of which alone it is
incumbent on him : and in the prefent ftate of the
world, it will require very great prudence and delicacy to manage it fo, that there fhall be a probability of its producing good effects. Serious inftructions fhould be brought in fparingly : feldom,
except when a very natural occafion offers, and in
a manner invites them. They fhould not be expreffed in a fententious and authoritative way,
which carries with it a forbidding air of folemnity
and affectation. They fhould not be infifted on at
large, fo as to turn them into formal or tedious
harangues ; but juft hinted at, and fuggefted with
the appearance of undefigning cafe and good humour. By this means they may be, on fome occafions, introduced to any perfon, not only without giving offence, but even fo as to be agreeable,
and fo as to be recollected afterwards, purfued
perhaps by the perfon himfelf, and applied to their
proper ufe. The more difficult this is, the more
folicitous we fhould be to contrive a proper method

of

of doing it, and the more careful to learn the re-quisite addrefs [x].

There is much lefs difficulty in introducing religious and moral fubjects among the lower ranks. Though they have often no great concern about such fubjects, yet their minds are not debauched with falfe politenefs, nor are they with-held by any capricious ideas of fafhion from propofing or liften-ing to them. They will think it very natural, and very right, for a minifter to pafs from ordinary talk upon common fubjects, to religious obferva-tions. He may make the tranfition with little ceremony; and he can never want occafions of doing fo. Whatever be the converfation into which he happens to enter with any of his parifhioners, he may find a handle for introducing fome inftructive topic, without even feeming to defign it, and of fuggefting remarks which will either improve their knowlege or influence their practice. And if it be once obferved, as it very foon will be, that a minifter is ready to enter into converfation of this kind, the people will willingly give him opportunities of inftructing them, and even afk his affiftance in explaining fomething which they find it difficult to underftand, or directing them in fomething about which they are at a lofs. When any topic is introduced, he may,

without

---

[x] Secker, Ch. 2. Cant.

without giving any offence to the common people, dwell upon it longer, inculcate it more profeffedly, and illuftrate it more formally and fully, than would be proper with thofe of higher rank.   But in what cafes he fhould do fo, and to what degree; and in what cafes he fhould fimply propofe, or only infinuate, inftruction, will depend on many particular circumftances, and muft be left to every man's own prudence.

There are very many religious fubjects which the moft ordinary converfation with his people gives a minifter a natural opportunity of introducing. Since all nature is the work of God, and all its operations are carried on by him as the firft caufe, a mountain or a valley, a river or a lake, a barren or a fertile field, the feafon of the year, the pro- grefs of vegetables, the nature and effects of the weather, and a thoufand other objects the moft common, with the converfation concerning them, into which perfons fall of courfe every day, natu- rally fuggeft to every thoughtful and well-difpofed perfon, fentiments of the divine perfections and providence; and therefore give a minifter the moft natural opportunity of fpeaking to any perfon on thefe important fubjects, and of making fuch re- flections as may give the ignorant jufter concep- tions and farther knowlege of them, render the thoughtlefs more attentive to them, or at any rate excite a livelier and a more practical fenfe of them. By a tranfition no wife forced, he may likewife

take

take occafion, from fuch common objects, for entering on other fubjects of religion, bearing fome
analogy to them, though not fo intimately connected with them.   Many of the fentiments of
Chrift's fermon on the mount, are drawn from the
objects which that fituation put into his view: a
city on a hill; perfons manuring the fields with
falt; the fun fhining on all the fields and gardens,
without diftinction, which fell within his extenfive
profpect; the fowls flying in the air, and the lilies
growing around him: he fpoke of good trees and
corrupt trees, of knowing men by their fruits, of
grapes not growing upon thorns, nor figs on
thiftles.   The gofpels contain many other inftances.

There are religious fubjects fuited to many of
the moft common incidents, and which may therefore be introduced on occafion of them.   Almoft
every thing that can furnifh a piece of news, has
fome connexion with human conduct, or with the
ways of Providence; and may be eafily turned to
infinuations or remarks, concerning prudence or
imprudence, faults or excellences of behaviour, the
caufes or the confequences of them, the feveral
phenomena of God's prefent government, the abufe
or the right improvement of them.   The actions
of men, or accidental and trivial emergences in
company, may be improved to ufeful purpofes.
From feeing fome perfons folicitous for the moft
honourable

honourable places at an entertainment, Chrift made an eafy tranfition to the propriety and advantages of humility; from the hofpitality of the entertainer, to the fuperior excellence of deeds of compaffion; and the feaft leading one of the company to reflect on the value of fpiritual enjoyments, Chrift thence took occafion to warn them of the danger of their excluding themfelves from thefe by rejecting the gofpel [y]. The fituation of any perfon whom a minifter meets with, or who happens to be fpoken of, gives an opportunity for familiar obfervations concerning the duties and the temptations of profperity or adverfity, or of fome peculiarity of circumftances.

A time of ficknefs or of any kind of diftrefs, a feafon or an inftance of mortality, the rife or the fall of a known individual, fuggeft even to the generality fome thoughts of the vanity of the world, the viciffitudes of human affairs, the fhortnefs and uncertainty of life, the approach of death: and thus give a minifter the moft obvious and natural occafions, very frequently recurring, of inftilling into any of his people who happen to fall in his way, fuch fentiments on thefe fubjects as may awaken attention to them, and have the beft influence on practice.

The

---

[y] Luke, xiv. 7, &c.

The birth of a child, or the fight of a family of children, gives a direct occafion of fuggefting obfervations concerning the proper methods of education, the duties of parents, the nature of baptifm, its defign, and the obligations which it lays men under to holinefs.

There are fubjects belonging to religion, and of great importance, which a minifter will not perhaps find either fo frequent or fo direct occafions of fliding infenfibly into, and in which it is, notwithftanding, neceffary fometimes to give inftruction: fuch as, the whole difpenfation of man's redemption, and all the peculiar doctrines of revelation. Thefe, whenever he judges it neceffary, he may very properly introduce without feeking for any occafion, or on a very flender occafion. But even thefe he will find occafions of introducing fo naturally as to take off the appearance of defign, when that appearance might do harm. Such objects or occurrences as would ferve for apt illuftrations of fuch fubjects, may, by a little fkill and addrefs, be fo managed as to furnifh a handle for paffing to them. On little children being brought to him, Chrift very naturally entered on the innocence, humility, and docility, which became his difciples, or prepared men for becoming fuch, and the privileges belonging to thofe who poffefs thefe qualities [z]. From meat and drink, he led the people's

---

[z] Mark, x. 13, &c.

K

people's thoughts to fpiritual nourifhment by means
of his doctrine, and participation in the bleffings of
his kingdom, expreffed in metaphors rifing out of
the occafion[a]. From the wafhing of the body, he
led them to the purification of the heart[b]. . Seeing
his difciples catching fifh, he paffed to the employment of bringing men to his religion, to the inter-
mixture of good and bad men in his church, and
to the final feparation of them at the day of judgment[c]. On obferving the indications of approaching fummer in the trees before him, he intimated
the approach of his kingdom, and the figns of it[d].
On feeing the fields ripe for harveft, he fpeaks of
the fpiritual harveft in which his difciples were to
be employed[e]. From Herod's imprudent expedi-
tion againft the fuperior forces of the king of
Arabia, and his confequent defeat, he takes occafion to fhew the danger of not confidering beforehand the difficulties of religion[f]. On the frequency
of robberies in a particular place and period, he
builds the beautiful and appofite parable of the
benevolent Samaritan[g].

Among religious and moral fubjects, that fhould
be preferred which is moft fuitable to the fituation
of the particular perfon to whom inftructions concerning

---

a John, vi. 47, &c.   b Luke, xi. 38, &c.
c Mat. xiii. 47, &c.   d Luke, xxi. 29, &c.
e Mat. ix. 37, &c.   f Luke, xiv. 31, &c.
g Luke, x. 30, &c.

cerning them are addreffed : and among fubjects
equally fuitable to his fituation, that fhould at any
time be chofen, which there is the moft natural
occafion of introducing. The manner both of
introducing and of inculcating inftructions, fhould
likewife be adapted to the character and cireum-
ftances of the perfon for whofe benefit they are
intended. Some private inftruction a minifter
ought to give to all who are committed to his
care : but to fome he will have accefs, and may
with propriety give it more frequently than to
others. It will be peculiarly ufeful to take every
opportunity of giving it to the young : their modefty will difpofe them to liften to it; and the
pliablenefs of their minds will contribute to its
having a great influence upon them [h].

Private inftruction may be given to perfons at
their work, by the road, or in any fituation. If a
minifter only keep it in his view as a part of his
duty, he may apply to fome perfon or other of his
parifh almoft every day, without any trouble or
inconvenience to himfelf. He may turn it into
little more than amufement. A walk or a ride
may be made the means of holding fome ufeful
converfation with fome of his people. This, he
fhould lay it down as a rule to himfelf not to omit
altogether

---

[h] Secker, Ch. 2. Cant.

altogether for any day, without a good reafon. I
mean not, that a minifter fhould converfe with his
people upon none but religious fubjects : what has
been faid concerning his feizing occafions for introducing them implies, on the contrary, that he
fhould often talk with them on other fubjects ; and
it is by entering freely into them, and purfuing
them, that he will be beft able to give them fuch a
turn as may moft favour the eafy and natural introduction of his inftructions. Neither do I mean,
that he ought at all times to turn his ordinary converfation with them into a religious ftrain, or to
moralize on whatever occurs or happens to be
faid. This would be ftiff and affected ; and it
would be forbidding and difgufting. But between
this extreme and the other extreme of neglecting
all ferious converfation, all application of common
and incidental things to purpofes of piety and
morality, there is certainly a proper mean : and
this mean is, to do fo on every fit occafion, and to
watch for occafions of doing fo where it is neceffary
or likely to prove ufeful.

A perfon may do a great deal, through the
courfe of his education and ftudies, in qualifying
himfelf for this method of private inftruction. In
order to this; he fhould be careful to ftore his mind
with juft and ftriking fentiments on all religious and
moral fubjects ; and to digeft them fo well, as to
be able to recollect them quickly when occafion
calls for them, and to exprefs them with eafe and
perfpicuity.

perfpicuity. He may likewife receive confiderable affiftance from books, even with refpect to the particular inftructions fuitable to common objects and incidents, and the proper manner of taking occafion from thefe to introduce them. There are many excellent books [i] on the works of nature confidered precifely as difplaying the perfections and providence of God; in which there are likewife fome inftances of tranfitions from thefe to other fubjects of religion. Acquaintance with fuch books will furnifh you with a variety of inftructive fentiments adapted to many common occafions, and point out natural methods of applying them when fuch occafions occur. There are alfo [k] books written with a profeffed defign to fpiritualize or to moralize the functions and occurrences of particular occupations, or particular fituations. Moft of thefe are exceptionable in refpect of the nature of the inftructions deduced, which are too often accommodated to the peculiarities of fome one party fyftem, and even that none of the beft; and fuch inftructions you fhould wholly and carefully avoid borrowing. Moft of them likewife are often too fanciful, forcing an application of things to purpofes to which they are not appofite; in this they

[i] Ray's Wifdom of God in the Creation. Derham's Phyfico-theology, and Aftro-theology. Niewentyt's Religious Philofopher. Spectacle de la Nature.

[k] Flavel's Hufbandry and Navigation fpiritualized.

they ought not to be imitated : at the fame time, a remoter relation or a lefs perfect analogy will juftify a tranfition from one fubject to another in the cafe of private converfation, than could render it allowable or prevent its appearing far-fetched in a written compofition. From fuch books, not-withftanding all their faults, much affiftance may, by a judicious and wary felection, be procured. In moft books on religious and moral fubjects, fentiments are frequently illuftrated by images and comparifons drawn from familiar natural objects or from the incidents of common life; and from every inftance of this, one may receive a hint for fome occafional inftruction : he has only to invert the order of the train of thought, to begin with that which furnifhes the image of comparifon, and from it to pafs to the religious fentiment; whatever is an apt illuftration of any fubject, may be im-proved into an occafion of naturally enough intro-ducing that fubject into converfation. You have accefs not only to fuch affiftances in preparing your-felves for giving private inftructions, but likewife to exercifes fit for beginning and forming a habit of fkill in giving them. You may take notice of any thing which falls in your way that would afford a minifter an opportunity for it, or you may fuppofe any fituation, any incident, or any converfation that you pleafe; and you may confider deliberately in what manner, if you fhould really meet with it, you could turn it into a religious channel, or in a familiar and eafy ftrain deduce ufeful inftructions

from

from it.: you may commit the whole to writing juft
as you think it ought to pafs or would naturally
pafs in the circumftances fuppofed : you may make
trials of this fort on a great variety of fubjects,
and in different manners ; fometimes only expreffing the fuppofed fituation, and hinting the
inftruction for which you would take occafion from
it ; fometimes extending the inftruction at greater
length ; and fometimes carrying on the whole
minutely in the way of dialogue. Such exercifes,
however unufual, may be very properly introduced into fchools of Theology, and will be very
ufeful. Each of you may attempt fomething of
this kind ; the choice of the occafion, the fubject,
and the manner of profecution, I leave entirely to
yourfelves, but defire that you may all give fome
fpecimen. It will require attention to, or reflection on, common objects and ordinary incidents ;
and in your firft effays it may require a good deal
of thought and ftudy, and even repeated efforts,
before you fucceed ; but accuracy of compofition
is totally unneceffary, and would rather be improper. You may write down many fuch fpecimens
in private, when you have leifure or inclination for
it, or when you meet with any ftriking occafion ;
and you may revife them afterwards both for cor-
rection or improvement, and for fixing them in
your thoughts. By this means you will foon be in
poffeffion of abundance of materials for private
inftruction on moft of the occafions that can occur
in a parifh ; and you will become gradually accuf-

tomed

tomed to difcern the proper occafions for giving
fuch inftruction, the nature of the inftructions
which will fuit them, and the beft ways of paffing
from the one to the other. You may do more;
you may fometimes have an opportunity of actually
giving inftruction to fuch as are younger or lefs
knowing than yourfelves; and will readily acknowlege themfelves your inferiors; and you may find
the moft natural and favourable opportunities of
giving it explicitly, or at leaft of fuggefting it,
without any rifk of incurring an imputation of
pedantry, affectation, or affuming. What it
is the duty of a minifter frequently to feek out
occafions of doing, it cannot be improper that
a candidate for the miniftry fhould with modefty
and delicacy attempt doing when the occafion
invites it.

Thus qualified, in the firft place, for giving private and occafional inftructions; and, next, diligent in giving them in the manner, at leaft on the
principles, which I have pointed out; a minifter
fhall be always doing fomething for promoting the
happinefs of mankind, by diffufing impreffions of
truth and goodnefs; and may conclude every day
with the pleafing reflection, that he has not loft it.
This employment will likewife have the ftrongeft
tendency to his own improvement in all goodnefs:
for by means of it, thofe moral and religious fentiments, maxims, motives, and confiderations, an
habitual fenfe of which is the fpring whence all
                                        virtuous

virtuous affections and actions flow, will be rendered familiar to him, will be always in readiness to come into his thoughts, to make a strong impreſſion on his heart, and to exert their influence in regulating his whole conduct.

SECT. III.

Of Private Exhortation.

EXHORTATION is often joined, in ſcripture, with teaching or inſtruction ; and often ſeparately recommended as a duty incumbent upon paſtors. " Give attendance to exhortation [l]. Exhort with " all long-ſuffering [m]. Theſe things ſpeak and " exhort [n]." There is the ſame evidence from ſcripture that it ſhould be performed privately as well as publicly ; and the ſame reaſons of neceſſity and of utility hold good for the performance of it.

To exhort men, is to excite them to the practice of their ſeveral duties. Teaching and exhortation, though different in idea, will run infenſibly into each other ; and it will be impoſſible to perform the one aright, without intermixing the other. As all the principles of true religion are of a practical nature,

---

[l] 1 Tim. iv. 13.　　[m] 2 Tim. iv. 2.　　[n] Tit. ii. 15.

nature, they cannot be properly illustrated without pointing out their influence on practice; and men cannot be urged to perform their duties, but by insisting on those principles of religion which are the proper motives to the performance of them. On this account, all the general observations which have been made, concerning the manner of intro-ducing and conducting private instruction, are equally applicable to private exhortation, and need not be repeated. But still these two duties are in some respects different, and therefore some peculiar observations may be made concerning this latter. A minister should endeavour almost every day to meet with some or other of his people, and take occasion to admonish and exhort them, to stir them up to the practice of some duty, to give them some plain directions for their conduct.

In order to perform this duty properly, it is first of all necessary that a minister discover the parti-cular situation and character of the person to whom he addresses himself, and that he adapt his admo-nitions carefully to them: for the same sort of exhortations does not suit all; and that may be useless or hurtful to one, which is profitable to another. As no two men are absolutely undistin-guishable in their faces, though every face be com-posed of the same features; so, though the powers of human nature, which are the ingredients in character, be possessed in common by all men, yet by means of the different degrees in which they are poſſeſſed; of the different form which they aſſume, and of the different ways in which they are combined, they produce ſuch an infinite variety of characters, that no two are perfectly alike. This renders it difficult to become acquainted with human characters, and requires the deepeſt inſight into human nature. But without this it is impoſſible to apply to men with propriety, or ſucceſs. One kind of vegetables requires one ſort of culture, and another a ſort totally different. One kind of food ſuits the conſtitution of one animal, but not that of another. What is wholeſome to a man of one temperament, would be almoſt poiſonous to a perſon of an oppoſite habit. In like manner, that may be a proper direction to one, which is entirely uſeleſs to another; and that may be a prevailing motive to one, which would have no weight with another. To pay a due regard to this, and to be aſſiduous in giving each perſon admonitions and directions peculiarly ſuited to himſelf, is to come up to the ſcripture characters of a paſtor. It is to be " a faithful and wiſe ſteward, ruling " over God's houſehold, and giving them their " portion of meat in due ſeaſon°." It is to be " a workman that needeth not to be aſhamed, " rightly dividing the word of truth ᵖ."

It is impoſſible, in diſcourſes of this kind, to point out all the variety of characters and ſituations

that

---

that you will meet with in a parifh, or to explain the proper method of applying to each. That I may not however leave you quite at a lofs, but at leaft give you fome hints to excite your own minds to purfue this fubject in a proper manner, I fhall mention a few inftances.

You muft admonifh young and old perfons in different ways. With refpect to the former, you may reafonably affume a confiderable degree of authority, and urge them, with a fort of feverity, to virtue and improvement. Age claims a refpect which is fcarcely confiftent with this in ordinary cafes, and will be moft effectually wrought upon by intreaty, and mild unaffuming addreffes; and therefore the apoftle himfelf directs Timothy not to " rebuke an elder, but to intreat him as a " father [q]." You muft admonifh the poor fo as to fhew them that you do not defpife them for their poverty, and fo as not to give them an uneafy feeling of it; and you muft endeavour to comfort them under it, to guard them againft the dejection, difcontent, peevifhnefs, and difhonefty, which are apt to arife from that ftate. The rich, on the other hand, are to be addreffed, fo as to fhew that you have no admiration or awe of their wealth; they are to be warned freely againft the luxury, pride, and confidence, to which their fituation

---

[q] 1 Tim. v. 1.

fituation leads, and urged ftrongly to that generofity, beneficence, and alms-giving, for which
their circumftances afford opportunities ; and
therefore the apoftle, giving Timothy directions
concerning his behaviour to them, does not fay
intreat, but " *charge* them that are rich in this
" world, that they be not high-minded ʳ," &c. It
can never be right to ftand in awe of their riches,
or to addrefs them in a manner that would feem to
imply this ; but it may be often prudent to foothe
them by the foftnefs of your exhortations, as David
calmed the evil fpirit of Saul by the charms of
mufic. Some men are naturally difpofed to giddinefs, levity, and thoughtlefs mirth ; to thefe the
language of fcripture is, " Wo unto you that
" laugh now, for ye fhall mourn and weep ˢ."
In conformity to this, a minifter muft often propofe to fuch the importance, the difficulties, and
the threatenings of religion, that they may be
excited to ferioufnefs. Others are naturally of a
forrowful and melancholy caft ; the pleafures and
the rewards of religion muft be frequently exhibited
to them, that they may be encouraged in well-
doing. Some are naturally forward and even
impudent, others are modeft and bafhful ; thefe
muft be treated in very different ways. The former can be affected only by fevere and peremptory
injunctions ; the latter will be touched with the
mildeft

ʳ 1 Tim. vi. 17, 18, 19.　　ˢ Luke, vi. 25.

mildeſt inſinuations. Some men are of a ſanguine
and confident temper; others, of a timorous
and diffident turn: the former are to be made fen-
ſible of their weakneſs, that their preſumption may
not precipitate them into ſin; the latter muſt be
rendered leſs ſenſible of it before they will ſo much
as attempt their duty. All motives which tend to
depreſs the mind are proper for the former; thoſe
which rouſe and invigorate it, for the latter. In a
word, the patient and impatient, the benevolent
and the envious, the meek and the paſſionate, the
humble and the proud, the reſolute and the
wavering, the active and the indolent, the peace-
able and the turbulent, the proſperous and the
afflicted, the maſter and the ſervant, the parent
and the child, the man who ſins deliberately and
he who is ſurpriſed into ſin by a ſudden paſſion or
the power of temptation, muſt be all treated in
very different manners. Both the nature of the
admonitions and exhortations which are given,
and the manner in which they are given, muſt
be varied according to every variety of temper and
ſituation in perſons. In order to be able thus to
vary them, a miniſter muſt obſerve carefully what
directions each of his people ſtands moſt in need
of, and how they are wrought upon and affected
in the ordinary concerns of life. Natural prudence
joined with careful experience will enable him by
degrees to give them all ſuch exhortations as they
ſtand in need of, in a proper manner. He ſhould
ſpare no pains in ſtudying the diverſity of human
characters,

characters, and the manner of application which each requires. The beft affiftance that you can obtain in this, is to attend carefully to the particular directions which the fcriptures any where give to different claffes of people, and to the manner in which they give them. By the careful ftudy of thefe, you will be able to make out for yourfelves rules for all the variety of matter and manner that can be needful in your private exhortations in any parifh ; and if you endeavour to render the rules which you thus deduce, familiar to yourfelves, efpecially by writing them down and reading them frequently over, you will not be wholly at a lofs for executing this part of your duty, even at your firft fettlement in a parifh, and a little experience will enable you to apply them to all particular cafes, readily and becomingly.

It will be proper to obferve farther, that though each peculiarity of character and fituation may require one manner of addrefs as moft fuitable to it, yet a minifter fhould not confine himfelf entirely to that one manner, but fhould imitate the apoftles, whom we find often foothing, intreating, befeeching, exhorting, commanding, threatening, thofe to whom they write, almoft in the fame breath and on the fame fubject. In like manner, a minifter fhould try every way with thofe with whom he converfes, touch as it were every ftring, ufe every topic, and every manner of addrefs, till at laft he hit on one which fhall be effectual. It will be peculiarly neceffary for a minifter to try this

method

method at firſt, till he become pretty well acquainted with the characters of his pariſhioners;
and the making frequent tiials in this way will
enable him by degrees to diſcover their characters
and the proper way of dealing with them. But
even after he has diſcovered this, it will be often
very proper to try the ſame variety of method;
for men are ſo capricious, and liable to ſo many
different humours, that what has great influence with them at one time, will have none at
another.

It will be of great importance for the right diſcharge of this duty, private exhortation, that a
miniſter obtain from people themſelves an account
of their peculiar temper, and of the difficulties
which they meet with in the virtuous conduct of
life. It is no eaſy matter to obtain this; for ſince
the particular confeſſion eſtabliſhed in the Popiſh
church, and productive of very ill effects, was
laid aſide, Chriſtians have run into an oppoſite
extreme, productive of almoſt as ill effects. Inſtead of laying open the ſtate of their ſouls to
their miniſters, they endeavour all they can to
conceal it from them; ſo far are they from
acquainting them with the vices to which they find
themſelves expoſed, or the temptations which they
find it difficult to reſiſt; from telling them, for
inſtance, that they find themſelves covetous, paſſionate, revengeful, envious, or the like; and
from aſking their advice concerning the means by
which they may withſtand theſe vices, and cultivate

vate the oppofite virtues. In order to avoid the inconvenience of this, a minifter fhould keep an eye on the conduct of his parifhioners in ordinary life, that he may obferve every opening that he can find into their characters. He fhould likewife encourage them in all the ways he can, to lay their hearts open to him, to confult him, to afk his advice in matters of practice. Befides, when he is engaged in converfation with them, if he poffefs the addrefs which is neceffary for the execution of his office (and this addrefs it is certainly his duty to ftudy), he will, by afking queftions, and by innumerable methods which occafion will fuggeft to him, difcover their character and fituation, in a great meafure whether they will or not. But if a minifter be really intent on difcovering the varieties of temper and circumftances among his people, he will perhaps find that it is owing as much to the minifter as to the people, that they are generally fo averfe, or at leaft fo carelefs in afking the advice of their paftor concerning every important ftep of their lives. If he fhould find this to be the cafe, if he fhould find them ready to inform him of their fituation, and to afk his advice, by his giving them proper encouragement to do it, he will thus obtain a very great advantage for admonifhing and exhorting them, fo as to promote their real improvement and falvation.

It was neceffary to confider thefe two duties, teaching and exhortation feparately, that you

might

might the better underſtand their nature; but I repeat, that they are not to be in fact disjoined in practice; every inſtruction ſhould end in exhortations or admonitions; · and every exhortation ſhould be ſupported with proper inſtructions. The apoſtles command miniſters both to " teach and to " exhort; *with all authority*." A miniſter ſhould always behave ſo as to command the reſpect of his people, and he ſhould maintain all the authority to which that entitles him, in his whole intercourſe with them. The exertion of ſome degree of this authority will often be neceſſary for keeping thoſe with whom he converſes, from declining the ſubjects which he chooſes to introduce, and running off to others which better ſuit their reliſh. The moſt effectual way to ſupport this authority, ſo as to gain attention to a man's private inſtructions and admonitions, is to ſhew that they proceed from a warm love to them, and a deep concern for their eternal intereſts.

I will conclude this ſubject with repeating, that a miniſter ſhould lay it down as a rule to ſpend ſome part of every day, except when a good reaſon prevents it, in giving private inſtructions and exhortations in this manner to ſome or other of his people, as he can meet with them. It will really be very little labour to him; it will rather be a pleaſure, if he be fired with the true ſpirit of his calling, and find his people docile and tractable, which if they ſhould not be at firſt, this

method

method will probably very foon render them. But if any man think the fpending a part of moft days in this manner an infupportable drudgery, let him recollect that the end of the miniftry is to render men fit for heaven ; let him judge whether all that we have prefcribed be more than fufficient for the attainment of this end. If he think it is, he has never confidered the difficulty and importance of the end ; and if he be not willing for the fake of it to take all the trouble that we have mentioned, he is not, till he change his fentiments, capable of fulfilling the miniftry of the gofpel; fo as to fave either himfelf or others.

Sect. IV.

Of Counfelling.

ANOTHER private duty of the paftoral office, which may indeed be regarded as a branch of the former, but is at the fame time fo peculiar in its nature as to deferve a feparate illuftration, is counfelling, or giving people advice in cafes of confcience, which they may propofe to their minifter. We have the example of the apoftles for this duty, particularly of the apoftle Paul, with refpect to diftinctions of meats and days [t], and with refpect to marriage.

---

[t] Rom. xiv.

riage ᵘ. We fhall content ourfelves with making a
very few obfervations on it, fuch chiefly as may
prevent the abufes of it.

When confcience or the moral faculty is exercifed about a man's own actions and temper, it
makes him folicitous to know beforehand how he
may act aright in particular circumftances, and
anxious afterwards to difcover whether he has
acted right; whether he ought to approve or condemn himfelf, and what judgment he may juftly
form concerning the general temper and ftate of
his foul. The reprefentation of the circumftances
on which this decifion depends, is termed a cafe of
confcience; a cafe in which a man wants to have
his confcience informed and directed. To counfel,
is to give fafe and feafonable advice in fuch a cafe,
to deal aright with men's confciences as to the
guilt of their fins. Before the Reformation, there
was a court for this very purpofe, called the Peni-
tential court, as well as another, the Ecclefiaftical
court, for judicial cafes. The latter had for its
object public offences; and for its end the enjoin-
ing of public penances for the fatisfaction of the
church, and had rules adapted to thefe; the former
regarded fuch cafes as were not public, aimed at
the private direction of penitents, and had rules
different from thofe of the other court, and adapted
to

ᵘ 1 Cor. vii.

to the peculiarity of its own object and end, but, chiefly calculated for proportioning the kind and degree of private penances to the nature of offences, the circumftances of perfons and actions, and the meafure of contrition. In the reformed churches, fuch courts are with good reafon abolifhed; and in ours, any formal abfolution by the minifter is in fuch cafes difcharged. But for every minifter it is neceffary to be able to fettle doubting confciences, to compofe the troubled, and to put men into the beft method of repenting, and avoiding fin for the future [x]. Cafes of confcience may be reduced to two general claffes; fuch as regard a man's conduct in a particular inftance, and fuch as regard the general ftate of a man's foul.

Firft, a man's confcience may be at a lofs to determine, what ought to be his conduct in fome particular fituation, or to decide upon reflection, whether he has acted right in that fituation. There is often real occafion for doubts on this fubject: for it is obfervable, that juftice is almoft the only virtue which admits of abfolutely precife and accurate rules. The rules of almoft all the reft are much more loofe and indeterminate; they admit of many exceptions, and require a variety of modifications, almoft as numerous as the circumftances

---

[x] Stillingfleet, vol. i. c. 3. p. 211.

cumftances in which they are to be reduced to
practice. The former are therefore compared,
by an ingenious author, to the rules of grammar,
which are determinate, and may be learned fo as
to be infallibly obferved in every cafe; the latter,
to thofe rules which critics lay down for the attainment of what is fublime and elegant in compofition, and which prefent us rather with a general
idea of the perfection we ought to aim at, than
afford us any certain and infallible directions for
acquiring it. A perfon therefore honeftly difpofed
to do his duty, may often be at a lofs to know
what piety, generofity, friendfhip, gratitude, requires of him in a particular fituation. The difficulty is increafed by this circumftance, that
written laws, whether divine or human, muft be
expreffed in general terms, and the application of
them to particular cafes muft be left to men themfelves. There is perhaps no virtue except juftice,
which admits of more precife rules than gratitude;
yet a very little reflection will make the difficulty
that we have hinted at, obvious. If a benefactor,
fuppofe, attended you in your ficknefs, ought you
to attend him in his? or can you fulfil the obligation of gratitude, by making a return of a different
kind? If you ought to attend him, how long
ought you to attend him? The fame time that he
attended you, or longer, and how much longer?
If your friend lent you money in your diftrefs,
ought you to lend him money in his? How
much ought you to lend him? When ought you
to

to lend it to him? and for how long a time? It is evident that no general rule can be laid down, by which a precife anfwer can, in all cafes, be given to any of thefe queftions. The difference between his character and yours, between his circumftances and yours, may be fuch, that you may be perfectly grateful, and yet juftly refufe to lend him any thing; and on the contrary, you may be willing to lend, or even to give him ten times the fum which he lent you, and yet juftly be accufed of the blackeft ingratitude, and of not having fulfilled the hundredth part of the obligation you lie under. This want of precifion in the rules of moft moral and chriftian virtues has difpofed perfons of tender confciences to defire determinate directions for their conduct in particular inftances, and has dif-pofed others to turn cafuiftry into a fcience for their direction. The cultivation of this fcience was greatly promoted in the middle and latter ages of the church, by the eftablifhed cuftom of auricular confeffion. By that inftitution the moft fecret actions, and even the thoughts of every perfon, which could be fufpected of receding, in the fmalleft degree, from the rules of chriftian purity and virtue, were to be revealed to the confeffor. The confeffor informed his penitents, whether, and in what refpect they had violated their duty, and what pennance it behoved them to undergo, before he could abfolve them in the name of the offended Deity. To be qualified to be a confeffor, was a neceffary part of the ftudy of divines; and

they

they were thence led to collect cafes of nice and delicate fituations, in which it is hard to determine how to act. Such collections they thought might be of ufe, both to the directors of confciences, and to thofe who were to be directed.

It happened, however, as might have been expected, that the want of precifion in the rules for the exercife of moſt virtues in particular fituations, which feemed to render cafuiſtry neceſſary, rendered it at the fame time imperfect, and in a great meaſure ufelefs; for it made it impoſſible to lay down exact and precife rules for the direction of every circumſtance of men's behaviour. It was hinted before, that one virtue, juſtice, admits of very exact rules. Thefe are fubject to no exceptions or modifications, but fuch as may be afcertained as accurately as the rules themfelves, and generally indeed flow from the very fame principles. What we ought in ſtrict juſtice to perform, how much we ought to perform, when and where we ought to perform it, the whole nature and circumftances of the action prefcribed, are all precifely fixed and determined. Accordingly, the whole of juriſprudence is, employed in determining the particular laws of juſtice; and as long as we keep to the precife principles and views of juriſprudence, it is eafy to determine them with abfolute certainty and perfect exactnefs. The principles of juriſprudence lead a perfon to confider, only what the man to whom the
obligation

obligation is due ought to think himfelf entitled
to exact by force, what every impartial fpectator
would approve of him for exacting, what a judge
or arbiter, to whom he had fubmitted his caufe,
and who had undertaken to do him juftice, ought
to oblige the other perfon to fuffer or to perform.
But even with refpect to juftice, cafuiftry does
not give fo clear decifions; it is not its aim to
teach a man how he muft act fo as to avoid deferving external punifhment, but how he muft act fo
as to be a good man, and to deferve praife by his
exact and fcrupulous behaviour. Cafuifts do not
confider fo much what it is that might properly be
exacted by force, as what it is that the perfon who
owes the obligation ought to think himfelf bound
to perform from the moft facred and fcrupulous
regard to the general rules of juftice, and from the
moft confcientious dread, either of wronging his
neighbour, or of violating the integrity of his own
character. To decide matters of conduct in this
point of view is of much greater delicacy, and the
decifion muft be more indeterminate. An inftance
that is very commonly debated will illuftrate this.
A highwayman, by the fear of death, obliges a tra-
veller to promife him a fum of money. Is fuch a
promife, extorted in this manner by unjuft force,
to be regarded as obligatory? Confider it merely
as a queftion of jurifprudence, the decifion can
admit of no doubt. It would be abfurd to fuppofe
that the highwayman can be entitled to ufe force
to conftrain the other to perform. To extort the

promife

promife was a crime that deferved fevere punifhment; and to extort the performance of it would
only be adding a new crime to the former. To
fuppofe that a judge ought to enforce the obligation of fuch promifes, or that a magiftrate ought to
allow them to fuftain action at law, would be the
moft ridiculous of all abfurdities. But if we confider it as a queftion of cafuiftry, as a cafe of confcience in which a good man wants direction, it will
not be fo eafily determined. Whether a man does
not owe fome regard even to a promife thus
unjuftly extorted, from a refpect to his own dignity and honour, from abhorrence of all treachery
and falfehood, may very readily be made a queftion,
and has divided the opinions of cafuifts. According to the fentiments of good men, fome regard is
due to fuch a promife: but it is impoffible to
determine how much, by any general rule that will
apply to all cafes without exception. If the decifions of cafuifts, even concerning cafes of juftice,
are thus neceffarily indeterminate, they muft be
much more fo with refpect to other virtues, which,
from their very nature, fcarcely admit of any precife and accurate rules. But though this circumftance renders cafuiftry, when formed into a fcience,
and reduced to a fyftem, in a great meafure preca-
rious and ufelefs, yet ftill it would be of great ufe
that people confulted their minifter in all points of
conduct that are of importance. They could
reprefent to him the prefent cafe in all its circumftances; and however difficult it is to form a
                                        general

general rule of conduct, yet it is eafy to give particular directions for one cafe. Though the decifions of cafuifts were juft, weak people could gain little advantage by confulting them, becaufe though multitudes of cafes are collected in them, yet there is an infinite variety of poffible circumftances, and it is a chance if one be found exactly parallel to the prefent. But a minifter of prudence and virtue may give them always a decifion precifely fuited to the prefent cafe, and can vary it according to every the minuteft variety of fituation; and thus accommodate it even to thofe virtues which admit leaft of precife and accurate general rules.

When a minifter is confulted beforehand, he fhould moft carefully avoid whatever can have the remoteft tendency to teach men to chicane with their own confciences, or to authorife by vain fubtleties innumerable evafive refinements with regard to the feveral articles of duty. In fact, this is the end to which cafuiftry has been often applied, not to direct the well-meaning to real virtue, but to enable the difhoneft to explain away their duty. He fhould make it his aim, not to inform men of the loweft degree of virtue that they may take up with, but to animate them to what is fublime and noble in goodnefs. He fhould not attempt to determine with a frivolous accuracy, but endeavour to excite commanding emotions, and to infufe a ftrong fpirit of virtue.

But,

But, as the world goes, a minifter cannot expect to be often confulted by his parifhioners, how they ought to act in particular cafes which are yet before them. Men are not very ready even to examine their own conduct before they act, much lefs to confult another about it. It is at that time of greateft importance, that we fhould have juft views of our actions; but paffion feldom allows us then to confider what we are doing, candidly and impartially. It is when the action is over, when the paffions which prompted to it have fubfided, that men begin candidly to confider their conduct. Then they often reflect on their violation of the laws of virtue, with remorfe, dread, and terror: and fometimes the confcioufnefs of having done wrong is fuch a load upon their minds, that they are eager to difburden themfelves to their minifter, and to know his opinion concerning that conduct which fills them with fevere compunction. In this cafe a minifter ought to reprefent their paft conduct to them in its true light, without either exaggerating or extenuating it. The former would only either irritate them to defend it, or fink them into defpair; and the latter would favour the partial views of it, which they are too apt to entertain of their own accord. It fhould be his chief bufinefs to prevent their confcioufnefs of guilt from producing vain regret, and to inftil fuch principles and refolutions as may fecure them from the like errors for the future. When they

feel

feel keen remorfe for fome heinous fin which they have committed, it muft be cherifhed by the minifter till it produce thorough repentance proportioned to the crime, and fo directed that it may moft effectually produce this. If their remorfe be in danger of degenerating into defpair, it is his bufinefs, without difguifing the real heinoufnefs of their fin, to inculcate the affurance which, notwithftanding that, they have of pardon on their amendment.

The fecond kind of cafes of confcience are thofe which regard the general ftate of men's fouls. It is natural that men fhould be folicitous to obtain fome degree of certainty, whether they be in a ftate of grace and reconciliation with God or not. But it is not always eafy, either for themfelves or others, to determine this. Though fome men may, on account of the great uniformity of their holinefs, obtain a confiderable degree of *affurance*, yet moft men, by reafon of the inconftancy of their good conduct, of the frequent repetition of fins which they have refolved to forfake, and of other caufes, can entertain only different degrees of *hope*, and ought not to be encouraged to more. There are feveral circumftances which increafe the difficulty of dealing with perfons who propofe cafes of this kind. We fhall mention a few of thefe, and make fome general obfervations on the fubject.

The

The doubts of men concerning their ftate are
generally very much heightened by a fyftem of
principles, exaggerated beyond the truth, with
which they are all connected, and on which they
depend. Some of the moft confiderable of them
are thefe. They carry the doctrine of original fin
fo far, as to imagine that all men are, for many
years of their lives, in a ftate of damnation, and
wholly deftitute of all grace; they think that this
ftate continues, till they be at a certain period in
a fenfible manner converted; by ftraining fome
fcripture metaphors, they reprefent converfion to
themfelves as attended with violent inward pangs,
and terrors of confiderable duration; they judge of
the fincerity of their converfion and regeneration
by the violence of thefe, more than by the general
tenor of their temper and conduct; when thefe
wear off, they are either filled with joy in the confidence of their being already regenerated, or elfe
plunged in doubts whether they do not ftill continue in a ftate of nature. It is neceffary that a
minifter know perfectly the fet of principles with
which a perfon's doubts are connected, before he
can argue with him; and that he do not attempt
directly to call them in queftion, even though he
fhould not be fatisfied of their truth, but rather
reafon upon them as much as he can. His chief
bufinefs fhould be, infenfibly to correct the extra-
vagancies of thefe principles, to direct men not to
judge by their inward pangs and forrows, which
are

are fallacious marks; to turn their attention to their habitual conduct and temper, as the only sure criterion. When he finds that their perplexity arises from their wanting to find in themselves some mysterious marks of grace, it should be his business to inculcate on them, that christian and moral virtues are both the only genuine fruits, and the only infallible marks of grace. By bringing men to estimate their state by this criterion, he will render the trial much less liable to ambiguity. It is likewise of importance that a minister, in cases of this kind, endeavour to give men right notions of conversion; for from wrong conceptions of it, many of their perplexities arise. In consequence of their exaggerations of the set of principles beforementioned, they consider regeneration as if it were a line, on the one side of which lies a state of damnation, but crossing it in a moment as it were, they are immediately in a state of grace and salvation, from which they can never fall. Regeneration must therefore be represented to them as a work that is not accomplished all at once, but carried on by slow degrees; so that it may be begun where it is yet very imperfect, and must be completed by strenuous diligence and the uniform practice of holiness. It must be urged, that they can never be sure of their conversion, till it has produced this effect; but that every degree of this effect is a sufficient ground of hope that it is begun: It is only by such a representation of things, that they can be guarded, on the one hand, against
despair,

defpair, from thinking themfelves wholly in a
ftate of nature; or, on the other hand, againft
fecurity or prefumption, from imagining that they
are all at once tranflated into that ftate of grace,
from which they are in no danger of apoftatizing.
It would be endlefs to mention all the difficulties
which arife from the perverfion of different principles of religion, or all the varieties which, from
this perverfion, occur in the cafes which will be
propofed to minifters. Prudence and reflection,
joined with experience, will be the beft help for
thefe.

It was already hinted, that one will not receive
a great deal of affiftance from the writings of
cafuifts, for the difcharge of this duty. But ftill
he may receive fome. He will however receive
greatly more from a thorough knowlege of the
fcriptures, from a diftinct comprehenfion of the
terms of the gofpel covenant, from an extenfive
view and a ftrong fenfe of the meafures of conduct
and the propriety of behaviour.

But we muft mention one circumftance, which
greatly increafes the difficulty of this part of a
minifter's bufinefs. It is this, that doubts or fears
are often joined with bodily diftemper, with melancholy. When this is the cafe, a doubt about the
nature of one action, fometimes comes to coincide
with a doubt about one's general ftate, as in the
inftance which is very common among melancholy
                                        perfons,

perfons ; .their fufpecting that they have been guilty of the fin againft the Holy Ghoft, and therefore incapable of forgivenefs. When perfons are fubject to a melancholy habit, it is not eafy to talk to them in any way that will have any good effect. I have been fometimes difpofed to fufpect, that it would be beft not to talk with them on religious fubjects at all : for their diftemper makes them mifunderftand every thing that is faid, and wreft even what is moft comfortable to a fenfe unfavourable. to themfelves. Imagination is fo ftrong in that difeafe, that they will be often fully convinced that a man has faid juft the reverfe of what he has faid, and, that the moft harmlefs things were intended as a plain hint to them that they are in a hopelefs ftate. There is nothing from which they will not take a handle to feed their diftemper, and fupport their apprehenfions. By this means, a minifter may increafe their diforder, while he is moft defirous to allay it. But, on the whole, I am inclined to the contrary opinion, that a minifter may, not often indeed, but when either the dif-ordered perfons, or even thofe about them, exprefs a folicitude for it, converfe with them with fome benefit. From his declining it, they might take occafion to draw conclufions more to their own difadvantage, than they could draw from any thing he would fay ; as, that he thought them unworthy of inftruction or advice, that he knew their ftate to be hopelefs, or the like. Though they will very probably wreft all that he fays into

M   a fenfe

a fenfe unfavourable to themfelves, ftill this is no worfe than would happen, though he abftained from converfing with them ; for the fame turn of imagination will lead them to run into fimilar conclufions from their own thoughts, or from the moft indifferent converfation. As there is always fome miftaken notion or another which breeds them uneafinefs, a minifter fhould endeavour to rectify it. This will very probably have little or no influence on them at the time ; but it may give them a handle for rectifying their own notions, when their difeafe begins to wear off. The talking with them on this fubject may feem to have a tendency to feed their diftemper ; but there is really a neceffity for humouring it in fome degree ; and the eafe which they receive from giving it fome vent at times, contributes more to wear it off, than keeping it always under reftraint. At the fame time, a minifter ought to endeavour to draw them off infenfibly from thofe fubjects which diftrefs and terrify them, to others more indifferent. It will not be eafy to do this ; for a melancholy imagination has a great degree of obftinacy in adhering to the fubjects which give it uneafinefs, and even perfifts in believing things that never had an exiftence, and in perfuading a perfon that he has been guilty of crimes which he never once thought of. It may, however, be in fome degree effected, by fhowing great fympathy with them, by humouring their caprices a little, and by other prudent methods. But when

perfons

perfons are in this diforder, which arifes chiefly from the body, it is above all of importance, that they be kept from being much alone, that they be diverted from thinking, and that they be prevailed upon to take moderate exercife. A minifter may be of ufe to them, by directing thofe about them to put them upon thefe : and by his authority with them from his character, and the influence which he may gain over them by infinuating converfation, a minifter may often be more fuccefsful in perfuading them to ufe thefe means of reftoring their health, than others could be.

To be often thus employed in directing the conduct of others in difficult emergencies, in teaching them what judgment they ought to form of their paft behaviour and their ftate, in diftinguifhing needlefs fcruples from confcientious care, in ftripping off falfe difguifes from what is really evil, has a plain tendency to difpofe a minifter himfelf to act with a conftant regard to the rules of duty, to live correctly, and frequently to review and examine his own temper and actions.

SECT. V.

Of vifiting the Afflicted.

THE confideration of that one kind of diftemper just mentioned, naturally leads us to another duty

of

of the paftoral care, Vifiting the afflicted, particularly the fick. Nature itfelf prompts all men
fo ftrongly to this, as might of itfelf convince us
that it is peculiarly the duty of a minifter. But
the fcripture likewife exprefsly makes it a part of
his duty, and directs Chriftians to call for him in
this fituation. " Is any fick among you?" fays
the apoftle James, " let him call for the elders of
" the church, and let them pray over him [y]."
It is a duty of common humanity to fympathize
with perfons in diftrefs, and to give them all the
relief which our prefence and the expreffion of our
fympathy can give; a minifter may likewife give
them ftill more important relief by his inftructions
and advices. Not only ficknefs, but every kind of
affliction, temporal loffes, or the death of relations,
is an occafion which merits the prefence and affiftance of a minifter. Adverfity of every kind
demands both fympathy and confolation; and to
" weep with- thofe who weep," and to comfort
them if poffible, is a noble employment. Profperity has a natural tendency to produce thoughtleffnefs and an unfeeling temper of mind, which
render men indifpofed for receiving good impreffions. Adverfity tends to correct this ftubborn-
nefs, to render the heart foft and pliable, to difpofe
it to ferious and ufeful reflections, and to fit it for
receiving a deep impreffion from religious inftructions

---

[y] James, v. 14.

tions and exhortations. A minifter fhould therefore regard the time of adverfity as a favourable
opportunity, which he fhould not fail to feize, of
doing fome good to thofe on whom all he could
fay formerly had very little influence. He may
employ this opportunity in giving them any ufeful
inftruétions, relating to the whole of their chriftian
duty; for they will then be more inclined to liften
to them, and to be fuitably affeéted with them, than
at other times. But it is more peculiarly proper
to fhow that all afflitions are appointed by the
powerful, wife, and good providence of God, and
that none of them can poffibly befal any man
without his permiffion; to explain the wife ends
for which they are appointed, and the ufeful purpofes to which men may render them fubfervient
to themfelves. Thefe are trite topics; it is taken
for granted that all men are acquainted with them,
and all imagine that they believe them. But it is
plain that they do not produce thofe effeéts upon
the temper of men, which they are naturally fitted
to produce; and therefore a minifter fhould inculcate them in fuch a way as is fitteft to make them
touch the heart. Adverfity of every kind contains
temptations to fome particular vices; a minifter
fhould make it a great part of his bufinefs, in converfing with the affliéled, to guard them againft
thefe vices, againft difcontent, repining, impatience, peevifhnefs. Adverfity demands fome
duties in a peculiar manner, and either difpofes to,
or gives opportunity for, the exertion of feveral

M 3   virtues;

virtues; it is the natural feafon of confideration, ferioufnefs, prayer, felf-examination, patience, refignation. To thefe a minifter fhould particularly exhort and excite thofe afflicted perfons whom he vifits. It muft however be remarked, that though it is the duty of a minifter to inculcate thefe things as much as poffible, yet great prudence is often neceffary in the manner of introducing them. When an affliction is of fuch a nature as to occafion violent forrow or great difquiet of mind, this muft be in fome degree abated, before men are capable of liftening to any thing. The weaknefs of nature feems to require fome vent for the firft tranfports of violent paffions; but its demand is much increafed by this circumftance, that the generality of men never think of reftraining any paffion, but accuftom themfelves to indulge the prefent impulfe or inclination, efpecially when it is ftrong and vehement. On this account, when a minifter has frequent and ready accefs to afflicted perfons, it will often be beft at firft to allow them to give fcope to their uneafinefs, only gently checking fuch expreffions of it as are quite extravagant, highly indecent, or plainly finful; and afterwards, as they become more compofed, to infinuate gradually ufeful inftructions and religious reflections, which may both contribute to compofe them more, and, by taking faft hold of their minds in their prefent pliable temper, remain with them, and actuate their future conduct. But he muft ftill take care, before that foftnefs and docility of mind

which

which fprings from affliction be worn off, or confiderably abated, to propofe to them, in the
ftrongeft manner, all the inftructions which he
thinks they ftand in need of, and will now receive
with greater advantage than at another time. If a
minifter will perform this part of his duty, he muft
generally do it without being afked; for it is not
entirely cuftomary to fend for a minifter on fuch
occafions: but, by going of his own accord, he
may furnifh his people with ufeful materials for
meditation in the time of their diftrefs, which may
likewife exert themfelves in directing their whole
future conduct.

Almoft the only fpecies of diftrefs in which
the generality think of defiring the prefence or
advice of their minifter, is ficknefs; and then too,
they are often very late of defiring it. They fometimes defer it till they have loft all hopes of recovery, and then fend for him, either to fit them for
heaven, as it were, by a charm, or to fee if he can
allay the terrors which have feized upon them in
the profpect of death. It is, at any rate, a difficult
work to deal with thofe who are juft ftepping into
eternity; but when this circumftance attends it, it
renders it much more difficult. In order to prevent it, a minifter fhould not ftay till he be fent
for; but as foon as he hears that any in his parifh
are fick, he fhould immediately go to them of his
own accord. By this means, he will have an
opportunity of examining and exhorting them,

M 4   while

while they are yet capable of fome compofure of
thought, and have fome time before them ; and
he will contribute to wear out an opinion which
feems to be too prevalent, that they need only a
prayer from a minifter in their laft moments.   By
this means too, he will moft effectually confult his
own eafe; for by vifiting the fick when he can
render it convenient for him, he will in fome meafure prevent his being fent for when it is lefs convenient.

In other churches, there is a particular office
for this duty prefcribed by authority : but even
this does not exhauft the duty.   " To run over
" fome prayers, and to take leave," is eafy, but
comes not up to the defign of thefe churches in
prefcribing it ; and the form itfelf fuppofes particular and fuitable addreffes by the minifter himfelf.
In all thefe addreffes he fhould apply himfelf particularly to the ftate and condition of the perfon
whom he vifits.

In every thing that a minifter fays to a fick perfon, he ought to keep three things fteadily in view ;
the influence which it may have on the perfon, if
dying; the influence which it may have on him,
if he fhould recover ; and the influence which it
may have upon perfons in health, who are about -
him.   Every thing that can have a bad influence
in any of thefe ways, muft be carefully avoided.,
A minifter muft guard the perfon himfelf againft.

ill-

ill-grounded hopes of mercy on the one hand, and
againſt deſpair on the other ; he muſt avoid giving
him any notions that could tempt him to careleſſ-
neſs and ſecurity, if he ſhould recover, or encourage him to truſt again to a death-bed repentance ;
and he muſt be anxiouſly on his guard againſt
dropping any thing that can lead ſpeƈtators in the
leaſt to flatter themſelves, that after having ſpent
their life in ſin, they may ſet all to rights by a few
tears, or confeſſions, or prayers, in their laſt hours.
Any man will very often find it difficult to guard
his thoughts and expreſſions ſo as to avoid all
theſe hazards ; and therefore every one ſhould
employ the moſt intenſe and deliberate meditation
about it.

There are many ſubjeƈts on which a miniſter
may properly inſiſt in all his exhortations to ſick
or dying perſons. He ſhould inculcate on them,
that diſeaſes are ordered, not by chance, but by
Divine Providence, either for puniſhment, for
correƈtion, or for our exerciſe in virtue ; and in
conſequence of this, encourage them to patience,
perſuade them to reſignation, exhort them to
examine their conduƈt, and to reſolve to amend
what has been faulty in it. He ſhould inſtruƈt
them in the nature of death, and inſtill into them
thoſe ſentiments of the vanity of preſent things, of
the folly of anxiety about them, of immodeiate love
to them, of endleſs endeavours or unlawful
methods to procure them, of abuſing them to bad
purpoſes,

purpofes, of finking ourfelves in fenfual pleafures,
which obvioufly arife from the confideration of the
nature of death, and which, if he can thoroughly
inftill them, will enable them either to leave thefe
things without regret if they fhould happen to
die, or to live above them if they fhould recover.
He fhould lead their view to the important confequences of death, as it is our entrance into an
eternal world ; that when they have now a near
profpect of it, they may be more fenfibly ftruck
with the folemnity of judgment, with the glories
of heaven, and with the terrors of hell, and feel
all their power. He fhould inftruct them in that
preparation which it will appear, from the view of
its nature, that death requires ; an habitual fuperiority to things external, difengagement from the
body and from fenfual pleafures, and fuch a conduct as naturally fprings from a firm faith in the
unfeen world. He fhould alfo explain to them
fully, and illuftrate with force, the nature of the
gofpel covenant ; the bleffings which God on his
part propofes to us, both thofe which he has
beftowed on us in this life as privileges which we
ought to improve, and by which we ought to be
excited to the practice of every chriftian virtue,
and thofe which he promifes in the future world
as the reward of chriftian obedience, and the improvement of grace already received ; and likewife the terms which God requires from us on our
part. As it is of the greateft confequence to preferve a full view of thefe through the whole of life,

. fo

fo it is of particular importance that perfons have a full and lively fenfe of them in the profpect of death, as they alone can direct their judgment concerning themfelves, and be a foundation either of fueh hopes as may comfort and encourage them, or of fuch fears as may roufe them to do all that is yet poffible for their fouls. If fick perfons difcover any thing which perplexes their minds, or any cafes in which they want to be refolved, a minifter ought to give them his counfel and affiftance honeftly; but he ought to avoid giving a pofitive determination about the final ftate of their fouls: as he cannot know the heart, he fhould content himfelf with calling upon them to finifh their duty, to do all the good they can in the time that remains, and to pray for pardon and acceptance, and with explaining the terms of falvation, fo as to give them the principles on which they themfelves may, from a careful and confcientious review of their temper and conduct, be enabled to judge concerning themfelves; but he has nothing to do to meddle with paffing a final fentence.

Sometimes a minifter is called to vifit a fick perfon, of whom he knows very little, and of whofe character and converfation he can obtain no information beforehand. In this cafe, all he can do is, " to lay before him what he ought to be, " and remind him to confult his confcience what
" he

" he has been ;" to reprefent, in a plain and
ftriking manner, the general confiderations which
have been already mentioned, and particularly the
terms of the gofpel covenant; to urge him to
apply thefe things to himfelf, according as his
confcience witneffes concerning the ftate of his
foul ; and to exhort him to examine himfelf, to
begin or perfect his repentance, to confefs his
fins, refolve againft indulging them hereafter, and
implore forgivenefs ; to be reconciled to his neighbours, and forgive his enemies, to make reftitution
to any whom he has wronged, to do all the acts of
piety and virtue for which he finds opportunity,
and above all, to take care not to fin towards the
end of life ; for if repentance on a death-bed be
very late for the fins of life, what time is left to
repent of fins committed on a death-bed ? Sometimes a minifter, who knew nothing of a perfon
before he went to vifit him, will, by converfing
with him, perceive fome openings into his character, and, by purfuing thefe, may draw out of
him a more thorough knowlege of his temper ;
and to this he fhould accommodate both his inftructions and exhortations. But as this may not
always happen, and as every one has not the
readinefs that is neceffary for fuiting himfelf to
what he difcovers concerning a man's character
immediately and wholly off hand, a minifter
fhould do every thing he can to obtain information concerning the character and conduct of
                                        perfons,

perfons, before he go to them in their ficknefs, that he may be able to apply himfelf fuitably to them.

Sometimes a minifter meets with fick perfons the whole tenor of whofe life gives him ground to believe that they are truly good. Some of thefe reap, in their laft hours the fruits of a well-fpent life ; he finds them rejoicing in the approbation of a good confcience, and in the hope of heaven. In this cafe, when there is reafon to judge that their joy and hope are well founded, a minifter has little to do but to rejoice with them, and to encourage them to thankfulnefs, and to that great act of faith and truft which muft be exerted in refigning the foul to its faithful Creator, as its guide into an unknown ftate. It will not however be improper, even in this cafe, to exhort them to examine themfelves over and over again, that they may be rendered ftill more certain of their ftate ; to repent ftill again particularly of all the fins which they can recollect ; to pray for the pardon of their daily infirmities, and of the fecret faults which they cannot recollect ; and to fill up the remainder of their lives with all the acts of virtue which they can crowd into it. But even of good perfons a minifter will find fome who are full of uneafinefs and fears. He fhould examine into the grounds of their fears. If he find that they do not proceed from the confcioufnefs of any habitual fins, or of inconftancy in religious practice, but only from a

7

ftrong

strong sense of the importance of the change of state at death, and of the possibility of their being mistaken in their judgment of themselves (and this alone will often occasion great uneasiness and discompofure in persons of timorous constitutions); then he ought to set himself particularly to strengthen their faith, and encourage their resignation, by reprefenting to them the goodness, compassion, and mercy of the divine nature, the display of it already made in the gospel difpensation, the tender care of God's providence, which they have experienced through life, the promises which he has made to his fincere servants of pardon and falvation, the security for the performance of these which arises both from the veracity of God, and from the blessings being already purchafed by Christ. In this manner he should raife them to hope, and endeavour to calm and compose them for the great change which they are soon to undergo. At the same time, it is proper to give them those exhortations which we have already hinted at with regard to other good men. All good men should be exhorted in sickness, to apply particularly to such exercises as are peculiarly fit to prepare them for death. Indeed, a good life is the only preparation for death. But though it is by far too late to begin our preparation for death when sickness is come on, and though such preparation can scarcely answer any good purpose; yet even they who have lived best will not find it unnecessary to apply more particularly to prepare for death when

when it feems to be approaching. They fhould
therefore be exhorted to draw off their thoughts
and affections from prefent things, to converfe
with themfelves more intenfely and uninterruptedly
than they had done before, that they may get
poffeffion of themfelves, that they may become
more acquainted and intimate with themfelves,
that they may fee whether there be any fin which
they have not yet thoroughly reformed, any injury
which they have not repaired, any quarrel which
they have not made up, any part of their duty in
which they have been negligent, any virtue which
they find weak ; and that they may fet about
putting all thefe things more perfectly to rights.
They fhould be exhorted to fpend a great part of
their time in acts of devotion, in prayer, in meditation, in praife, that they may thus be raifed above
the world, and formed to the temper and employment of heaven.

But the work of a minifter is both moft difagreeable and moft difficult when he finds thofe
upon a fick bed whofe paft conduct and temper
make it extremely probable, or next to certain, that
they are vicious and wicked, that they have the
work of their falvation yet to begin. There is
fcarcely any ground to hope for their perfecting
their repentance, or fecuring their falvation; and
yet it would be a melancholy work for a minifter
barely to tell them this and leave them ; and it
might render them defperate, and make them,
through

through defpair, die obftinate in their fins. " If
" he 'find them'fo ignorant as not to know what
" faith and repentance mean ; if they have led fo
" carelefs lives in this world, as fcaice ever to
" have had a ferious thought of another ; what is
" to be done? can he do nothing but pray by
" them, and fo difmifs them into their eternal
" ftate ? It is certainly a very unpromifing
" attempt, to teach men how to begin to live,
" when they are ready to die, or to make them
" fenfible of their fins in the moment of death,
" when they never before beftowed a thought upon
" them ; yet a minifter fhould do what he can, by
" his warm and ferious difcourfe, to inform and
" awaken the confciences even of fuch [z]." He
will find fome great finners infenfible and unconcerned even in the views of death. They will
only acknowlege that they are finners, as well as,
all other men, but they truft to the mercies of God
and the merits of Chrift. To fuch he muft reprefent the terrors of the wrath to come, and imprefs
them with lively apprehenfions of it. In order to
make them fenfible that they are in danger of it,
he muft endeavour to make them fenfible of their
particular fins, by leading them to difcover them
themfelves, and by charging them with fuch as he
knows they have been guilty of ; and he muft
expofe the falfe grounds of hope on which they
build,

---

[z] Stillingfleet, vol. i. p. 54, &c.

build their confidence, and fhow them the indifpenfable neceffity of repentance and holinefs.
But if he fhould even fucceed in awakening the
confciences of habitual finners, or if he fhould
find fuch finners, as he fometimes will, feized
with terror in the profpect of death, and the minifter called to give them comfort, what can he
then do? He fees confufion in their faces, and
can difcern the violent throes of a guilty confcience, and the torturing fears of a fad hereafter;
he knows that all their terrors are too juft, and
that it is fcarcely poffible that they can now fincerely repent. But with what reluctance muft he
fpeak the fevere truths which yet are fit for them
to hear? Shall he, therefore, immediately apply
to them all the promifes of the gofpel, merely becaufe they are alarmed at the near approach of
death and judgment? Whatever pain it give himfelf, he muft beware of fpeaking peace too haftily
to their fouls. He fhould endeavour to prevent
abfolute defpair, but he muft do no more to comfort them; for the more they hope, it may for the
moft part be juftly faid, the worfe they are. With
regard to all wicked perfons, it is the bufinefs of
a minifter, to prefs them to repent upon a fick
bed as the beft thing they can do, though the fuccefs of it be far from certain; to point out the acts
of repentance of which they are ftill capable, and
put them upon performing them; to exhort them
to forrow for their fins, to confefs them to God,
to refolve againft continuing in them if they fhould

N   recover;

recover; to pray earneſtly for mercy and for true repentance; to negleft no aft of virtue for which they have opportunity; in a word, to do all that they can in the ſhort time that yet remains. He ſhould inform them, that if their ſalvation be yet poſſible, it can be only in this way.

Sometimes a ſickneſs is of ſo long duration, that perſons have time, during the courſe of it, to give ſtrong marks of their repentance, patience, and piety. Theſe may be encouraged to ſome degree of humble hope, though not without a mixture of fear. But in every other caſe, a miniſter ought not to give a perſon who has lived a wicked life, any poſitive ground of hope, on account of the forced and imperfeft repentance which takes its riſe only on a ſick bed from the fears of hell. Nothing can have more pernicious conſequences; it makes the perſons themſelves, if they die, periſh in ſecurity; it encourages them, if they recover, to return to their ſins, in hopes of receiving as quick and eaſy an abſolution when they come again to be laid on a ſick bed; and it leads all who witneſs it, to what they are too prone to of themſelves, to put off religion to the laſt, when they ſee that all may be made up ſo eaſily by a few ſighs or tears in the concluding hours of life, when they are not fit for ſinning. All the promiſes of the goſpel-covenant are made only to them who lead a holy life; and ſince theſe promiſes are the only foundation of our faith and hope in Chriſt, we

cannot

cannot give encouragement beyond them to thofe who have lived a wicked life, and only begin to repent of it in the hour of death. A minifter, therefore, can warrantably only do fome of the following things. He may urge a finner to all the repentance that he can perform, as the only poffible, though now a very uncertain remedy, and to refign the event to the mercies of God in Chrift Jefus, fince he has not ground for truft or confidence. Or, he may reprefent to him the terms of the gofpel-covenant, and leave the application to himfelf; but tell him withal, that the application muft be difficult and uncertain. Or, he may tell him, that his repentance will be accepted if it be fincere and genuine; but inform him at the fame time, that whether it be, in his circumftances, fincere or not, neither the minifter, nor the perfon himfelf, but God alone, can certainly know. How can it be afcertained that a perfon is fincere in his repentance, who is out of a capacity of giving proof of its fincerity by amendment of life? How can it be afcertained either to himfelf or others, without its being at all tried? And how can it be tried, when he is juft going out of the ftate of trial? When we reflect how fmall a proportion of thofe who make a fhow of repentance on a fick bed, and afterwards recover, live like penitents, and lead truly holy lives, we may be convinced that a death-bed repentance gives no ground for higher hopes than we have reprefented. But though a minifter can give fo little comfort, and

though

though it be fo extremely doubtful whether all the
repentance to which he can bring wicked men
upon a fick bed will be available to their falvation,
yet his vifits to fuch are not altogether ufelefs.   If
they fhould recover, the fenfe of the dangerous
ftate in which they were, and the fentiments which
have been rendered familiar to them during their
ficknefs, may, perhaps, be the beginnings of a
new life, and the principles of a thorough amendment.   In order to promote this the more, a minifter fhould urge the fick perfons whom he vifits,
to make folemn vows of amending the vices to
which they have been formerly addicted, of practifing the duties which they have hitherto neglected;
and he fhould exact particular promifes on thefe
heads.   Whenever they recover, he fhould put
them in mind of thefe, oblige them to renew them,
recommend it to them to repeat them often.   If
he obferve them tranfgreffing them in any inftance,
he fhould reprove them, for it.   If they appear to
throw off all regard to them, as is too often the
cafe, then he may fafely affure them, that if they
had died in their ficknefs, as their repentance was
not fincere, they muft infallibly have perifhed;
and he ought to warn them beforehand, that if
they perfift in a courfe of vice till they again fall
upon a fick bed, all the ftrongeft fhow of repentance and ferioufnefs which they can then put on,
will be of no advantage to their falvation.   Such
awful denunciations may, perhaps, awaken them;
but though they fhould not, the minifter has done

                                                        his

his duty by making them, and their guilt refts upon their own heads.

There is a middle clafs of perfons, the incon-ftant and wavering. With thefe, alfo, it is not eafy to know how to deal, in ficknefs and the profpect of death. It is not eafy to judge, whether all the infirmities which have attended them, be confiftent with fincerity on the whole; whether their frequent relapfes after repentance be con-fiftent with the truth of that repentance; whether their fins be confiftent with a ftate of grace and the hope of heaven; whether they are failings, or were committed in oppofition to fuch a meafure of con-viction and power of refiftance as makes them wilful and prefumptuous [a]? All that a minifter can do in this cafe, is to reprefent the real doctrine of fcripture concerning univerfal and ftedfaft obe-dience, and to enforce the deep repentance con-feffedly requifite, in fuch a manner as neither on the one hand to difcourage hope, nor on the other to encourage confidence.

It is cuftomary, not only to admonifh fick per-fons, but alfo to pray with them; and it is indeed proper, though the prayers of a minifter be often regarded too much in a fuperftitious light. Any of the proper materials of devotion are, no doubt, proper

---

[a] Stillingfleet, Eccl. Cafes, vol. i. p. 57.

proper materials of prayer on fuch occafions; but
fome fubjects of devotion have a peculiar propriety;
as expreffions of the holinefs and the mercy of
God; of his perfection, and fuperiority to all evil;
of his eternal and immutable happinefs; of his
univerfal authority and providence, by which he
difpofes all things, and without which nothing can
befall us, nor a hair of our heads fall to the
ground; of our dependence upon him, and of the
frailty of our nature; of his tender care, pity, and
indulgence to good men; of the merciful ends for
which he afflicts, and the good fruits which we
may derive from afflictions, by bearing and improving them aright; expreffions of gratitude to
God for the mercies which he continually beftows,
even in the midft of adverfity, but efpecially for
the mediation of Chrift and the gofpel covenant,
which is the only foundation of hope to fallen
creatures; for the glorious bleffings that are pro-
mifed in it; and for the reafonable and eafy terms
which are required; joined with expreffions of our
full perfuafion, that we can be accepted only on
thefe terms, and that neither the mercies of God,
nor the purchafe of Chrift, will be extended to any
who remain unpenitent in fin; petitions for a deep
fenfe of our obligations as Chriftians; for patience
to bear afflictions; for grace to make a proper ufe
of them; for the pardon of fin according to the
gofpel terms; for the recovery of the fick perfon;
for bringing him to repentance, or for perfecting
his fanctification; for mercy to his foul if he die,

6

for

for the peculiar-care of God in the moment of death, and in conducting him into the unseen world; for grace to lead all to a sense of the certainty and importance of death, and to a constant preparation for it. These and other similar sentiments, which will naturally occur, have plainly a particular propriety in prayers for sick persons.

It has been already remarked, that in all admonitions to sick persons, a regard should be had to spectators. And it is often one of the most useful purposes of visiting sick persons, to give those that are about them such admonitions as naturally arise from the occasion. They may very probably have a peculiar degree of force, when they are preached from a sick bed as a text. It will be very proper to impress them with a sense of their mortality, of the uncertainty of life, and to press them to a speedy and timeous preparation for death. The particular situation of the sick person will suggest particular considerations which may be proposed to them. A good man, composed and joyful in the view of death, may be represented to them as a living and striking example of the blessedness of religion and goodness. From seeing a good man in some degree of fear, they may be warned, how much juster ground of fear they have, whose consciences tell them that they have led worse lives. The agonies of a dying sinner supply a strong picture of the misery of vice, which may alarm the most insensible. The vain hopes of a wicked man

give

give a proper handle to reprefent the obduracy which fprings from continnance in fin, depriving men of all fenfe both of guilt and of danger. Every other peculiarity in the fituation of a fick perfon will, in like manner, fuggeft fome fuitable exhortation to fpectators. In every cafe, it is proper for a minifter to comfort the relations, and to inculcate on them refignation.

This duty of the paftoral office is both important and of a very delicate nature. We have, therefore, been the more particular in explaining it. But, after all, there will fo many minute varieties arife in particular cafes, that, notwithftanding all the directions that can be given, there will remain great need for prudence and attention. Not only the ufefulnefs of thefe labours to others fhould recommend them to the careful practice of a minifter, but likewife the influence which the right performance of them will have on the improvement of his own heart. Nothing can have a ftronger tendency to excite men to all holinefs, than the frequent occafions which minifters have of going into the houfe of mourning, and converfing with the fick. They are a continual prefervative againft the infection and corruptions of profperity. To fee virtue fupporting thofe who have been fteady in the practice of it, in their lateft moments, under the agonies of pain, and enabling them to triumph in the profpect of death, is naturally a ftrong incitement to virtue. To fee a

fmall

fmall degree of confcious vice difquieting a good man, muft excite a minifter to the greateft vigilance. To fee the horrors of vice taking faft hold on the fturdieft finners, can fcarcely fail of deterring him from fin. Opportunities of this kind returning fo often to a minifter, that the impreffion made by one inftance can fcarce decay, till it be revived and ftrengthened by another, muft form him to virtue, if he be not deftitute of all principles of reformation. And every minifter fhould be careful to execute thefe duties in fuch a manner as not to lofe the advantages which they afford for his own improvement.

SECT. VI.

Of Reproving.

ANOTHER duty of the paftoral office is to reprove and rebuke fuch as are faulty in their moral conduct. This is always difagreeable to a man of modefty and goodnefs ; but reproofs and rebukes are often neceffary and ufeful for reforming finners; and whenever they are fo, the fcripture makes it the indifpenfable duty of a minifter to tender them. Thus the apoftle commands Timothy to " reprove " and rebuke with all long-fuffering and doctrine [b],"

to

b 2 Tim. iv. 2.

to expose to wicked persons the baseness of their conduct, and admonish them to amend. And he commands Titus to " rebuke sharply [c] " certain unruly persons, and in general to " rebuke," as well as to " speak and exhort with all autho- " rity [d] ."

To rebuke in such a manner as may give a probability of its answering a good end, will gene- rally require a considerable degree of prudence and address, and will always require care to suit it both to the nature of the offence, and to the cir- cumstances in which the rebuke is given.

Sometimes things worthy of rebuke are done by persons in the presence of a minister. Oaths and imprecations are sometimes uttered; senti- ments are expressed and avowed, that tend to pol- lute the imaginations, or corrupt the hearts of men; and sometimes even topics are enlarged upon, which are irreligious, immoral, or indecent. It is always necessary for a minister, in this case, to show his disapprobation; but great prudence is necessary in choosing the proper way of show- ing it.

There are some cases of this kind, in which a grave rebuke, and serious arguments, to show the

badness

---

[c] Tit. i. 13.   [d] Tit. ii. 15.

badnefs of the conduct, will be both proper and
effectual. When the offenders are of the lower
fort, fo that they and all others muft acknowlege
the minifter's fuperiority to them; or when they
are not hardened in vice, but appear to have run
into the indecency more through inadvertence than
bad difpofition, this method of difapprobation is
generally proper. A man of prudence will, from
his knowlege of the circumftances of each particular cafe, judge when it is proper to apply it,
that is, when it is likely to do good. But it is
plain that there are many cafes, in which this
method would do harm inftead of good; and as
rebukes are ufeful only for the end they anfwer,
it can never be incumbent on a minifter to ufe them
in thefe cafes. Yet ftill, as a fubordinate end of
them is to warn others, and prevent their being
infected, a minifter fhould ufe fome other method
of fhowing his diffatisfaction. Sometimes a hint
dropped with good humour, from which the perfon himfelf may eafily infer the indecency of his
conduct, and the minifter's fenfe of it, or a ftory
ferving this purpofe, will have a very good effect.
At the fame time that it fhows a man's fenfe of the
indecency of the conduct, it fhows an unwillingnefs to find fault, and a tendernefs and deference
for the perfon, which cannot fail to touch thofe
who have any degree of ingenuity, though they
would have perhaps been irritated, and rendered
obftinate in defending themfelves, by a plain
reproof. Sometimes a minifter may plainly per-

ceive,

ceive, that even this would provoke the offender
to proceed to greater outrages. In that cafe he
may fometimes fucceed, by turning the converfation to fome more innocent and ufeful topic.
By this means, he will at leaft prevent the repetition and continuance of the offence; and very
probably the offender may, if not immediately,
yet afterwards, perceive the meaning of the
tranfition, and be gained by the gentlenefs which
attended it. If a perfon be fo obdurate, that none
of thefe methods can influence him, a minifter may
fufficiently fhow his difapprobation of the indecency
to the reft of the company, by preferving filence of
an expreffive kind. But if the indecency rife high,
and cannot be checked by any of thefe methods,
a minifter fhould withdraw from the company, and
not give even the degree of feeming approbation,
which might perhaps be inferred merely from his
prefence. There is another way which may fometimes be tried with good fuccefs. If the indecency
be fuch, that a minifter can at all bear to witnefs
it, he may feem to let it pafs in the company
unobferved, and take the firft opportunity which
occurs conveniently to mention it to the offender
in private. In this fituation he will not be fo
ready to grow obftinate in defending it; he will
be more eafily convinced of its impropriety; he
will be apter to acknowlege the fault, and may
poffibly afterwards himfelf inform the company of
the difapprobation he met with; at any rate,
the tendernefs which is in this way fhown to his
reputation,

reputation, muft, if he have any degree either of fenfe or goodnefs, prevent his being provoked by the admonition.

It muft be left wholly to a minifter's own prudence to difcover which of thefe methods of reproof fuits every particular cafe. But ftill it muft be remembered, that a minifter ought in no cafe to fhow the leaft appearance of approving any thing that is indecent or immoral, or even an unconcernednefs about it. A great degree of modefty may tempt a minifter to this ; but it is a falfe and exceffive modefty : and however amiable this quality is in itfelf, yet whenever it hinders a man from doing his duty, or makes him afhamed of adhering to ftrict virtue, it becomes a real vice. A minifter fhould fet himfelf to conquer it, and to obtain fuch a degree of affurance, as may both enable him to do his duty when the interefts of virtue and religion are concerned, and to do it with that eafe and addrefs which may render it fuccefsful. If an excefs of modefty cannot excufe a minifter from performing this part of his duty, much lefs can a fervile complaifance to rank and fortune, which is vicious in itfelf. Indeed, a neglect of this duty can never fail to bring upon a minifter fufpicion of his being indifferent about virtue, to diminifh his authority and influence, to expofe him to contempt, and to bring the whole order into difrepute. I fhall only remark farther, that as rebuking feems in its very nature to imply

a claim

a claim to fuperiority, the greateſt care muſt be
uſed to take off, as much as poſſible, this appearance, by the manner of giving it, without the
moſt diſtant approach to paſſion, pertneſs, infolence, or aſſuming, with the ſtrongeſt marks of
meekneſs and reſpect.

But it is not only offences committed in a
miniſter's company, that are the proper ſubjects of
rebuke. A miniſter muſt admoniſh his pariſhioners, for whatever faults he either learns from
others, or diſcovers by his own converſation with
them, to prevail in their temper or their conduct.
Heinous crimes require ſevere rebukes; and even
ſlighter deviations from virtue muſt be reproved,
that both the perſons themſelves may be reclaimed
from them, and the contagion kept from ſeizing
others. But theſe two different ſorts of faults
muſt not be treated in the ſame way. The apoſtle
Jude points out the diſtinction which ſhould be
made between them: " of ſome have compaſſion,
" and others ſave with fear, pulling them out of
" the fire[e]." Gentler remedies muſt be applied
to the leſſer irregularities of the ſoul. But the
deeper pollutions of the ſoul, like the more dangerous wounds of the body, muſt be ſearched and
probed, and have more painful remedies applied to
them. Again, all ſorts of perſons muſt be admo-
niſhed

---

[e] Jude, xxii. 23.

nifhed and rebuked, when their conduct deserves
it, but not all in the fame manner. The fame
apoftle Paul, who commands Timothy and Titus
fo often to reprove, yet directs the former,
" rebuke [not an elder, but intreat him as a
father ᶠ." This direction is applicable to all fuperiors, whether in age, education, rank, or fortune. According to the natural fentiments of
mankind, all thefe qualities produce a kind of
fuperiority; and deference and refpect is our duty
to all fuperiors; a duty the obligation of which
their faults cannot extinguifh. When the offender
is plainly our inferior, we have a natural authority
which gives us a right to addrefs him without much
ceremony. It is generally fufficient with fuch
to profefs our concern for them, our fincere intention of their good, and immediately to enter on the
part of their conduct that is blameable : their fenfe
of their inferiority will keep them from taking
offence at the freedom. It is generally neceffary
to reprefent the fault to them fully and in ftrong
colours; for their want of improvement would
prevent their underftanding your meaning, if you
fhould touch it more flightly, or endeavour to
point out its evil by hints. It is often likewife
proper to condemn it with ftrong expreffions of
authority and difpleafure, though always without
anger or paffion; for the lower forts of men have
fo

ᶠ 1 Tim. v. 1.

fo little of delicate feeling, that without this they
will fcarce think you in earneft. But it will eafily
appear that this method of addrefs would be often
improper to perfons of fuperior quality or abilities.
It would fcarcely be confiftent with the deference
and refpect due to them ; and therefore, in reproving their faults in this manner, a minifter would
really tranfgrefs his own duty. Rebukes are not
enjoined for their own fake, but for the fake of the
good effects which they produce; and-there is the
greateft probability of their being ufeful to fuperiors, by their being managed in another way. It
is often proper to wait or to feek for an occafion
which will naturally introduce a rebuke, that
you may not feem to be fond of finding fault. It
is often proper not to dwell long on the fault, but
to give a few hints of its bafenefs ; for fuperior
parts always, and often even the improvement
which arifes from the converfation of the higher
ranks, give a penetration and acutenefs which
enable men to take a hint ; and if they do, it will
have this advantage, that their conviction will
fpring chiefly from their own reflections in purfuing it. It is generally proper to avoid an appearance of difpleafure, becaufe perfons of better rank
will probably be offended with it ; and therefore it
will defeat the end of the rebuke. And that can
never be juftified by the dignity or authority of a
minifter, which arifes only from the good and
important end of his office. He never defcends
from his dignity, nay he fupports it moft truly,
when

When he fubmits to the likelieft means of doing good. It will be fometimes the beft way, efpecially with regard to leffer faults, to exprefs a general cenfure, or to give an oblique infinuation againft them, without directly charging them upon the perfon. This will be fufficient with fome difcerning and ingenuous perfons; and whenever it is fufficient, it is the moft eligible, and will be the moft fuccefsful method. Sometimes alfo, a man's vices may be reproved, by condemning the fame or fimilar ones in another perfon. The parable by which Nathan reproved David, is an inftance of this. Many of our Saviour's parables too are reproofs of his hearers. This method is always inoffenfive, and will often be extremely convincing and effectual. The guilty perfon will often feel ftrong fentiments of difapprobation againft his own vices, when they are reprefented as belonging to another; and, by fhowing him that his own conduct is fimilar, thefe fentiments, when they are already raifed, may be eafily transferred to himfelf, and converted into remorfe.

It has been already remarked, that the only end of rebukes is amendment; therefore a minifter muft not think that he has difcharged his duty, merely by telling a perfon his faults. He muft obferve what effect the rebuke produces; if it produce not amendment, he muft repeat it; if it produce this, he fhould encourage the perfon to perfift and to improve. Attention to the defign and ufe of reproof will likewife direct a minifter

confi-

confiderably in many circumftances relating to the manner of rebuking. 'One fhould give cautions oftener, than rebukes; always, when they are likely to anfwer the purpofe. When a rebuke is neceffary, it fhould not be given harfhly; with concern, not with anger. Some perfons might be apt to find fault, merely to give vent to their own fpleen and ill-nature; and when reproof proceeds from this principle, it can fcarcely fail to be given in a haughty, fupercilious, or paffionate manner. Attention to its defign will effectually check this; for a fufpicion of pique, or fpleen, or humour is.fo fure to render reproof ineffectual, that it is generally eligible to let it alone altogether, when it is likely, from particular circumftances, to give rife to this fufpicion. Every reproof ought, on the contrary, to bear all the marks of tendernefs, meeknefs, and friendfhip, and even to be accompanied with warm expreffions of benevolence and concern. It is generally beft that rebukes be given fecretly and kept fecret; for this will give them a ftrong appearance of foftnefs and meeknefs, will fhow a tendernefs to the perfon's reputation, and, by this means, will gain upon him. A.man diflikes to be condemned in the prefence of others, and often thinks himfelf obliged in honour to attempt to juftify himfelf, though he be really fenfible of his faults. The difpofition to this will be prevented, or at leaft diminifhed, by the fecrecy of the rebuke. This fpirit will, indeed, fo far prevail fometimes, that an offender will attempt to excufe his fault even to a minifter alone, when he

- is

is notwithftanding fenfible of it. On this account,
a minifter cannot always conclude that his reproof
has been entirely ufelefs, even when the perfon's
pride would not fuffer him to acknowlege his fault;
for it may, notwithftanding, be remembered afterwards, and produce fome effect upon him. It is
of importance to choofe fit times for admonifhing
and rebuking; for a perfon will often bear at one
time what he would not at another. A perfon
may be bettered by a rebuke given when he is eafy
and in good humour, who would have been provoked by it, if it had been given when he was
perplexed or out of humour with fomething which
difcompofed him. A perfon will liften to a rebuke, when, by any emergence, he is put into a
ferions, and thoughtful temper, who would have
paid no regard to it in an hour of gaiety and diffipation. Sometimes the approach of a communion
will give a minifter a favourable opportunity of reproving men for their vices, and of urging them
to forfake them, that he may not be obliged to
exclude them. Sometimes he may take occafion,
from their defiring to have their children baptized,
to admonifh them of fome faults, particularly of
fuch as look like a renouncing of their Chriftian
profeffion, and reprefent the neceffity of amending
them, in order to their being reckoned Chriftians
themfelves, or having their children intitled to
baptifm. However delicate a matter it is to give
reproof, yet, if a minifter have prudence, and
beftow the neceffary reflection, he may almoft

always

always fall on some method so soft and inoffensive, as even to affect the worst men, at least as not to irritate and do harm. This is often the ill effect of rebukes indiscreetly managed. Some men, whose zeal is greater than their prudence, think, themselves obliged to treat all in precisely the same way, and imagine that any other conduct would show a faulty respect of persons. Pride and conceit are, sometimes, in this case mistaken for zeal. But even when the conduct proceeds from real zeal, it is from zeal ill-conducted, and defeating itself. I therefore repeat, that reproof is only useful on account of its end, and therefore should be always managed in the way that is fittest for producing reformation.

A minister ought to maintain an exact impartiality to all, and to show no respect to the great and rich, more than to the meanest. But this does not require that he should behave to them in precisely the same way. On the contrary, to treat them in the same way would be absolutely wrong. It must be remembered, that the great and primary end of rebuking men is always their reformation, and that, of consequence, it is strictly the duty of a minister to rebuke only in such a way, as is most likely to answer this end. Now not only the different tempers, but also the different educations, ranks, and circumstances of men, render different methods of reproof fittest to reform them, and render a method of reproof, which will have great
force

force with one, abfolutely unfit to work on another.
A minifter who is careful to find out the proper
manner, and to apply it, not only is not guilty of
partiality, though it be very oppofite to the kind
which he fometimes ufes on fimilar occafions, but
really could not difcharge his duty without it. A
minifter fhould rebuke all ranks impartially and
without refpeét of perfons; but he is impartial
only then, when he rebukes each in the way that
is likelieft to work on him, however different that
way be from what he finds it proper to ufe to another; and not to make this difference, would
really be a fpecies of partiality. It is in vain to
fay that a minifter cannot exoner his confcience,
without ufing an uniform method of reproof with
all different ranks; for confcience requires, not
only that he fhould warn all, but likewife that he
fhould be careful to do it in the moft effeétual
way. But ftill, a minifter is under a real and indifpenfable obligation to rebuke all offenders, as
long as there is any hope of them, in that way
which he judges will be moft effeétual with each.
There may be fome, indeed, fo very profligate,
that to reprove them will only make us the objeéts
of their fcorn and hatred. When we are fure
that this is the cafe, our Saviour has excufed us
from meddling with them, when he fays, " Give
" not that which is holy unto the dogs, neither
" caft ye your pearls before fwine, left they tram-
" ple them under their feet, and turn again and

O 3 " rend

" rend' you ᵉ:" But a minifter ought not haftily
and rafhly to take it for granted, that men are thus
abandoned; indolence or indifference will often
plead this excufe, when there is no real ground
for it; but before men be thus given over as incorrigible, a minifter muft have the ftrongeft and
moft fatisfying and inconteftable proofs of their
being really fo; if he has not thefe, he is inex-
cufeable for neglecting to watch all opportunities
to reprove them. When it is plain that they are
incorrigible, a minifter fhould, as much as poffible,
fhun their company; whenever he does not think
himfelf obliged to this, he fhould reckon himfelf
obliged to rebuke them. It may be likewife proper, fometimes to warn others to beware of the
infection of their example; this may fet them a
thinking, and produce their amendment.

It is a natural remark on this fubject, that a
minifter ought not to frequent the company of
any, whofe conduct contains many things worthy
of rebuke. Not to rebuke them, will defervedly
deftroy his authority; and if he rebuke them always when there is occafion, he cannot continue
long fond of their company, nor they of his.

ᵉ Mat. vii. 6.

SECT. VII.

Of Convincing.

THERE is another duty of the paftoral office fomewhat a-kin to reproving, I mean Convincing. Rebuking regards the practice of men; Convincing regards their principles. Paul exhorts a minifter to " hold faft the faithful word,. that he " may be able, by found doctrine, both to exhort " and to convince the gainfayers [h]." To the fame purpofe is what he writes to Timothy: " The fervant of the Lord muft not ftrive, but be " gentle unto all men, apt to teach, patient, in " meeknefs inftructing thofe that oppofe them- " felves, if God peradventure will give them " repentançe to the acknowleging of the truth [i]." A minifter may fometimes have occafion to convince thofe of our own communion, of particular errors which they may have embraced; and fometimes he will have occafion to confute and convince thofe who are not of our perfuafion. We need not confider thefe two feparately; for they are diftinguifhed only by a greater or a lefs degree of difference of opinion; and the means of convincing

---

[h] Tit. i. 9. ― [i] 2 Tim. ii. 24, 25.

convincing both are the fame; for a minifter has no dictatorial power over the former any more than the latter; he is no lord over God's heritage, nor has any right to dominion over the faith of Chriftians. His whole power is minifterial; the only inftruments he muft ufe for accomplifhing any of the ends of his office, are inftruction, reafoning, perfuafion. A minifter fhould take every fit opportunity of endeavouring to convince thofe whom he knows to entertain errors. The more dangerous any error is, that is, the more immediately it influences practice, the more earneft and affiduous he fhould be in endeavouring to reclaim people from it. In order to be able to attempt this, it is neceffary that a minifter be thoroughly acquainted with the fubject in difpute, and with the principles and fpirit of thofe whom he endeavours to convince. In the prefent diftracted ftate of Chriftianity, there are many different forts who are involved in error, as infidels, papifts, feceders, methodifts, quakers, &c. fome of which a minifter will moft readily meet with in fome fituations, and others in another. He ought to qualify himfelf for dealing particularly with thofe who are to be found in his parifh. In endeavouring to convince them, he fhould ufe only folid argument and calm reafoning; for unfair arts in making profelytes are perfectly unjuftifiable; they may fometimes entrap the weak, but if they are detected, they will only confirm men in their own way, and expofe the perfon who ufed them to juft abhorrence; and any

degree

degree of heat and paffion will look either as if a man had an ill caufe, or as if his defire to convince them arofe only from his own humour and defire of conqueft. Before a minifter can expect to gain on thofe who differ from him, he muft fhow them that he loves them and wifhes them fincerely well, by ufing them with all kindnefs, by doing them obliging offices, by betraying no difpofition to put them to any inconvenience on account of their difference of fentiment, by rejoicing in the toleration they enjoy, and the liberty they have of profeffing their belief according to their confciences; in a word, by all the methods of charity, meeknefs, and moderation. This will difpofe them to liften to his arguments. To give thefe their full weight, he muft firft ftudy to combat the perverfenefs of their wills, their prejudices, the defire of victory and applaufe, their pre-engagement in a party, and their fhame and unwillingnefs to yield; and ftrive to render them meek and pliable, and fincerely defirous to know the truth. When this is obtained, they will either be more eafily convinced, or more excufeable, if through weaknefs they ftill continue in their errors [k]. He fhould, by friendly difcourfe, difcover what led them into their errors, and then he will know better how to lead them out again. A minifter ought not to defpair of convincing diffenters, or persons

---

[k] Scougal.

perfons in an error, upon a few unfuccefsful attempts. Men's principles really depend fo much on their education, that it is not to be expected that a hafty conference or a fhort difpute fhould prevail with thofe who have been long habituated to faife principles, and fucked them in with their nurfe's milk, to abandon them all at once. They muft be treated with great patience and long-fuffering, and wrought upon by arguments frequently repeated. A minifter muft vifit them often in a fpirit of love, and offer them conferences. He may likewife direct them to fuch books as are fitteft for rectifying their miftakes, that they may read and weigh them at leifure.

The emiffaries of the church of Rome fometimes make an impreffion on thofe whom they want to convert, by this argument, that it is fafeft to join their church, becaufe Proteftants themfelves allow the poffibility of falvation in it, whereas Papifts allow no poffibility of falvation out of it. This may have weight with very weak perfons; but a fmall degree of underftanding may fatisfy a man, that an uncharitable, judging, damning fpirit, is no probable mark of the true Chriftian church. A minifter ought not to adopt this conduct, or to attempt to magnify the differences between fects and parties, in order to make profelytes. Indeed, the errors of fome parties are fo grofs, and have fo direct an influence on practice, that it needs no exaggeration to fhow perfons the neceffity of quitting

ting them. Infidelity, for inftance, implies a total rejection of Chriftianity, and therefore muft be attended with the moft dreadful hazard. In Popery, Chriftianity is fo corrupted and over-clouded with idolatry, fuperftition, and tyranny, as renders it very difficult for thofe of that commu-nion to direct their endeavours to true holinefs. Quakers reject many of the effential inftitutions of the gofpel. Some parties, as feceders and inde-pendents, adopt antinomianifm, and thus make void the law by faith. Some parties too are ruled by a bitter fpirit, inconfiftent with that love which is the end of the commandment, which is our Saviour's new and peculiar commandment, which is greater than faith and hope; and they thus deftroy Chriftian charity. A minifter may juftly reprefent fuch errors as thefe as highly dangerous, and fhould fet himfelf with a proportionable zeal to correct them in thofe in his parifh who may be infected with them. There are other differences among Proteftants, which have not fo great influ-ence on practice; and therefore are of lefs confe-quence. A minifter fhould not attempt to magnify thefe. On the contrary, he fhould fhow how infufficient they are to interrupt the courfe of Chriftian love, or to produce divifion; how juftly, notwithftanding them, Chriftians may live in com-munion together; and therefore urge them to maintain the unity of the church, not to rent it, not unneceffarily to make a fchifm or feparation from that profeffion which is eftablifhed in the country.

country. But he muſt always carefully avoid laying great ſtreſs on party diſtinctions, and incul- cate the far ſuperior importance of real holineſs and goodneſs. While he allows that they may be ſaved, notwithſtanding their preſent errors, which they hold honeſtly and miſtake for truth, if they be really holy; he muſt inculcate on them, that though they renounce theſe errors, though their opinions be true in all reſpects, yet they can- not be ſaved without holineſs. Though he ſhould proſelyte a thouſand to his own party, he muſt think that he has done nothing, till he make them likewiſe truly religious and holy; for without this, no man can be ſaved in any religion. Better perſuade one perſon to be truly holy, than bring over ten thouſand to the pureſt ſect among Chriſtians.

There are ſome caſes, in which convincing, as well as rebuking, ceaſes to be a miniſter's duty. He muſt always ſtrenuouſly oppoſe all notions which directly tend to promote licentiouſneſs and vice, that if he cannot reclaim thoſe who have embraced them, he may at leaſt prevent others from being infected with them. But there are many differences of opinion about leſſer matters, which, as they are unavoidable, can ſcarce be ſaid to deſerve great regard. Beſides, whenever per- ſons are ſo much under the power of prejudice, as to be bigotted in their own way, all a miniſter's pains would be in vain. It will often happen, that

all

all his arguments cannot convince thofe with whom he difputes. When they are honeft in their belief, and live as becomes Chriftians, he fhould not, on this account, ceafe to treat them with the greateft kindnefs and regard; he will thus fhow them, that the love of truth, not defire of conqueft, was his motive in endeavouring to convince them.

SECT. VIII.

Of reconciling Differences.

IT is often another duty incumbent on a minifter to endeavour to reconcile differences, and extinguifh animofities among his parifhioners. Warm benevolence will lead every good man to do his utmoft to promote peace and concord; and our Saviour has ftrongly recommended this exercife of benevolence, by pronouncing " the peace-makers " bleffed, for they," fays he, " fhall be called the " children of God[1]." It is indeed neceffary for all men, but efpecially for a minifter, becaufe the confequences of his giving fuch offence will be worfe, not to be forward or over-bufy in meddling in the affairs or quarrels of others. It often happens, that a perfon by this offends one, or, it may be,

---

[1] Mat. v. 9.

be, both parties; and if a minister offend, a person
by being thought to be partial against him, it will
probably be for ever out-of his power to be useful
to him. For this reason, a minister should always
avoid 'deciding the differences of his people, as a
judge or arbiter; for if either party should be dif-
pleafed with his sentence, it will produce reflections
on his character for integrity; and these must
always diminish his esteem. All his endeavours to
reconcile differences must be of a more private
nature, and in a way more suited to his profession.
In addressing himself to either party, without
blaming him as if he were absolutely in the wrong,
or even supposing him to be as much injured as he
thinks himself, he may yet inculcate the obligation
of forgiveness, and display the beauty of placability. And resentment tends so much to aggravate
the faults which are the objects of it, and makes
men so unwilling to consider things in a fair light,
that we may almost promise, that if a minister can
once convince the persons who are at variance,
that it is their duty to forgive, and bring them to
wish that they were able to practise it, and thus
awaken that general benevolence which resentment
had extinguished, they will of themselves perceive,
that their passions have represented the grounds of
their difference as much more considerable than
they really are, and be almost ashamed of their
diffension. Men often come to this when their
resentment cools; and the only thing which prevents their reconciliation is a shyness to make the
firft

firſt advances, or an uncertainty in each, whether the other party be as much diſpoſed to it as himſelf. A miniſter may often be of uſe to them in this ſituation, by aſſuring them of each other's good diſpoſition, and by uſing other prudent means of bringing them together.

Sect. IX.

Of Care of the Poor.

It is incumbent on a miniſter, to ſearch out the poor and indigent in his pariſh, and to contrive means for ſupplying them. While the idle, the impudent, and clamorous poor make their neceſſities known, and obtain relief, there are many honeſt, modeſt, and induſtrious perſons, who are contented to pine in poverty and ſtraits, rather than make their ſituation known. Theſe are the propereſt objects of charity, whom every pious Chriſtian ſhould ſearch out, and relieve according to his ability: but this is peculiarly the duty of a miniſter.

In the beginning of the Chriſtian church, when the rich ſold their poſſeſſions for the common ſupport of the brethren, they brought the price to the apoſtles, who took care of the diſtribution, according to every man's need [m]; and one of them, Peter,
inflicted

---

[m] Acts, iv. 35.

inflicted death on Ananias and Sapphira, for defrauding the poor [n]. And though afterwards, when the number of the difciples increafed, the apoftles appointed deacons to have the immediate care of the poor, while they gave themfelves up wholly " to prayer and to the miniftry of the word [o] ;" yet we find that the apoftles thought themfelves ftill obliged to intereft themfelves very particularly in obtaining provifion for the poor, on many different occafions. Paul and Barnabas were careful to carry relief, from the church at Antioch, to the Chriftians in Judea, in the profpect of the great dearth of which Agabus had prophefied [p]. Paul had not only undertaken the diftribution of the liberal charity, which the Macedonians had given for the relief of the faints at Jerufalem, but likewife by their example, and by many other arguments, he excites the Corinthians to contribute largely for the fame purpofe [q].

If a minifter be affiduous in the practice of the feveral duties which have been already explained, he will thence derive great advantages for the difcharge of this duty. His converfing with his people and inftructing them in private, will give him many opportunities of difcovering their fituation, without his feeming to inquire into it. And his
fhowing

---

[n] Acts, v.
[o] Acts, vi. 4.
[p] Acts, xi. 27, &c.
[q] 2 Cor. viii. 1, &c.

showing all the concern he can, to supply their wants and mend their situation, will increase their confidence in him, and add new authority and weight to all his instructions and advices. They will easily believe that he sincerely wishes well to their souls, who is anxious for their bodies, and that all his exhortations proceed from his real sense of their being absolutely necessary for them.

There are many different ways which a minister may take, for supplying the poor in his parish, according to the variety of their rank and circumstances. These he must attend to with prudence; otherwise, what he designs well, may offend and irritate, by the manner in which it is bestowed. There are some, whom he may all at once, without any ceremony, either supply out of his own charity, as he is able, or recommend to the charitable funds of the parish. Many, who would have been backward to apply for relief, will yet readily and thankfully accept of it, even in this ordinary way, when it is procured to them without its being asked. But many stand really in need of relief, who yet, on account of their rank or other circumstances, will not care to receive it in this public way. To these, a minister may sometimes convey his own charity privately. Sometimes he may obtain for them relief, from persons who are disposed to bestow, and able to bestow more liberally than he himself can afford, and who will, either by him, or by other means, convey it to

P them

them in a private and inoffenfive way. When a minifter can neither afford himfelf to give, nor procure from other private perfons for them, that relief which their fituation demands; and when, at the fame time, they could not bear to be regarded as objects of public charity, it may be poffible, in fome cafes, for him to procure fomething from the public charitable funds, to be privately beftowed by himfelf. But this fhould not be often attempted. Men are fo apt to mifconftrue the actions of minifters, and it is of fo great moment that they fhould not lie open to any fufpicion of mifapplying charitable funds, that it will be generally moft prudent for them not to defire to diftribute any part of them, but to perfons whom they exprefsly name. Individuals may, perhaps, fometimes fuffer by this referve; but by neglecting it, a minifter's own reputation, and confequently his ufefulnefs, may be wholly ruined. There are often perfons in a parifh who cannot be faid to be indigent, or to ftand in need of alms, who yet would often receive great advantage by having the ufe of a little money at particular junctures. A minifter may fometimes do important fervice to whole families, by lending fmall fums, without intereft, to fuch honeft and induftrious perfons, to affift them in particular emergencies, or to enable them to catch occafions of profit. A man ought not indeed to ftraiten his own family in order to do this, and many minifters are in fo narrow circumftances, that they can fcarcely do it at all, without ftraitening them. But, if a mi-

niſter

nifter have a little money, he may, in this way, at the expence of a very few fhillings, and with the rifk of a very few pounds, not only make feveral families happy, but obtain both the love and efteem of many in his parifh, and greatly increafe his power of being ufeful.

It is certainly the duty of a minifter, to take care of the charitable funds of the parifh, both that they be preferved, and that they be well applied. The want of knowlege in bufinefs may fometimes lead to errors in the former cafe; but confcience requires that all poffible pains fhould be taken to fupply that want by proper advice: to expofe what is given for the fupport of the poor, knowingly to any rifk of being loft, would be bafe. In apply-ing them, the leading principle fhould be, to caufe them to do as much good, relieve as much diftrefs, and promote as much happinefs, as poffible. If this be kept in view, it will give direction in moft of the particular cafes which occur.

CHAP. II.

Private Duties respecting lesser Societies.

THE duties of a minister which we have hitherto confidered are, in the ftricteft fenfe, private, becaufe feparate and diftinct individuals are the objects of them. There are other duties of the paftoral office which are of a private nature, yet have bodies of men for their objects, or, at leaft, are, from their nature, performed in the prefence of families, or of a number together. We fhall now proceed to thefe which are of a middle kind between the moft private and the moft public duties of the minifterial office.

SECT. I.

Of Vifitation of Families.

THE firft duty of this kind is Vifitation of families, when a minifter goes through his parifh, affembling each family by themfelves, or two or three families together. In this round through his parifh, a minifter may do feveral things which are extremely ufeful, and which this is the beft opportunity of doing. At this time, a minifter forms a roll or catalogue of his parifhioners, according

to

to which he calls them to be catechifed, and by
which he may know whether they all attend him.
This, of itfelf, is far from being ufelefs, as it will
be a check on thofe who, through a confcioufnefs
of ignorance, an averfenefs to learn, or any other
bad principle, might be prone to avoid examination. At this time, likewife, a minifter may moft
conveniently obtain the knowlege of ftrangers who
have come into his parifh from other places, and
enquire into their characters and their atteftations.
This will be often of ufe for preventing diforderly
perfons, who might corrupt others by their vices,
from fettling in a parifh. As our Saviour, when
he fent forth, firft, his twelve apoftles, and afterwards, the feventy difciples, to preach the gofpel,
commanded them, into whatever houfe they went,
to fay, " Peace be to this houfe;" fo a minifter
ought to join with his vifit to any family, fincere
devotion and earneft prayer, particularly for the
fpiritual and temporal happinefs of that family.
A minifter may likewife render this part of his
labour fubfervient to other good purpofes, particularly to recommending fuch duties as are properly
economical, or relative to a family. This will be
a proper opportunity of inftructing them in the
nature, and exciting them to the practice, of all
the relative duties. He may enquire how the
bufband and wife behave to each other, give them
directions for the practice of their feveral duties,
point out to them many faults of conduct, which
would not perhaps have been attended to by them-

P 3   felves,

felves, which yet are both tranfgreffions of their duty, and will diminifh their happinefs in each other, and their authority in the family. He may examine the mafters and the fervants, how they treat each other, direct the former to kindnefs, and the latter to obedience and fidelity. He may inculcate on parents the obligation of taking care of the virtuous education of their children, give them familiar directions about the right manner of it, warn them againft the faults that are generally fallen into, fhow them the neceffity of training them to induftry, and fitting them for fome lawful calling. He fhould recommend family religion, particularly the reading of the fcriptures, and infpecting the behaviour of all within the houfe. A vifit to a family is one of the propereft opportunities of giving inftructions, exhortations, or reproofs, on fuch fubjects as thefe.

It happens often, efpecially in country parifhes, that feveral families are convened together. In this cafe, befides what has been already mentioned, a minifter has a fit opportunity of enquiring, on what terms they live with one another, of examining into the grounds of any differences which prevail among them, and into the occafions, which, from their fituation, produce difputes more frequently among them; and he may contribute greatly to eftablifh good neighbourhood and harmony, by directing them how to avoid thefe contentions, by reconciling their differences, and urg-

ing

ing the obligation of Chriſtian concord. This may likewiſe be a fit opportunity of exciting them to brotherly admonition. As it is the duty, not only of miniſters, but of all Chriſtians, to exhort one another on proper occaſions, a miniſter may direct neighbours to keep an eye on the conduct of each other, to admoniſh each other privately whenever they find one another guilty of a fault, or wanting in any duty. By this means, they may be ren- dered uſeful monitors to each other; the more knowing may contribute to the inſtruction of the ignorant, and the regular and virtuous to the amendment of thoſe who are not ſo well diſpoſed. A miniſter may render viſitation of families ſtill farther uſeful, by accompanying it with catechiſing. This might make it tedious and laborious in very large and populous pariſhes; but in ſmall pariſhes, and even in all except the very largeſt, it may be eaſily accompliſhed in ſo moderate a time as no man will grudge, who enters into the ſpirit of his employment. By this means, a pariſh may be catechiſed twice, with very little additional trouble to the miniſter.

Viſiting families begins to be neglected by ſome miniſters, as a leſs uſeful part of their employment; but they who neglect it, ſeem not to attend to the good purpoſes to which it may be rendered ſub- ſervient. It ſeems to be naturally implied in teach- ing " from houſe to houſe;" it is expreſsly en- -joined by the laws of our church; and a miniſter

who

who firſt performs it, or thinks of performing it in ſo careleſs and formal a manner as to render it uſeleſs, and then neglects it becauſe he finds it uſeleſs, is plainly wanting in his duty, and omits one thing, by which he might, in a great degree, and in ſome peculiar ways, promote the good of his people. This part of a miniſter's work ſhould generally be performed once every year; and that ſeaſon ſhould be choſen for it when the people are moſt at home, when they are leaſt engaged in work, and can attend with leaſt inconvenience; a ſeaſon of this ſort in the ſummer will be moſt commodious for the miniſter, who is obliged to go through the whole pariſh. As the intermiſſions of labour are not very long, a miniſter ſhould contrive, as much as poſſible, to viſit his whole pariſh during the continuance of them; but he ſhould, at the ſame time, not hurry it ſo much, as to oblige him to go through it in a ſuperficial or merely formal way. If a pariſh be ſo very large, as to render it neceſſary, either to viſit it haſtily, or to encroach upon the buſy ſeaſons of the year, it may be proper, either to viſit the whole pariſh, in the way we have deſcribed, one year, and catechiſe, without viſiting it, the next; or, every year to viſit one half, and catechiſe the other.

Sect. II.

Of Catechifing.

THIS brings us to the next duty, Catechifing. This has been confidered in all ages as the propereft method of communicating the knowlege of every fubject. A particular fpecies of it was the only method which Socrates ufed for either confuting errors, or leading men to the knowlege of the truth. It is plain from fcripture, that this method was ufed for bringing converts to the knowlege of the gofpel. Luke tells Theophilus, that he wrote his gofpel on purpofe that he " might know the " certainty of thofe things wherein he had been " *inftructed* ;" it is in the greek, περι ὡν κατηχήθης, wherein he had been *catechifed*, or inftructed by catechifing '. It is faid, that Apollos was " in- " *ftructed* in the way of the Lord ';" the greek word κατηχημενος fignified initiated, or informed by catechifing. As this is indeed one of the pro- pereft methods of inftructing, efpecially the young and the ignorant, it is to be confidered as recom- mended by all the exhortations which are given minifters to " teach." We know that it has been always ufed in the Chriftian church, and that con-

verts

' Luke, i. 4.   ' Acts, xviii. 25.

verts to Chriſtianity were, by this method, very carefully inſtructed in the nature of that religion, before they were baptized, and on this account were, during the time that paſſed before their baptiſm, called Catechumens. This method of inſtruction has many advantages. It keeps up the attention much better than a continued diſcourſe. It gives opportunity of obſerving how far a ſubject is underſtood, and of illuſtrating it till it be underſtood. It tends to make things better retained. It ſerves to explain thoſe terms which often occur in preaching, and which, however familiar they may be to the preacher, might be dark to many of the hearers, or be miſunderſtood by them; and will thus prove an excellent preparation for their attending to ſermons with underſtanding and advantage. But its obligation and utility will be eaſily acknowleged; it is more neceſſary to conſider the beſt manner of performing it.

We have already mentioned, that catechiſing may be very properly joined with viſitation of families; not that, when it is thus joined, it ſhould be thought ſufficient. It ought to be likewiſe performed by itſelf. Sometimes a miniſter may find it convenient to do this likewiſe, by aſſembling ſeveral families together in their own neighbourhood; but generally it is moſt convenient to call them to the church, or to his own houſe; the fatigue of coming once is inconſiderable to each of them, whereas it would be a great toil for him to go through

through them all. The winter months, when they are little taken up with their bufinefs, will be generally found moft convenient for this, and are for the moft part chofen. It is fometimes, too, eligible to fpend a part of Sunday afternoon in catechifing, efpecially in the fpring, immediately before afternoon fermon be begun, and in autumn, immediately after it is given over. A great many can then attend without any interruption to their work, and receive at leaft, from hearing others examined, fome inftruction in the principles of religion.

It is by no means fufficient, that the people be able to fay a catechifm by rote; they are perfectly ignorant till they know the meaning of all the words and propofitions in it; and the abfurd anfwers which the common people often give to the queftions of the moft common catechifm, fhow that they may have the whole by heart, without really underftanding any part of the fubject of it. A minifter's chief care therefore ought to be, to bring them, not to repeat, but to underftand the catechifm; and this may be done almoft with the ftupideft, by means of plain explications and eafy illuftrations. Anfwering to the queftions of a catechifm fhould not be made a mere exercife of memory; it may be no more, even when they underftand what they repeat. It fhould be made, as much as poffible, an exercife of judgment. In order to this, fuch queftions fhould be put, as may

lead

lead them gradually to difcover of themfelves, and to give in their own words the anfwer which they fhould have given, and about which they were at a lofs.   This method of leading men, by well-contrived queftions, from fome eafy and known principle to the difcovery which we want them to make, is properly the Socratic method of inftruction.   It requires fome genius and dexterity in the queftioner to purfue this method on any fubject ; but if he be capable of it, it will render catechifing an agreeable and entertaining exercife to himfelf; whereas, in the way it is commonly managed, it is a dry and tedious labour.   It will likewife be highly profitable for the learner.   It will make thofe whofe memory is naturally weak, to attain almoft as much real knowlege, as they who have ftronger memories : it will render their conceptions diftinct and determinate : and when they are thus led to deduce all their knowlege from eafy principles, conviction will neceffarily attend all their conceptions.   They will comprehend religion, and, at the fame time, perceive the truth of its feveral parts. This manner of examination which we propofe, will probably be eafily comprehended by all of you, however difficult it may fometimes be to reduce it to practice.

It is a fault in moft catechifms, that they abound too much in technical and fyftematic terms.   This is one great occafion both of people's getting them merely by rote, and of their not underftanding

15   them.

them. It were much better that thefe terms were
confined altogether to controverfial writings, and
ufed neither in fermons nor in catechifms. But as
they are often 'ufed in both, they fhould, in catechifing, be explained in as eafy and familiar a
manner as poffible, that, when they occur in
preaching, they may not be unintelligible. It is
likewife a fault in moft catechifms, that the principles of religion, and the precepts of it, are kept
too much diftinct, and laid down in different parts.
By this means the practical tendency of the chriftian
doctrines does not appear; their connection with
holinefs is not pointed out; the duties of religion
are explained, but they are not enforced by the
proper motives. Thefe inconveniences fhould be
remedied in catechifing. No queftion relating to
any doctrine of religion fhould be difmiffed, without fhowing its influence on practice, and the
force with which it recommends holinefs. In
examining, again, on every queftion relating to
duty, the peculiar obligations of that duty fhould
be brought into view. All this may be accomplifhed by proper queftions put in the way that we
have already defcribed. But with thefe, it will be
very proper, that a minifter frequently intermix
fhort exhortations to the due improvement of the
principles of religion, by the careful practice of
every duty.

It is but a fmall part of a catechifm that a minifter can afk at every particular perfon; yet the
defign

defign of catechifing is to inftruct perfons in the whole fcheme of religion. In order to effect this, a minifter muft call as many together to be cate-chifed, as he can go through, without either ren-dering the examination of each fuperficial, or immo-derately fatiguing himfelf. The increafe of labour at every particular meeting will be compenfated, in fome degree, by the fmaller number of meetings. He muft endeavour at each meeting to go through the whole catechifm; by which means, all who are prefent may be inftructed in all the parts of religion. In order to make room for this, it will be proper to pafs flightly over fuch things as are of leffer moment, and to dwell chiefly on thofe things of which the people feem moft ignorant, or which are of greateft importance, and moft immediately connected with practice.

The duty of catechifing fhould be diligently practifed, efpecially with regard to the young. It is by this means that they can beft learn the great articles of the chriftian religion: if they do not learn them then, they will fcarce ever learn them thoroughly; but if they then learn them, they will keep a faft hold of them to the end of their lives. It is with the young that moft benefit may be expected from it; their minds are open to truth, and pliable to goodnefs; on thofe who are already confirmed either in ignorance or in vice, it cannot be expected that fo great an impreffion will be made.

Sect. III.

Of Fellowſhip Meetings.

We ſhall next make a few obſervations on a cuſtom which prevails in ſome places, but is not univerſal, that of holding fellowſhip meetings. It cannot be doubted, that meetings of private Chriſtians, either among themſelves, or with their miniſter, if they were managed aright, and judiciouſly employed in devotion and in exciting one another to love and good works, might be attended with very conſiderable advantages. But at the ſame time it is plain from experience, that they have ſeldom been managed aright, and that they have in fact generally been attended with real inconvenience. They are too much confined, as all who chooſe are not admitted to them, though their morals may be unexceptionable. They are chiefly compoſed of perſons who are diſpoſed to idleneſs, and think they cannot mind religion, without neglecting their worldly buſineſs and many of the ſocial duties of life; of ſuch perſons as are conceited of their knowlege, on account of their dipping into abſtruſe and diſputable ſubjects, or of their peculiar ſanctity, on account of the orthodoxy of their opinions; of ſuch perſons as place almoſt the whole of religion in a punctual obſervance of the ceremonial duties of it, and thus ſubſtitute

ſuperſtition

superstition in the place of holiness; of such persons as are under the influence of a weak and ignorant enthusiasm; and, in a word, of such as think they derive great merit from their attending such meetings, and on that account regard themselves as the only godly persons, and despise others, who are perhaps much better and more virtuous than they. The consequence of persons of such characters meeting together is generally to promote their spirit of superstition, to foster their enthusiasm, to flatter their hypocrisy, to cherish their conceit and spiritual pride, and their pharisaical contempt of others. When they are met, the spirit that reigns in them will make their conversation tend rather to pervert, than to improve, their religious sentiments: their spirit, joined with their ignorance, will render their devotions often full of absurdities and extravagance. This has been so generally the effect of these meetings, the abuse of them has been so frequent, that it appears to me, they should rather be shunned upon the whole, than courted by a minister. If they have not been customary in his parish, it will be better not to introduce them. All the good effects that could be expected from them will be much more certainly and more effectually promoted by the occasional private instructions and exhortations which we have formerly recommended, and by exciting those who live in the same neighbourhood to converse about religion, and admonish each other, in the way that we have already hinted.

And

and they will be promoted by this means, without
the danger of thofe abufes which have often arifen
from formal meetings. If a minifter find that
meetings of this fort have been already introduced
into his parifh, it can feldom be prudent to attempt
to difcourage, or to abolifh them, all at once.
This would only irritate the people, and in a great
meafure deftroy the minifter's ufefulnefs. If he
fhould refufe to attend them, the people would
hold them by themfelves, and be apt to proceed
to a greater height of extravagance, than if he
were prefent. He ought therefore to fet himfelf
to eftablifh fuch regulations, as may tend to prevent the abufes of them, and render them fubfervient to a good purpofe. He fhould take care to
be always prefent at them himfelf. He fhould
appoint them to be held at fuch times as may not
interfere, either with their worldly bufinefs, or
with other duties. He fhould take care that they
be not confined to a particular fet of people of a
pharifaical fpirit, but that all who are unexceptionable in their morals have free accefs to them.
He fhould take care that all fubjects to be difcourfed
on be propofed at a previous meeting. He fhould
hinder every fubject from being introduced, that
tends to lead men into ufelefs fpeculations, intri-
cate difputes, or fuperftitious and enthufiaftical
notions. He fhould allow only fuch fubjects to be
introduced, as have a real tendency to make men
wifer and better, by either explaining or enforcing
the duties of religion; and he ought to lead them

R

to

to confider them in thofe views in which they
tend moft ftrongly to produce this effect, and to
keep them to this way of confidering them. He
ſhould recommend it to the people to confider the
fubject carefully by themfelves, before they venture
to fpeak on it in the prefence of others. When
any of them vent any thing abfurd or enthufiaftic,
they ſhould be immediately checked and corrected.
None ſhould pray, but thofe who are defired by
the minifter; and when they utter any thing extravagant in prayer, it ſhould not only be pointed out
to them, but they ſhould be hindered from attempting it again for fome time, till they learn to think
more foberly and juftly. The minifter ſhould
always be careful to inculcate on them, that they
are no better than their neighbours merely for
attending thefe meetings; that they are only ufeful
fo far as they are means of rendering them more
virtuous in their ordinary conduct. By fuch
means as chefe, a minifter of prudence may, in a
great meafure, prevent the abufe of fellowſhip
meetings, and turn them to real advantage: and
when he finds that they are already introduced into
a parifh, and that the people are fond of them, it
will generally be better to model them, in this way,
into an ufeful form, than to attempt abolifhing
them altogether.

SECT. IV.

Of Marrying.

To thefe duties we may add Marrying; but it will not require many words. It is by law committed to minifters, and from its folemn and important nature, there are good reafons why it fhould be fo.

It is their duty to do all they can to prevent marriages in any way improper, by advice and perfuafion. If thefe prove ineffectual, and if the impropriety lie only in fome imprudence, or fome inequality between the parties, the minifter muft allow them to judge for themfelves; to refufe to marry them, would be affuming an authority to which he has no right. But there may be improprieties of fuch a kind and degree, as to juftify or even require this; for inftance, if one of the parties be under age, and plainly drawn in by the art of the other, it would be a juft reflection on a minifter to folemnize their marriage. Some marriages are fo confeffedly unlawful, that not to refufe abfolutely to celebrate them would be highly criminal.

A minifter may be fometimes defired to celebrate marriages which are in themfelves unexcep-

tionable,

tionable, in an irregular manner, or without the ordinary forms of proclamation. There no doubt are cafes in which the omiffion of thefe cannot be attended with any bad, confequences. Yet it is fafeft for a minifter fteadily to adhere to them. There can never almoft be a good reafon for feek-ing to difpenfe with them; it is a caprice which deferves no encouragement; it it really penal, though there may be no danger of the penalty being actually demanded. Such cafes may be pleaded as a precedent for his conduct in others, where it is not fo clear that bad confequences may not follow; and by refufing in thefe, he incurs the charge of inconfiftence and partiality, or by com-plying, does what he thinks improper, or even hazardous.

The form of marriage includes fome inftructions concerning its nature and duties, and the marriage vow, with prayer before and after. All this is fo fimple, that it muft be unneceffary to enlarge upon it.

SECT. V.

Of fubordinate Duties.

IF the feveral private duties, refpecting both individuals and focieties, which we have hitherto illuftrated, be really incumbent on a minifter, it

will

will follow, that whatever is absolutely neceſſary
to the performance of them is in the ſame degree
incumbent on him, and that he is under ſome
obligation to whatever can contribute to his performing them in the beſt manner. Hence are derived ſeveral ſecondary or ſubordinate duties of the
paſtoral office, the conſideration of which will
ſerve for a proper concluſion of this part of the
ſubject.

The firſt of them is conſtant reſidence. If there
be no expreſs command in ſcripture, impoſing this
as a neceſſary duty, the reaſon is admitted even by
the Popiſh caſuiſts to be, that the nature of the
office implies it, becauſe it cannot be executed
without it; and every paſtor being obliged to execute his office, is of courſe obliged to reſidence
as indiſpenſable for that purpoſe. In the primitive
ages, the paſtors of every church reſided in it, except when they were driven away by perſecution;
and even by this they were not eaſily prevailed
upon to deſert it. In the original eſtabliſhment of
parochial churches in every nation, the incumbents
were looked upon as ſtrictly obliged to reſide; and
it was on the ſuppoſition of their being ſo, that
glebes and houſes were provided for them, in order
to render their reſidence commodious. After corruptions in religion began to prevail, paſtors ſometimes indulged themſelves in abſence from their
charges, for taking care of ſome worldly occupations in which they were engaged, or for attend-

ance

ance at the courts of emperors and kings : and in
the farther progrefs of thefe corruptions, the fame
perfon poffeffed himfelf of two or more churches
or parifhes, in one only of which he could re-
fide. Thefe practices were, however, very generally condemned as grofs abufes ; and, from
their firft appearance, even prohibited by the canons of fucceffive councils. Thefe canons began,
in courfe of time, to admit fome exceptions ; firft,
by allowing one man to hold two churches when
a fufficient number of fit perfons could not be
found for providing each with a feparate paftor ;
next, when one church was fo poor as not to
afford a competent and fufficient maintenance ;
afterwards for reafons far lefs reafonable, as in favour of perfons of high birth, or eminently learned,
or dignified in Univerfities, who, on difpenfations
being granted by the Pope, might hold a plurality
of benefices. By means of thefe exceptions, along
with the facility of procuring difpenfations, the
abufe rofe to fo great a height, that many remote
benefices were often accumulated in one perfon ;
for remedying which, the Council of Trent made
feveral decrees ; and though thefe did not take
away all difpenfations, they have rendered applications for them, and confequently both non-refi-
dence and pluralities, lefs frequent in the church
of Rome than they formerly were. In England,
a law had paffed fome time before that council,
and before the eftablifhment of the Reformation,
which, by admitting the exceptions introduced in
the

the moſt 'corrupt ages, gave them a ſanction in
that church: and it has never been formally re-
pealed. Under the authority of it, non-reſidence,
on account of pluralities as well as on other pretences, continues to prevail; though it has always
been condemned by many, and pronounced to be
contrary to the declared ſenſe of the church, particularly in its public offices, and unjuſtifiable in
point of conſcience[t]. Reſidence being indiſpenſably required in our church, it is unneceſſary for
me to inculcate the obligation of a miniſter to reſide ordinarily in his pariſh. Care of health, neceſſary buſineſs, and other duties of different kinds,
may, doubtleſs, prevent reſidence in the ſtricteſt
ſenſe continual, and juſtify abſence for a ſhort, and
ſometimes a longer time: but even ſuch induce-
ments ſhould be complied with ſparingly, not ea-
gerly catched at. Without living much at home,
a miniſter cannot perform the ſeveral duties of his
office, which recur almoſt every day, in ſuch a
manner as can either give full ſatisfaction to his
own mind, or yield the greateſt benefit to his
people. To wander often abroad on needleſs viſits
or amuſement, expoſes a miniſter to the contempt
of his people, alienates their affections, and impairs
his

---

[t] Stillingfleet, Ecclef. Caſ. 1. p. 23. Caſ. 2. p. 158. Caſ. 3.
p. 213. Burnet's Paſt. Care, ch. v. vi. Secker, Charge 1.
Cant.

his ufefulnefs. But to be always at hand, to advife, direct, and inform them, to comfort the
afflicted and difeafed, to awe the diforderly, to
give countenance to the well-behaved, to reconcile
their differences, to promote friendly offices, to
procure relief for the indigent, to anfwer quickly
and regularly the feveral calls which they may
have occafion to make upon him, will endear a
minifter to his people, and add an incredible force
to all his inftructions [u].

On the fame principles it is the duty of a minifter, to keep himfelf as much as poffible difen-
gaged from all occupations except thofe belonging
to his office : for the proper and careful performance of its duties, together with the ftudies requifite for that purpofe, and the attention which his
own worldly affairs render indifpenfable, will be
fufficient to fill up all his time. No doubt there
are cafes which ought to be excepted. Teaching
in any ufeful line is congenial to the proper bufinefs of a clergyman; fome clergymen are well
qualified for it, and in fituations which put it in
their power; and by engaging in it no farther than
is really confiftent with all their paftoral duties,
they may not only innocently render their condition more comfortable, but employ their time
laudably,

---

[u] Stillingfleet, Ecclef. Caf 1. p. 23. Caf. 2. p. 158. Caf. 3.
p. 213. Secker, Charge 1. Cant.

laudably, improve themselves, be highly useful to society, and even be kept more constantly at hand for attendance upon their parochial functions. If a clergyman understand medicine, he may practise it in his neighbourhood to a certain degree, without drawing him off from these functions: and by this may not only better his circumstances, and do much good to the bodies of men, but also give assistance to such as could not otherwise have procured it, multiply his opportunities of addressing his people as a minister, and render them well disposed to listen to his addresses on subjects of religion. Some degree of attention to business, particularly in the way of agriculture, the situation of most clergymen renders necessary: but it can never be proper to extend it beyond what is necessary. If they engage so far in any secular employment as to be immersed in it, they cannot have leisure for all the duties which are incumbent on them, they will contract a turn of mind unfavourable to their always entering heartily into them, and there is a risk, that it may put them on doing some things which will not be deemed perfectly consistent with the purity and dignity of their character, and which will, on that account, render them less acceptable and useful in their proper station [v].

That a minister may perform the several duties which we have enumerated, it is plainly necessary

for

---

[v] Stillingfleet, Ecclef. Caf. 2. p. 157.

for him to be often in the company of his people,
and to live in familiarity with them: and his performing thefe duties, on all fit occafions, when he
is in their company, will prevent all bad confequences from his familiarity. To be often in their
company, joining in their amufements, falling in
with the trifling, or conniving at the blameable
converfation in which they frequently engage, will
very eafily produce an exceffive familiarity of the
worft tendency. It cannot fail to deftroy that refpect and efteem which it is abfolutely neceffary for
him to maintain, in order to give weight to his
miniftrations. But when, inftead of that, he takes
every opportunity of introducing ufeful converfation, of enlarging and correcting their knowlege,
of exciting them to their duty and directing them
in it, of giving them confolation, of doing them
good offices; he may be very often in their company, not only without breeding any inconvenient
familiarity, but fo as to raife their efteem, and increafe their love to him. If fome of them fhould
have even entertained prejudices againft him, he
will, by this means, moft effectually wear them
off: when they find him thus folicitous for their
improvement and falvation, they will drop them of
their own accord; and labour to make amends for
them, by the warmth of their affection.

CHAP. III.

Public Duties, respecting a whole Parish.

Sect. I.

Of Preaching.

AS we are now come to the public duties of the
pastoral office, we shall begin with Preaching,
both because it will require a fuller consideration than
the rest, and because, being one very considerable
mean of instruction, it is nearest akin to the private duties, which we have hitherto chiefly illustrated. Preaching is so natural a method of teaching, is so often enjoined in the New Testament,
and is so fully recommended by the example of
our Saviour and his apostles, that it has always
been acknowleged an important part of the office
of a minister; and therefore it will be unnecessary
to spend time in proving that it is incumbent on
him. Nor do we propose to lay before you a
complete system of the rules of preaching, deduced from the general principles of composition,
or traced up to their source in the constitution of
human nature. We shall content ourselves with
proposing some of the principal rules of it, in
such a way as may both convince you of their
justness,

juftnefs, and render them eafily applicable to practice.

We fhall not attempt any precife general definition of Preaching; it might be difficult to contrive
one which would fully take in all its varieties; and
the confideration of thefe varieties will fuperfede
the neceffity of it.   It is plain that Preaching is the
delivering a difcourfe, which tends to promote the
falvation of mankind, by inftructing them in the
knowlege of their duty, and exciting them to the
practice of it, and to the love of goodnefs.   This
being its defign, " it is certainly," to ufe the
words of Bifhop Burnet, " a noble and profitable
" exercife, if rightly gone about; of great ufe both
" to the prieft and people, by obliging the one to
" much ftudy and labour, and by fetting before
" the other full and copious difcoveries of divine
" matters, opening them clearly, and preffing
" them weightily upon them.   It has alfo now
" gained fuch efteem in the world, that a clergy-
" man cannot maintain his credit, nor bring his
" people to a conftant attendance on the worfhip
" of God, unlefs he is happy in thefe perform-
" ances w."

The general end of Preaching, the promoting
the religious and moral improvement of mankind, all preachers have profeffed to aim at,
though they have taken very different methods,
and

---

w Burnet's Paftoral Care, ch. ix.

and the fashion of Preaching has, like all other fashions, undergone many changes. In the beginning of Chriftianity, Preaching was extremely fimple; it confifted almoft wholly of plain practical exhortations; it has fince been fometimes joined with all the ornaments of rhetoric, and fometimes with all the fubtlety of fcholaftic philofophy. In the dark ages, it was little elfe than panegyric on the Romifh faints: after the Reformation, it was employed about the doctrines and duties of religion, but with too great a mixture of controverfy: the feveral changes which it has fince undergone, may be traced in the fermons to which there is eafy accefs. It would be curious and entertaining to trace it through the various forms it has affumed, and to point out its moft confiderable revolutions. But a complete hiftory of this would be long; and fo far as it is either neceffary or proper to hint at it, we fhall have occafion to take notice of fome of the moft remarkable forms of Preaching, in illuftrating its particular rules.

Preaching is one fort of public fpeaking; the eloquence of the pulpit is one branch of eloquence. A preacher differs from one who fpeaks in the fenate or at the bar, only in the fubject which he treats, and in the end which he purfues. Thefe differences will occafion fome varieties in the manner of fpeaking which he is to ufe; but ftill the peculiar rules of Preaching arife from the general

principles

principles of eloquence, the fame principles which
are the fource of all other forts of compofition.
A particular comparifon of the eloquence of the
pulpit with that of the bar or the fenate, in order
to difcover their agreements and their differences,
would be curious, and might illuftrate all of them ;
but it is not fo abfolutely neceffary to our prefent
defign, as to require our entering on a full difcuf-
fion of it.   We fhall only remark in general, that
on account of their agreements and analogy,
many of the rules laid down by the ancients for
the bar or the fenate, are applicable to the pulpit ;
but in applying them to it, judgement muft be
employed, on account of the circumftances in
which they differ.   It would be eafy, from the
comparifon we have hinted at, to deduce the fuperior importance of chriftian oratory to all other
kinds, both in refpect of its fubject and its end ;
to point out the advantages which the chriftian
orator has above all others, from the fublimity and
moment of the topics on which he infifts, and of
the motives which he urges ; and to fhow the difadvantages under which he lies, in comparifon with
others, particularly from the fpiritual nature of the
fubjects on which he infifts, and from its being his
bufinefs to excite men, not to fome one action,
which may be performed immediately, but to a
general courfe of behaviour.   But thefe things you
will be able to profecute, if you find it neceffary,
by yourfelves.

The

The ancient rhetoricians diftinguifhed orations into three kinds, the nature and rules of which they delivered very particularly: 1. Deliberative, which were employed about fomething future, about what was to be done; and for thefe, there were frequent opportunities in the fenate and popular affemblies in Greece and $R_o m_e$, where public meafures were concerted and refolved upon. Such orations aimed either at *perfuading* to, or *diffuading* from, certain actions or conduct; and the topics on which they turned were, the honour or difhonour, the juftice or injuftice, the advantage or difadvantage, of the meafures propofed. Many fermons might be reduced to this clafs; all fuch as aim at perfuading to virtue in general, or to any particular virtue, from its obligations, its excellence, its advantages here and hereafter, or at diffuading from vice, by the oppofite topics. 2. Judicial, which regarded the paft, and belonged to the criminal courts; they were employed in accufing or in defending, and made ufe both of facts and arguments for thefe purpofes. Sermons which are employed in defending any character approved in fcripture from objections that have been raifed againft it, are of the fame kind with judicial orations. So are all fermons, in fome meafure, whofe bufinefs it is to vindicate religion in general, or any particular doctrine or duty which has been attacked as unreafonable, abfurd, unworthy of God, hurtful to men; or to expofe any error or vice which has been recommended under the oppo-

fite

fite views; only thefe latter have things for their objects, not, like the former, perfons. 3. Demonftrative, which relate to fomething prefent, and are employed either in praife or blame. They were employed in panegyrics on the excellence of perfons, characters, conduct, laws, forms of government, or whatever could admit of an enccmium; and likewife, in invectives againft perfons or things of an oppofite nature. Of this kind were all their funeral orations on eminent perfons, orations in meetings for the choice of fit perfons for offices, or for continuing or repealing laws. To this clafs may be reduced fermons on the excellence of any great character recorded in fcripture, on the excellence of Chriftianity, or of any particular doctrine or virtue, or on the deformity of vice. As the beft rules for eloquence are to be found in the writings of the ancient rhetoricians, and as they apply their rules particularly to orations, according to this divifion of them, it may be ufeful for you to confider, how far, and in what refpects, fermons are analogous to thefe fpecies of orations; for fo far as they are, all the rules of the ancients regarding each kind, will be applicable for your direction in the compofition of fermons. But this divifion is plainly adapted to the feveral ends of fpeaking and forts of difcourfes, for which the conftitutions of Greece and Rome gave opportunity; it gives not the moft natural view of the variety of pulpit difcourfes, though it may be in fome meafure accommodated

to

to this; and therefore we shall arrange them under a different division.

As eloquence, considered in its largest extent, is the art of speaking so as to attain the end which a man pursues; so from the variety of the ends which may be attained by speaking, the most natural division of eloquence may be deduced. Now a man can scarcely be supposed to aim at any end, but one or other of these; to instruct, to convince, to please, to move, or to persuade. A man who aims at instructing or at convincing, addresses himself, though in different ways, to the understanding; he who aims at pleasing, addresses himself to the imagination; he who wants to move, to the passions; and he who wants to persuade, to the will. All these ends are allowed in some sort of composition or another; and from that end, the rules of that composition, which are no more than the proper means of promoting its main design, flow as from their source. But, from the nature of Preaching, all these ends are scarcely allowable in it. Some of them can never be in it pursued for their own sakes, or ultimately, though they may be used as means to something farther; and therefore will not come in, in determining the kinds of pulpit discourses.

To please, is an end which can scarcely ever be ultimate to a preacher. A poet may be allowed to rest in pleasing his readers, by presenting to their

imagina-

imaginations all that is sublime and beautiful, by the
novelty of his thoughts, and the harmony of his
numbers. This is indeed the sole end of pure
poetry or description, as distinguished from other
kinds of composition; and it aims at nothing but
in subservience to this end. If it convey just and
striking sentiments, if it move the passions, and
agitate the soul with various emotions, it is only
as a mean to prevent disgust, and to heighten the
delight. But it is only a small part even of poetry,
that rests wholly satisfied with giving pleasure. The
epic, the tragic, and all the greater kinds of
poetry, aim at something beyond it, and aim at
giving pleasure only as subordinate to instructing,
moving, or persuading. And if poets themselves
generally aim at a farther end than pleasure or
amusement, much more ought an orator constantly
to look beyond it : or, if it were allowable for the
orator at the bar or in the senate sometimes to aim
only at pleasing, at exciting the admiration of
men, at setting off his own ingenuity and parts,
and raising his reputation ; yet even on that supposition it could not be allowable in the preacher.
His function is so important, the character he
sustains is so grave and sacred, the subjects of
which he treats are so momentous, that it is inex-
cuseable to spend any part of the time which men
allow for their being instructed in religion, and
excited to the duties of it, in merely amusing
them with ingenious thoughts and gaudy figures.
If a preacher only dazzle his hearers with the

brightness

brightnefs of his fentiments, the vivacity of his turns, or the beauty and propriety of his language, he is a mere declaimer. A preacher ought never to be actuated by a fond defire to pleafe, in any of his performances. All true eloquence is fit to pleafe ; but pleafing is not its true or ultimate end. It may however be allowed, that there is one way in which the chriftian orator may properly enough aim at pleafing; he may endeavour to raife admiration of a virtuous character or action. Admiration is one fpecies of pleafure ; it is not, properly fpeaking, a paffion, but a fentiment belonging to the imagination ; and the raifing of admiration is the only way in which a preacher can be allowed, profeffedly and mainly, to addrefs the imagination of his hearers.

It is very feldom too, that moving can be the ultimate end of a pulpit difcourfe. It is indeed often neceffary to move the paffions in Preaching, but not merely for the fake of moving them. The paffions are the great fprings of action : in order to perfuade men to any courfe, it is always neceffary that the paffions be moved, engaged, and directed to their proper objects; but they may fometimes be moved, without tending in any degree to perfuafion ; and when this is the cafe, to move them is not properly Preaching. There is but one cafe in which a fermon can properly reft in this ; when it is defigned to excite certain affections, which are to be immediately exerted in the performance of

fome

fome religious duty. When a fermon is intended
to be a preparation for the right performance of that
religious duty, it may be allowable to point the
whole of it at raifing, to a great degree of fervour,
the devout affections fuitable to that duty. Of this
kind is what is called an Action fermon. But
even in this cafe, as the devout affections which
fhould be raifed tend directly to practice; as the
raifing them, to a confiderable height tends to
render them habitually prevalent; and as the religious duty in which they are exerted is a noble inftrument of virtuous practice, and directly fubfervient to it; the difcourfe may be confidered as not
wholly refting in moving the paffions, but tends in
fome meafure to perfuafion, and therefore may be
included in that clafs, of which this is the main
and ultimate end. Thus, in dividing pulpit
difcourfes, it is not neceffary to make a diftinct
branch of thofe which aim at moving the
paffions.

On thefe principles, we may divide all pulpit
difcourfes into four kinds: 1. Such as aim at
inftruction or explication. 2. Such as aim at
convincing men of truth. 3. Such as aim at
raifing admiration of a virtuous character or
action. 4. Such as aim at perfuading men to
goodnefs.

ART. I. *Of Inſtructive or Explicatory Diſcourſes.*

THE firſt ſort of pulpit diſcourſes are inſtructive
or explicatory diſcourſes. They are addreſſed to
the underſtanding, to our powers of perception or
apprehenſion. Their deſign is ſimply to make the
hearers comprehend or know the nature and extent of the ſubject. They may be reduced to different kinds, according to the different ſubjects
which it properly belongs to a preacher to explain.
Theſe ſubjects are three : 1. A paſſage of ſcripture. 2. A doctrine or duty of religion, 3. A
character.

1. As the Chriſtian religion is contained in the
ſcriptures, and as it is proper that every Chriſtian
ſhould be able to read the ſcriptures with under-
ſtauding, the explication of a particular paſſage
of ſcripture is often a fit ſubject of a diſcourſe from
the pulpit. This kind of diſcourſe is already
marked out by the name of a Lecture, though we
muſt extend this name a little beyond ordinary
uſe, in order to take in all the diſcourſes that properly belong to this head. It is commonly reckoned a diſcourſe on a large paſſage of ſcripture ;
for the moſt part, it ſhould be ſo ; but the extent
of the paſſage is not eſſential to the idea of a lecture. A lecture is any diſcourſe deſigned to explain the import of a particular paſſage of ſcripture. Now, ſome paſſages of ſcripture are diffi-

cult ;

cult; others are eafy and practical. Hence will arife two kinds of lectures, which we may call, for diftinction, critical, and practical.

The main defign of a critical lecture is to give a diftinct view of the meaning of a paffage of fcripture. In order to explain it, it is firft of all neceffary, to find out the general defign and fcope of the paffage; for a clear view of this will throw great light upon all the parts; and by exhibiting a diftinct comprehenfion of this to the audience, they will be enabled to enter into all the particular illuftrations, and to perceive their whole force. If, for example, a Pfalm be the fubject of lecture; when we can find out the author of it, the occafion on which he compofed it, his fituation when he compofed it, what he had in view by it; this will of itfelf often illuftrate many of the expreffions, fhow the propriety of the fentiments, give them a peculiar force and beauty, and render the whole a lively picture of the author's foul, of the different emotions to which he was fubject, of their conflicts with each other, and of the fentiments and affections which prevailed and chiefly influenced him. Whatever place of fcripture be pitched on, there is the fame need for confidering the fcope and occafion. It were eafy to point out many paffages in the Gofpels, where a different view of the general defign will lead to very different explications of the particulars; and where, without fixing on the defign, it is impoffible to give

any

any tolerable, or confiftent explication of them at all. In the Epiftles, it is ftill more neceffary; for fometimes a whole Epiftle, and always a large portion of an Epiftle, is a chain of reafoning all tending to one point, either confirming or illuf- trating it; and not to confider it in this light, is to mifs the whole meaning of the writer. You need only look into any good commentator on any paragraph of an Epiftle, to be convinced how much the underftanding, and, by confequence, the ex- plaining of it depends on perceiving the general fcope. There are indeed fome parts of fcripture in which no connection is preferved, but almoft all the fentences are unconnected, as particularly the book of Proverbs; and there it is fufficient to attend-to the fcope of each diftinct aphorifm.

It will follow from the obfervation that has been already made, that it is proper to lecture on the fcriptures in the order in which they lie, or on a book regularly from beginning to end; except the Pfalms, which being feparate pieces, and not ranged in the order in which they were written, may be explained with equal propriety in almoft any order; for each may be confidered as a diftinct book. But in other parts of fcripture, it is by thus going re- gularly through a whole book that we can follow the fcope of the author, and unfold it gradually to the hearers, with all that is faid in order to pro- mote it. In going through any book of fcripture, one will fometimes come to verfes which are plain

enough

enough to be underftood by all.   It is enough to
read thefe, without attempting any explication of
them ; for this would both wafte time needlefsly,
and make the people imagine, either that they were
obfcure, or that the preacher trifled. If a verfe
contain any expreffions that are obfcure, it is neceffary,. in explaining it, to afcertain the meaning
of thefe expreffions, either from other places of
fcripture where they are ufed, or by other eafy and
convincing means. If any of the· expreffions be
metaphorical, it is proper to point out from what
the metaphor is taken, what is the force of it, and
how it is applied to the prefent fubject.   The·
meaning of every difficult expreffion fhould be reprefented in as plain terms as poffible. This is
often .the firft ftep towards an explication of· a
verfe.   But a preacher muft not reft here ; for it
is not enough to find out the meaning of a fingle
expreffion ; it is neceffary to fhow the force which
it has in that particular place, and how, in conjunction with the other expreffions, it tends to
.make up the meaning of the whole.   It is a great
.fault in, lecturing, to enlarge on every fingle expreffion, as if it were, a complete fenfe, and to
raife doctrines and obfervations from it in this way.
This is not to analize the fcripture, but to mangle
it ; it is not to explain it, but to play with it, to
fpeak about it and about it, to wreft and diftort it.
When any obfcure expreffions which occur in a
verfe are explained, it is next proper, putting the
explication of them, or plainer words in the place

- of

of them, to exprefs the fenfe of the whole verfe or
whole claufe, as clearly, as fhortly, and as ftrik-
ingly as poffible. If the verfe be a fimple, complete, and unconnected fenfe, no more is neceffary
for the explication of it. If it be a propofition
laid down to be proved or illuftrated, this muft be
exprefsly taken notice of, that it may be kept in
view, and that the.view of it may throw light on
all the arguments or illuftrations produced in fupport of it. If it be a part of a chain of reafoning,
or an argument or illuftration of any particular
point, then, after the general fenfe of it is un-
folded, its force for proving the point in hand, or
its influence in illuftrating it, muft be fhown; for
this is abfolutely neceffary for explaining it as it
there ftands. It often happens in fcripture, that a
particular paffage expreffes fome affection or temper of the perfon who writes it. In this cafe, it
cannot be truly explained by unfolding, in the
cleareft manner, the import of every expreffion.
This would be only to reprefent the dead carcafe
of the fentiment, but to mifs the foul or fpirit of
it. A preacher fhould endeavour to paint the
affection expreffed, to the life, and to transfufe it
into his hearers. This is the cafe particularly
in the Pfalms, and in all the places of fcripture
which are devotional. This is no more than entering into the fpirit of the author, which is con-
feffedly, in every cafe, neceffary for explaining
him. In lectures to a congregation, a difplay of
critical

critical knowlege is always improper; it is enough
that the preacher proceed upon the principles of
genuine criticifm; he fhould feldom lay open thefe
principles to the congregation, for they cannot
enter into them, and will rather be perplexed by
them. For the fame reafon, it is improper to
mention a number of different explications of a
paffage. It is generally beft to give them the explication that appears to be moft probable, without
troubling them with any other, which would both
confound them, and perhaps lead them to think
the fenfe of fcripture uncertain. In lecturing,
every thing fhould be expreffed as fhortly as poffible, for thus it will be beft remembered; and as
clearly as poffible, for this is neceffary to explication, the chief means of promoting which is perfpicuity.

A lecture is a difcourfe which admits very little
ornament, very little of addrefs either to the imagination or the paffions. But it fometimes even
requires a little of both. As much as is neceffary
to preferve attention is abfolutely requifite, and attention can fcarcely be preferved, where neither
the imagination is in any degree gratified, nor the
paffions roufed. But fometimes the nature of the
paffage to be explained, demands more. When
it abounds with images, for inftance, it is beft explained by unfolding them, and making them
more ftriking to the fancy. When it expreffes

4

any

any paffion or temper, it is beft explained by difplaying that, and infufing it by fympathy into the
hearers.

The lectures which we have termed critical,
may be fubdivided into two forts : 1. Such as are
explications of a large portion of fcripture. Thefe
are now commonly called lectures. They are the
more neceffary in our church, becaufe they are
now the only thing we have in place of public
reading of the fcriptures, which, in oppofition to
our own directory, they have unhappily juftled
out. In difcourfes of this fort, it was formerly
remarked to be proper, to explain a book regularly throughout. For every diftinct lecture, a
diftinct and complete paragraph or fenfe fhould be
chofen. It is always proper to add to the explication of the verfes, fuch practical reflections and
exhortations as naturally arife from them. Thefe
ought not, in general, to be mixed with the explication, becaufe it would break the connection,
and keep the force of the whole from being perceived. It is better to fubjoin them to the explication ; for thus it will beft appear that they are
founded in the paffage, and they can be profecuted
together, and without interruption. It fometimes
happens, that one paragraph is too fhort for a
lecture, and that two or three can be comprehended in it. Then, the reflections arifing from
one of the paragraphs may be fubjoined immediately to the explication of that paragraph, before
proceeding

proceeding to the explication of another. For, such a difcourfe is, in reality, two or more diftinct lectures put together.   2. Such as are explications of one verfe or two, which contain fome confiderable difficulties.   Thefe are lectures, according to the definition we have given; for their defign is the explication of a part of fcripture; and all the rules which we have laid down, are as applicable to them as to the former fort.   An Exercife and addition is a difcourfe of this fort, when it is properly purfued; not fpent in an ufelefs grammatical analyfis of the words, but employed in a true critical explication of them.   Only it is plain, that when fuch a difcourfe is brought to the pulpit, it muft not be filled with the words of the original language.   Making allowance for this circumftance, many of Clarke's difcourfes are of this fort, and very proper models for them.   In a difcourfe of this kind, the meaning of the words fhould be firft cleared up; then, the doctrine which they truly contain, fhould be propofed and briefly illuftrated; and then, the ufe and improvement of that doctrine fhould be fhortly pointed out.   The proper fubject for fuch a difcourfe is a text, which at once is difficult, and contains fome important and ufeful doctrine.   Difcourfes of this fort will naturally be interfperfed with thofe of the former kind; for in every book, one will now and then meet with a difficult verfe, which requires a particular explication.   And as, on the one hand, it is contrary to the defign of lecturing to fpend more
time

time than is neceffary in explaining a clear paffage;
fo, on the other hand, it would be wrong, when
a difficult paffage occurs, not to allow it the time
that is really neceffary for explaining it.

Every part of fcripture is intended either to
illuftrate and enforce our duty, or to explain and
confirm fome doctrine of religion; and as all the
doctrines of religion are fubfervient to practice,
and are propofed as motives to our duty, we may
juftly fay that every part of fcripture is fit to influence our practice. On this account practical
reflections are, as we have obferved, an effential
part even of a critical lecture. But there are many
paffages of fcripture which are extremely plain in
themfelves, and need very little explication: thefe
are the proper fubjects for that fpecies of lecturing
which we have termed practical. Some of the
rules of critical lectures, already laid down, are
likewife applicable to thefe: for inftance, it is
neceffary to obferve the general defign and fcope
of the paffage. Even in a plain paffage, there are
generally fome expreffions that need to be explained. Thefe fhould be firft of all explained,
according to the rules already mentioned. After
this, the practical obfervations which arife from
the paffage, fhould be profecuted. In profecuting
them, two things are neceffary; firft, to fhow that
each obfervation is founded on the paffage; and
next, to illuftrate the obfervation itfelf, and apply
it to practice. There are many parts of fcripture

fit

fit for fuch lectures.   Thus many hiftorical paffages
are fo eafy, that very little is neceffary for clearing
up the narration ; and that little may often be beft
done by giving the fubftance of the hiftory in
modern language, and even with greater brevity
than it lies in the paffage.   After that is done; a
preacher fhould point out, with what view fuch a
paffage of hiftory is recorded, to what end we may,
apply it, what leffons we may learn from it ; and
in pointing out this, may very properly fpend the
greateft part of the difcourfe.   The parables of our
Saviour alfo are extremely proper fubjects of practical lectures.   It is at leaft, in general, proper firft
to explain the whole ftory or fimilitude in its literal
fenfe, fo far as it needs to be explained, that thus
the whole import of it may be feen at once.   This
literal explication of the verfes will generally be
extremely fhort.   But it is beft to give it altogether;
it will afford an opportunity of fhowing the propriety, the beauty, and the real occafion of many
of the circumftances which are fuppofed or related ; it will likewife tend to prevent a fault which
is very common in explaining parables, but a fault
which ought to be carefully avoided ; I mean, the
drawing a moral from every circumftance or incident of the parable.   This fault has in a great meafure arifen from giving the meaning and intention
of the parable as one proceeded, verfe by verfe,
which obliged him to contrive fomething defigned
by every circumftance ; though it is plain that
many circumftances are added, merely to render
                                                  the

the literal ftory probable, or for ornament, but have nothing anfwering to them in the moral. And it were eafy to give many inftances of ftrange myftical explications which have been devifed from fome circumftances of our Saviour's, parables. In general, it is proper firft of all to explain. the parable itfelf, as if it were a literal ftory, and had no farther meaning, fo far as it needs explication in this way; and it is proper that this be a con-tinued explication, not interrupted by pointing out the meaning of any part of it, at leaft in moft cafes. After this is done, we muft next explain the real defign and intention of the fimilitude, and propofe the inftructions which it was defigned to convey. When thefe are propofed after the whole explication, the fame fault muft be avoided which we have already taken notice of. We are often, efpecially young men, apt to be greatly pleafed. with finding fome myftical fenfe in every circum-ftance. To allegorife them all has an appearance of ingenuity, and therefore gratifies; but it is always merely fanciful and uncertain, and there-fore fhould be avoided. It is always faulty to refine in this manner, to found doctrines or to fqueeze maxims from every incident in a figurative difcourfe. It is neceffary to diftinguifh the cir-cumftances which are brought in merely to fill up or adorn the narration, from thofe which are effen-tial to the parable. Attention to the occafion of the parable, or to the run of the incidents, or to the reflections made on it, will enable us to diftinguifh

guifh between thefe. We muft draw the moral only from the latter, and inculcate the inftruction which the parable was plainly defigned to convey. As all our Saviour's parables weie originally addreffed to the Jews, moft of them were defigned to convey fome inftruction, which their particular circumftances rendered neceffary. It is proper always to take notice what this inftruction was, becaufe the view of it adds greatly to the force and beauty of the parable. Sometimes it will be beft to exhibit the whole import of the parable with refpect to the Jews together, and afterwards to fhow what inftruction it conveys to all Chriftians. Sometimes again, when the inftructions conveyed by a parable are pretty much diftinct, it will be better to confider each inftruction feparately, as directed firft to the Jews, and then as applicable to Chriftians. But ftill, whichever of thefe ways be chofen, the principal part of a lecture on a parable fhould be inculcating on the auditory the inftructions which it conveys. In profecuting the inftructions that arife from a parable, it has always a peculiar beauty, to introduce only fuch allufions, fimilitudes, and illuftrations, as have an analogy to the circumftances of the parable. This prevents a confufion of metaphors and figures: it makes the whole appear to rife naturally from the parable: it ferves to inculcate the whole with the greater force. You will find models of the manner of explaining parables which we have recommended, in Tillotfon's difcourfes on the parable of the ten virgins,

virgins, and the parable of the rich man and Lazarus. I fhall mention only one other fubject proper for this fort of lecture, which we have termed practical, the book of Proverbs. Some of the apothegms there need a critical explication; but in explaining all of them, the principal thing to be done is to reprefent the fentiment or maxim which each contains, in a ftrong and ftriking light, fo that it may affect and touch the hearers. And as they are all feparate practical fayings, there is fcarcely any need of general reflections at the end of a lecture on feveral of them.

A practical, as well as a critical lecture, may be fometimes made on a fingle verfe, or a fmall portion of fcripture. A difcourfe on a fingle verfe is always properly a practical lecture, when it is not a profecution of fome one fubject, but is intended to explain or enforce all the inftructions which are implied in the feveral members of the verfe. Thus every difcourfe, profecuted in what is called the textual method, is properly a lecture, either of the critical or the practical fort, or often a mixture of both. A fermon, as diftinguifhed from thefe, is the profecution of fome one fubject, in fome or other of the ways that will be afterwards explained.

2. Lectures are confined to an explication of the fcriptures; but there are other fubjects which it is neceffary to explain. A fecond kind of explicatory

catory

catory difcourfes is fuch as are intended to open up
or illuftrate a particular doctrine or duty of religion. It is abfolutely neceffary that a doctrine be
underftood, before it can be believed. It is abfolutely neceffary that a duty be underftood, before
it can be practifed. It is therefore proper that
difcourfes be often employed in explaining both.
A fubject of this kind is either fimple or complex ;
a regard muft be had to this diftinction in explaining it.

Some fimple fubjects are at the fame time fo
eafy and well known, that any explication of them
is unneceffary ; it cannot make them plainer ; and
in that cafe, it would be mere trifling. All our
natural paffions, as joy, grief, love, hatred, are
known to every one by immediate feeling, and
cannot be made clearer by any verbal explication ;
all that can be done is to refer the hearers to what
they feel. In difcourfing on thefe paffions, it may
indeed be neceffary and proper to point out the
feveral views which the fcripture gives of them,
the objects which it prefents to them, the good
purpofes which they anfwer, or the abufes to
which they are liable ; but all this is different from
explaining the paffion itfelf. When a fimple fubject
needs explication, or can be made clearer by it,
the explication may be performed by a definition
marking precifely what it is. The rules of definition are given in logic, and have their foundation
in nature. 1. It fhould be fhort. 2. It fhould
be

be perſpicuous; and therefore both obſcure and metaphorical terms ſhould be avoided in it.   3. It ſhould be exact, ſo that the definition may be ſub-ſtituted for the name of the thing defined; it muſt on the one hand exhauſt the ſubject, and, on the other hand, include nothing but what belongs to it.   A ſimple ſubject may be farther explained, by diſtinguiſhing it from ſome other with which it is naturally connected or nearly allied, and with which it may therefore readily be confounded. Thus kindneſs, meekneſs, and placability, are virtues near a-kin, and yet really diſtinct.   A per-ſon may have a very warm and affectionate diſpo-ſition, and yet not poſſeſs meekneſs, which is a calmneſs in oppoſition to anger, and not eaſily ruffled even by great provocations; and a man may poſſeſs this temper, and yet not be placable, but unrelenting, when once provoked. Things which have no natural connection often acquire an artificial connection, or become ſo related in the opinions of men, that they are as readily con-founded as if they had been naturally connected; and conſequently it is as neceſſary to diſtinguiſh them.   The power of education, cuſtom, example, the ignorance, the weakneſs, and the paſſions of men, lead them to form many unjuſt aſſociations; and on no ſubject more frequently than on religion and morality, where it is alſo moſt dangerous. To break theſe aſſociations, to ſeparate things which are totally diſtinct and yet often confounded, is a point of great importance in diſcourſes calcu-

lated

lated for the religious improvement of mankind.
Thus religion is often confounded with fuperftition; yet they are very different. Superftition
reprefents God as a capricious being, pleafed with
infignificant ceremonies and abftinence from indifferent things, and fevere on the neglect of them.
True religion muft be carefully diftinguifhed from
this; it is the very reverfe; it confifts in having
juft conceptions of the divine nature and perfections, in exercifing fuch devout affections as
correfpond to thefe, and in exerting them both in
external devotion and obedience to his will. Thus
zeal for truth and goodnefs, and virtuous indignation againft vice, are often confounded with,
and therefore muft be explained as perfectly diftinct
from, a fettled fournefs or violence of temper, and
hatred of men's perfons for difference in opinions
or ceremonies. In the imaginations of fome,
pride, which confifts in a high opinion of one's
own talents and endowments, and leads to refent
the fentiments of others concerning him, when
they fall below this ftandard, is connected and
confounded with greatnefs of mind, which is
totally different, which confifts in a freedom from
all mean paffions, little defigns, and interefted
views. On the other hand, humility is by fome
confounded with littlenefs of foul and meannefs of
fpirit; but no two things are more different. Humility arifes from a juft fenfe of our own imperfection, of the narrownefs of our underftanding, of
the defects of our knowlege, of the weaknefs of

                                                    our

our virtues; and it is never found except in thofe who have conceived a high ftandard of perfection and virtue, and who, from frequent felf-reflection, are confcious that they fall below it. But the forming of fuch a high ftandard is fo far from having any tendency to produce meannefs or littlenefs of mind, that on the contrary, it has the ftrongeft tendency to wear it off, to exalt our aims, to cherifh whatever is great or worthy, and to raife us gradually nearer to the ftandard which we have conceived. Thus again, envy and emulation are often confounded, and muft be diftinguifhed; the former is an uneafinefs at the fuperiority of others, producing a defire that they may be brought down to our level, or below it; the latter is a noble ardour for attaining excellence, leading us only to improve ourfelves. A fimple fubject may be explained, not only by a definition, and by diftinguifhing it from others with which it is apt to be confounded, but alfo by defcription. A thing that cannot be defined, may notwithftanding be defcribed; and after a fubject has been defined, it may be illuftrated. A fubject may be defcribed or illuftrated in many different ways. Many things are very properly defcribed by their effects. The divine perfections cannot be conceived by us abftractly, as they exift in God; they are conceived only by means of their effects, and as fhowing themfelves in thefe; and it is by properly pointing out their effects in the works and ways of God, that they can be explained. In ex-

plaining

plaining a thing by its effects, the most striking
and interesting of them should be selected; this
will render the explication animated and spirited.
Such principal and leading effects likewise should
be chosen, as include or suggest many particulars;
this will prevent tediousness of illustration, and
render it full in a consistence with brevity. In
particular, any virtue or vice cannot be more properly explained, than by pointing out how it shows
itself in human life. This may be done by examples taken from history, especially from the sacred
history; or it may be done by pointing out how it
shows itself in the different situations of life; for
instance, humility may be explained, by pointing
out how it will lead us to behave to those who are
our inferiors, our equals, or our superiors, in
knowlege, in religious improvement, in rank, in
age, or in character; this will give a full and the
most practical view of the subject. A simple subject may be farther explained by comparison with
others nearly related to it, or in any respect analogous to it, but better known, or better defined.
A subject may likewise be illustrated by contrasting
it with its opposite; for opposites set by one another, mutually illustrate and throw light on each
other. Humility and pride, temperance and intemperance, piety and impiety, when opposed in
their natures and their effects, on the persons
themselves or on others, will by this means be
better understood. It must be observed, that all
these methods of explication are not necessarily to
be

be united on every fubject; but a perfon's own judgement muft direct him, which of them is proper on each particular fubject, as he has occafion to treat it.

The fecond kind of fubjects for explication is complex, or fuch a fubject as is made up of different parts into which it may be diftinguifhed. In this cafe, whether a doctrine or a duty be the fubject to be explained, it is firft of all neceffary for the explication, that the feveral parts or branches of it be pointed out diftinctly, and in a natural order. Diftinctnefs and order are neceffary in every kind of difcourfe; but they are above all neceffary here, where information is the ultimate end. If the parts be confufedly jumbled together, or if the fubject be not diftributed into its natural and complete members, or if the feveral members be not exhibited in their natural order and fucceffion, the difcourfe can convey only an imperfect, or a confufed idea of the doctrine or the duty. The principal rules of a juft divifion are three. 1. It fhould be complete; the feveral parts taken together fhould exhauft the fubject. For example, if we fhould divide all practical religion into the duties which we owe to God, and thofe which we owe to our neighbour, the divifion would be faulty; for there is a third clafs diftinct from both thefe, the duties which we owe to ourfelves. 2. In a juft divifion, all the parts fhould be diftinct and feparate, fo that no one of them be included in another.

other. 3. The parts fhould fucceed each other in a natural order; the fimpleft and moft fundamental going before the others, and rifing ftep by ftep through thefe others. For example, in explaining the love of God in the moft extenfive fenfe, to find out the natural order of the parts, we may reflect on what paffes in our minds towards a perfon whom we efteem and love, a perfon of high abilities with whom we are connected by fome degree of dependence, and from whofe favour we expect fome advantages. To fuch an one we will feel, 1. High efteem of his talents and virtues; 2. A propenfity to think often and to fpeak honourably of them; 3. Defire of his happinefs and joy in it; 4. Defire of his approbation and pleafure in poffeffing it; 5. Gratitude for his favours; 6. Confidence in him. This may be eafily tranfferred to God. If the firft of thefe were placed any where elfe, the divifion would be confufed; for efteem is the foundation of all the reft. When the fubject is thus properly divided into its parts, each part fhould be profecuted according to the rules already mentioned for the explication of a fimple fubject.

It were eafy to produce many examples both of a proper and improper order in explaining doctrines or duties. But you will eafily be convinced of the neceffity of the former, and of the inconveniences of the latter, without our fpending time in producing examples. The beft means of leading you

into

into a proper order in compoſing on any particular ſubject, is a thorough underſtanding of that ſubject, and of the dependence of its ſeveral parts. This will enable you to throw them into that order, in which they will reflect greateſt light on one another. On ſome ſubjects, however, different orders in arranging the parts may be equally natural, and each may have ſome advantages. For example, in explaining religion in general, as conſiſting of three kinds of duties, we may begin with the duties to ourſelves, which are ſimple and eaſily comprehended; as ſelf-government, or a due command of our ſenſual appetites, ſo that they may not lead us into gratifications prejudicial to our health, vigour, reputation, or fortune; and of anger, reſentment, and other paſſions deſtructive of the peace of our minds; attention to the improvement of our rational powers, and the proſecution of our moſt important, our ſpiritual and eternal intereſt. Next, the duties which ariſe from our connection with other men, with individuals, with a family, or with larger ſocieties. Next, the duties incumbent on us as members of the mediatorial kingdom of Chriſt. And laſtly, thoſe which belong to us as creatures, as ſubjects of God's rational kingdom. Or, we may obſerve the contrary order, beginning with our duties to God, and deſcending to the inferior duties. The former gives the moſt eaſy view of the ſubject, as the firſt ſteps are ſimple, and prepare the way for the comprehenſion of the ſucceeding ones; the latter may

give

give the completeft view of 'each part, as founded
in the authority of God. , The former would be
the proper order in inftruefting a perfon totally unacquainted with the fubjeft; for it would be impoffible to give him an idea of love, reverence,
and gratitude to God, without having firft taught
him to obferve the motions of his heart towards
men ; the latter, will, perhaps, give the moft folid
and comprehenfive view of the fubjeft, to one who
has already a general acquaintance with it.

When I fpeak of diftributing the fubjeft to be
explained, into its natural members, I do not
mean to recommend a multiplicity of dry divifions
and fubdivifions. This cuftom, unknown to the
ancient orators, and to all the Chriftian preachers ·
of the firft ages, was introduced by the fcholaftics.
It often gives only a feeming order to the difcourfe,
but really mangles and breaks it; by following
it too much, a preacher does not, like a fkilful
anatomift, feparate his difcourfe into its proper
parts ; but, like a butcher, cuts it out into a number of pieces. A divifion is more neceffary in an
explicatory fermon, than in any other. But even
here, a fimple and natural divifion of the doftrine
or duty into its general parts is fufficient ; and fubdivifions generally break the fubjeft and clog the
memory. It is much better that without them
every part be placed in its natural fituation. Both
in dividing and in profecuting the explication of a
fubjeft, all fcholaftic terms and method fhould be
avoided.

avoided. A preacher fhould not explain a doctrine or duty, by the technical terms of metaphyficians, but as much as poffible, in the language of common fenfe, and in the words of fcripture. He fhould not divide it in the forced method of the logical topics, but in the natural way that will convey fuch a conception of it, as may tend to influence practice.

The defign of an explicatory difcourfe being to inform the underftanding, there can be in it no direct or profeffed proofs of the truth of the doctrine, or arguments for the duty, which is the fubject of it; the whole is defigned for explication. By confidering, therefore, what is implied in explication, or what is neceffary for accomplifhing it, we may perceive the nature of an explicatory difcourfe. Now, it is plain that every particular included in a doctrine or duty, muft be clearly expreffed, and fpread out as it were. It muft likewife be fhown, that every particular introduced, is really included in that doctrine or duty; and that it arifes from the preceding and is fubfervient to the fucceeding parts of it; and thus, reafoning is introduced on the feveral particulars of a doctrine or duty, even in an explicatory difcourfe, though not on the truth of the general doctrine, or obligation of the whole duty.

Explication, from its very nature, admits very little of addrefs to the imagination or the paffions.

But

But it does not exclude it altogether. Even in explaining a doctrine, comparisons, metaphors, and all other figures which serve for illustration, are very naturally introduced. The explication of a duty admits something more. It is the design of an explicatory sermon, not so much to give a dry analysis of a duty, which would enable a moralist to comprehend distinctly all that it includes, as to give a striking view of it in its whole extent, fit to influence the practice. It is its design, not so much to inform persons of what they did not know before, as to give them a lively sense of the nature of a duty generally understood. In order to answer this end, every thing that is said must be addressed, though not to the passions, yet to the feelings of mankind. This is what is properly termed, sentiment; a notion or opinion set in such a light as to touch the feelings, particularly any of the internal or reflex senses of human nature. Every thing that is said in explaining a duty should be set in such a light as to touch the consciences of the hearers, with a sense of its beauty, propriety or obligation. This can scarcely fail to happen, if the sentiments themselves be just and true, and be expressed by the preacher so as to show that he feels them himself. For then the hearers will, by sympathy with him, conceive them strongly; and a strong conception of any duty will always produce a perception of its obligation or propriety.

3. There

3. There is likewise a third fort of explicatory difcourfes, in which the fubject to be explained is a particular character. The two former kinds are very common; this kind is more rare, but may be fometimes ufed with great advantage. Butler's fermon on the character of Balaam is an example of it. Human characters are very complicated, and frequently compofed of very inconfiftent principles, of which one actuates a perfon in fome parts of his conduct, and another in other parts; and fometimes all of them influence him in fome degree, in the fame action. Hence it becomes often difficult to form a juft idea of a man's true character. Now the defign of fuch a difcourfe as we have mentioned is, to unravel a particular character, and point out the operation of the different principles which are compounded in it. A character which is to be explained, ought always to be that of fome perfon who is defcribed, or whofe hiftory is recorded, in fcripture: for otherwife, it will not be fo familiar, nor can be rendered fo familiar to the audience, as to make them enter into it, or eafily apprehend it. It is proper to give a view of the hiftory of the perfon whofe character we defign to explain, fo far as it can throw any light upon his real character; for as it is from actions that a character appears, fo the hiftory of a perfon's actions is the only means by which we can inveftigate his character, and the principles by which he is actuated. With the hiftory of a perfon's particular actions muft be joined an

6   account

account of the principle and temper which each of
them difcovers or proceeds from, and the ftate of
mind which they fhow a perfon to have been in at
the time of doing them.   By this means the hearers
will be affifted in forming a juft, and at the fame
time a lively conception of the feveral principles
which form the chara&er.   This will prepare the,
way for reprefenting, in an intelligible and ftriking
manner, the whole chara&er at once, with all the
complication and oppofition of principles which it
appears to contain.   The pi&ure of the moft
remarkable features in a chara&er fhould be
attended with fuch obfervations as may account for
it, and explain the combination of principles, and
the degree of influence which they have in the
condu&.   When the chara&er of a particular
perfon, defcribed in fcripture, is thus plainly reprefented as fhowing itfelf in his particular circumftances, the hearers will, of themfelves, in fome
meafure, be able to difcern how far it refembles
their own.   But, in order to enable them the
better to difcern it, and to render the defcription
more ufeful, it will be proper to reprefent the
chara&er in a more general way, or rather to fhow
it in a variety of lights; to point out the different
forms which it affumes, the different ways in which
it influences the condu&, the different degrees in
which it betrays itfelf in common life.   This will
bring it home to the hearers, and apply it dire&ly
to their inftru&ion.

Sermons of this fort will require a great knowlege of human nature; but if they be properly
executed, they may often be extremely ufeful.
By being employed about the character of an individual, they will give both a plain and a ftriking
view of what is the fubject of them. By analyfing
that character, either as it is maintained through
life, or as it is difplayed in a particular action,
they will lay open fome of the moft fecret windings
of the human heart, fome of thofe turns of mind
and temper, which have the moft extenfive influence upon the fentiments and practice of men.

There are many proper fubjects for fuch difcourfes
to be found in holy writ; as, for example, the fituation of David's mind in the matter of Uriah, the
character of the proud pharifee in our Saviour's
.parable, and in a word, all fuch paffages as give
an opportunity of pointing out any combination of
principles, any contraft of paffions, or any fecret
and fubtle workings of human nature, in the
perfon to whom they refer.

So much for thofe difcourfes which reft in explication or inftruction, and are addreffed purely and
ultimately to the underftanding. We fhall conclude with obferving concerning all explicatory
difcourfes, that, as their ultimate end is information or inftruction, fo their prevailing character
ought to be perfpicuity. It is only by this, that
their end can be promoted; and in order to
obtain

obtain this, the fentiments muſt be juſt and natural, difpofed in a fimple and regular order, fet off with apt and obvious illuſtrations, and expreſſed in words plain and common in themfelves, and, as much as poffible, familiar to the hearers. The beſt way of attaining this perfpicuity is to keep it conſtantly in view, while we are compofing, as our principal aim, to be underſtood by the hearers. This will prevent our aiming at an oſtentation of ingenuity and learning, and will make all our efforts to centre in giving a clear view of the ſubjeſt. In order to this, the firſt requifite is, that we have a clear idea of it ourfelves. This requires both a confiderable exaſtnefs and extent of general knowlege, and a careful preparation for every particular ſubjeſt.

ART. II. *Of Conviſtive or Probatory Difcourfes.*

The fecond kind of pulpit difcourfe is that which has for its end the proof of the truth of fome doſtrine of religion. This may be called a conviſtive or probatory difcourfe. It is addreſſed to reafon, or to thofe powers of the mind, by which we perceive evidence, and diſtinguiſh truth from falfehood. There are many of the truths of religion, which all Chriſtians believe ; but it is often proper to exhibit the proofs even of thefe : for though men do not difbelieve them, a clear view of their evidence will render their belief firmer : though their belief be firm, yet a ſtrong perception

of

of their evidence will render its influence upon the conduct greater. Thus the proofs of a God, of a Providence, of a future judgment, are very proper fubjects of fermons to a chriftian audience, who do not doubt of any of thefe doctrines. As the design of preaching on them is, not fo much to convince men of what they do not believe, as to ftrengthen the influence of a belief which they have already, a preacher is not confined altogether to the abftract and cool method of argumentation, but may very allowably throw in whatever tends to make the force of the argument better felt, or to render it fitter to touch the heart. In fuch fermons, therefore, a degree of ornament may be admitted, which would be very unfuitable to a philofophical examination of the evidence of principles. Were a metaphyfician, for example, to produce a proof of the being of God, he would fatisfy himfelf with giving a plain and conclufive argument for it; but a preacher fhould fet that argument in a more popular light, exhibiting it in fuch a way that it may produce a fenfe of the divine exiftence, fit to remain with men, and to influence them in life. In order to this, he muft turn every part of it into fentiment; he muft fhow that he has himfelf a ftrong conviction of it, which may infect them with the fame by fympathy; he muft not urge the argument in general, but muft in every part of it give a view of fome particular exiftence, and a lively picture of the impreffions of the creator which it bears; the fame proof

which

which he reprefents fo as fully to convince the
underftanding, he muft make to ftrike the imagination, and to touch the heart. Whatever be the
truth propofed to be proved, the chriftian orator
will find means of fetting the proofs of it in this
ftriking, light. It would be abfurd to attempt a
formal proof that all men are mortal; yet it is very
neceffary, to infift on the certainty of death, to
give men a ftriking fenfe of it, and to detect thofe
caufes which make it have fo little influence on the
generality.

Even in the moft abftract reafoning, it is wrong
to ftay to obviate every trifling objection that may
be formed againft the reafoning. It retards the
progrefs, breaks the argument, and diftracts the
attention. But it is ftill more improper, when the
defign of a fermon is to ftrengthen men's conviction
of a truth which they believed before, and to
render that conviction fitter for influencing practice. In this, cafe, to introduce every objection,
and ftop to anfwer it, muft perfectly chill the
argument, muft wholly interrupt the courfe of the
thought, and render it unfit to operate either on
the imagination or the paffions. Befides, as a
great part of mankind are incapable of balancing
evidence, or of weighing objections and anfwers
againft each other, and perceiving the preponde-
rance of evidence, the multiplying of objections
in preaching will tend much more to perplex or
raife doubts, than to remove them and ftrengthen,
conviction.

conviction. They fhould therefore be very fparingly introduced in fuch probatory difcourfes as are intended to give men a ftrong conviction or a lively fenfe of truths which they already believe. And by far the greateft part of probatory difcourfes from the pulpit ought to be of this kind. The doctrines which a preacher ought certainly to treat moft frequently, are the great and important truths of natural and revealed religion. Thefe are univerfally believed by thofe to whom he has occafion to preach. The greateft part even of the controverfies that have been raifed about thefe, among the different fects of Chriftians, has regarded the manner of explaining them, rather than the truth of the doctrines themfelves. Yet it is neceffary to remind men of the evidences of thefe doctrines, otherwife their affent to them will be very weak. But it is proper to handle them in the popular, fentimental, and ftriking manner, which we have pointed out, not in the accurate, dry method of ratiocination, which would be proper for the conviction of a perfon who difbelieved them.

But though this be the kind of probatory difcourfes for which a preacher will have moft frequent occafion; yet it may fometimes be neceffary to prove doctrines which are really denied by fome of his hearers. When doctrines of real importance are denied, or doctrines truly pernicious and of a bad tendency in life are propagated, it becomes a very proper

end

end of preaching, to prove the former, and to confute the latter. There will be need for difcourfes of this fort much more frequently in fome congregations than in others; and different fituations will point out different fubjects as fit to be handled in this way. But whatever be the fituation in which a minifter be placed, he fhould be careful to preach in this way no more than is abfolutely neceffary; for to dwell on the dry eviction of mere fpeculative and controverted points, tends to draw men too much off from practice, to lead them to place religion in fpeculation, and to render them fond of queftions and fruitlefs difputes.

In fuch difcourfes two different methods may be ufed; the analytical, and fynthetical. In the former, the point to be proved is not explicitly propofed, but the principles from which it is deducible are laid down and purfued through their feveral confequences, till at laft the point in view appears to be evidently deducible from them. This method is not very common in fermons, and is indeed difficult; but it is very proper when the hearers are prejudiced, and leads them on, without fufpicion, from one acknowleged truth to another, till at laft the conclufion breaks in unexpectedly upon them. In the fynthetical method, which is the moft common, a propofition is explicitly laid down, and the arguments for it profefledly urged. This kind likewife admits two different methods, anfwering to the two kinds of demonftration in mathe-

mathematical ſubjeƈts, the direƈt, and·the indireƈt. In the former, the preacher confirms the truth, by piopoſing the arguments for it in· their natural order, by which they add· greateſt weight to one another. He ſhould propoſe· them in that point of view, in which they are leaſt liable to the exceptions which are made againſt them. · When they cannot be·ſet in ſuch a light as to be evidently not expoſed to theſe exceptions, he muſt take notice of ſuch exceptions as are moſt material, and ſhow that they are invalid, and that the argument againſt which they ſeem to lie, is concluſive notwithſtanding them.

Sometimes again, a probatory diſcourſe· may proceed in the indireƈt method of reaſoning. This will be the caſe, when the preacher's aim is chiefly· to confute error. Sometimes a falſe opinion-is advanced, and by merely ſhowing that the arguments produced for it are really inconcluſive, the oppoſite truth will be ſufficiently ſupported. Sometimes a truth is not direƈtly denied; but it is thought to be attended with ſuch difficulties, or liable, to ſuch objeƈtions, as weaken men's conviƈtion of it, and make them doubtful or ſceptical about it. In either of theſe caſes, the moſt natural way of producing a conviƈtion of the truth, is to proceed in the indireƈt way; to propoſe the ſeveral arguments by which the falſe opinion is ſupported, to ſhow that they are not ſufficient to prove it, that notwithſtanding them, men may re-

main

main convinced of the oppofite truth. It will thus
depend on the nature of the truth that is denied,
on the manner in which it is denied, and on the
particular difpofition of the hearers, whether it
will be moft effectually fupported by reafoning in
the direct and oftenfive, or in the indirect and apo-
gogical method. To thefe circumftances: the
preacher fhould attend, and by them he fhould be
directed to the one method or the other; always
taking care to choofe what will be moft effectual
in the particular cafe.

   In mathematical fubjects, either of the kinds of
demonftration is fufficient of itfelf; if either be
ufed, it would be fuperfluous to add another of
the fame kind, or to fubjoin a demonftration of
the other kind. But religious and moral fubjects
are widely different. Their evidence generally not
only arifes from feveral arguments joined together,
but alfo, there are at leaft appearances of argument againft them. On this account, in moft
fubjects of preaching, both the methods of eviction
that have been mentioned, may be very properly
united in probatory difcourfes from the pulpit.
When the difcourfe proceeds chiefly in direct confirmation of the truth, by propofing the feveral
arguments that fupport it, it is highly proper, not
only to remove the exceptions brought to weaken
the feveral arguments, which will be beft done in
profecuting the particular argument againft which
they are pointed; but alfo, after all the arguments
                                          have

have been profecuted in this manner, it will be very fit for the farther confirmation of the truth, to anfwer the arguments which are produced on the other fide, and to fhow either that they have no real force, or that they have not force enough to counterbalance the arguments which have been propofed before. In like manner, when the dif-, courfe has proceeded chiefly in the indirect way; after having infifted on all the arguments for the falfe opinion, and fhown them to be inconclufive, it will add great weight to the reafoning to fhow next, that not only is there no folid argument for it, but that there are alfo ftrong arguments againft it; that not only is there no valid objection againft the truth, but alfo the ftrongeft evidences for it. Hence, every probatory difcourfe, intended to evince a truth difbelieved or doubted by the hearers, will properly proceed both by confirmation and confutation; and the kinds of fuch difcourfes will be diftinguifhed chiefly by the order in which thefe fucceed each other.

Thus probatory difcourfes are of two kinds; fuch as are defigned to produce a fenfe of truths already believed, and fuch as are defigned to beget belief of truths formerly denied or doubted; and the latter hold chiefly either of confirmation or of confutation. We may reduce to this head a third fort of difcourfes; fuch as are employed in inveftigation, or in tracing out the caufes of things; as, Why Chriftianity has not, in fact, a

greater

greater influence on the reformation of mankind.;
Why men are fo apt to place religion in externals;
and the like. For though fuch difcourfes are not
employed in proving a particular propofition by
arguments, they confift principally of reafoning,
in order to convince men that the caufes affigned
do really produce the effects taken notice of. But
as the end of all thefe forts is the fame, conviction,
fo there are many rules common to them all, re-
fulting from this their common end. Thefe are,
in general, the rules of right reafoning, which
ought to be delivered fully in that part of philofophy which profeffes to teach the art of reafoning.
We cannot here enlarge upon them all; but fhall
only hint at a few of the moft confiderable of
them.

It is neceffary to attend, whether the point to be
proved is fimple or complex; if it be complex,
its feveral parts muft be kept in view, and the
arguments fupporting them, according to their
natural order, be regularly propofed. The arguments which prove only one part of the propofition, muft be carefully feparated from thofe which
prove the whole, and reduced to different claffes.
If thofe which directly prove the feveral parts of
the propofition, be firft urged according to the
natural order of thefe parts; fuch arguments as
confirm the whole, will, by coming after them, be
well underftood, and will, as it were, collect into
a point, and concentrate the conviction produced
by

by them. In other cases, it may have a good effect to begin with the general arguments, and then, such as particularly prove the several parts, will spread out and illuminate the conviction produced by the former. If the general truth to be proved is pretty well understood in the grofs, and the general arguments for it are very plain, this latter is perhaps preferable; if that truth be but indistinctly, or imperfectly conceived by the hearers, or if the general arguments for it be complex, the former manner will be most eligible.

In order to reason well on any subject, it is first of all necessary, that a man know what kind of proof or evidence that subject admits of; otherwise, he will be in danger of falling into a wrong track, and of searching out improper arguments. On this account, that part of logic which distinguishes evidence with accuracy into its different kinds, and afcertains the proper province of each kind, is of the greatest importance, and is indeed a proper preparation for reasoning of every fort. Now, all the subjects, of which a preacher has occasion to attempt the proof, are reducible to two kinds; such as are to be proved by reason, and such as are to be proved by revelation. He should content himself with whichever of these kinds the present subject admits of; for to apply them indiscriminately to all subjects, would be perfectly abfurd. In proving a truth difcoverable by reafon,

fon, he muſt confider what is the peculiar kind of proof ſuited to that truth, and exhibit it. In proving a truth by revelation, care muſt be taken to argue, not from the ſound, but the real meaning. It is proper to ſhow that the expreſſions in a text, which ſeem to imply a proof of it, have that ſenſe which renders them a proof of it in other texts; and that they are determined to this ſenſe by the context and ſtrain of writing in that particular text. When a truth admits a proper proof only from reaſon, yet that proof, or ſome ſteps of it, may very well be expreſſed in the words of ſcripture. When a truth is to be proved only by revelation, it may yet be very properly illuſtrated from ſuppoſitions of reaſon. Some truths may be proved both by reaſon and revelation; then, each part of the proof ſhould be proſecuted according to its peculiar rules. In proving from reaſon, all abſtruſe, far-fetched, and complex arguments ſhould be avoided, for they will be neither intelligible nor convincing. In proving from ſcripture, only plain texts and fully to the purpoſe ſhould be uſed; obſcure texts would need long explication before they could be applied, and ambiguous ones will promote doubt, inſtead of diſpelling it. In proving from either, only ſuch arguments ſhould be uſed as are truly concluſive; a few of theſe will be ſufficient to produce conviction; but a weak argument always debilitates the ſtronger ones. Every argument, from whatever

ever, fource it be derived, fhould be exhibited as
fhortly as can, be, without detracting from its
force; for thus its whole force will be beft reprefented at once. Care fhould likewife be taken
not to urge too great a multiplicity of arguments,
for this would only confound the judgement and
burden the memory. It is much better to make
a felection of thofe which will be moft eafily comprehended, and are moft undoubtedly conclufive;
thefe will be fufficient to produce conviction, and
more would rather tire, than ftrengthen the conviction. In other cafes, it may be proper to diftribute the arguments into different claffes, which,
like a projection in architecture, will take off from
the ill effect of the number, and enable the mind
to comprehend them without difficulty or difguft.
All the doctrines of true religion are of a practical
nature, and ought to be always reprefented as
fubfervient to practice. Even in a difcourfe therefore, intended mainly for proving a doctrine, its
influence on practice ought to be pointed out.
When the difcourfe is of the firft kind, defigned
to produce a ftrong fenfe of a doctrine already
believed, it has been formerly obferved, that the
whole argument fhould be carried on in fuch a
way as to touch the heart. But befides this, every
probatory difcourfe fhould conclude with pointing
out its influence on practice. Sometimes this may
be done, by enforcing from it fome one virtue to
which it is principally fubfervient. Sometimes,
when the doctrine proved, enforces equally feveral

veral duties, the obligation which it lays us under
to all thefe; may be pointed out in diftinct inferences or deductions.

ART. III.   *Of Panegyrical or Demonftrative Difcourfes.*

THE third fort of difcourfes are fuch as are addreffed to the imagination, and are intended to
raife admiration. A preacher may, without de-
viating from the end of his vocation, endeavour to
enrapture his audience with this pleafure. The
reafon is, that admiration tends naturally and immediately to produce imitation, and to excite noble
ambition and emulation. The preacher feems to
aim only at making a character admired; he em-
ploys all the means which can promote this end;
but he feeks the admiration of his hearers only for
the fake of its neceffary confequences; yet as nothing farther is requifite for fecuring-thefe, but
exciting admiration, this may juftly be confidered
as the diftinguifhing aim of fuch difcourfes.

The ancient Rhetoricians take notice of this
fpecies of difcourfes, and call them Panegyrical or
Demonftrative. They allow two forts of them;
one employed in praifing, another in blaming.
Cbriftian charity fcarcely allows one of the latter
fort to be brought to the pulpit; it feems to forbid
making it the whole purpofe of a difcourfe, to defcribe and exaggerate, as it were, all the vices of
one particular perfon. It is more fuitable, to reprefent,

prefent, in the faireft point of view, eminent virtue
and goodnefs. There are many fubjects on which
fuch difcourfes, may be properly compofed by a
Proteftant preacher; as the life of our Saviour,
and the lives of thofe holy men whofe hiftory is
recorded in fcripture. We are exprefsly commanded to follow thefe examples; and therefore
it muft be highly proper to propofe their examples
to a chriftian audience.

A demonftrative difcourfe bears fome analogy
to the laft kind of explicatory difcourfe which was
explained, as a character is the fubject of both.
But they are confiderably different. The defign
of the one is from the actions to deduce a diftinct
analyfis of the character; the defign of the other
is to reprefent the character and the actions in fuch
a light as may moft effectually promote imitation.
The true way of doing this is to paint the whole
man, and to fet him before the hearer's eyes,
fpeaking and acting. In defcribing the courfe of
his life, the preacher fhould chiefly point out thofe
paffages in which his virtues beft appeared. He
fhould recount his laudable actions: this gives
force to a panegyric; this is what inftructs people,
and makes an impreffion on their minds. This is
to paint a perfon to the life, and fhows what he was
in every period, in every condition, and in the
moft remarkable junctures of his life. At the
fame time, a demonftrative difcourfe fhould not be
a fimple narration. It is enough to felect the
chief

chief facts, and reprefent them in a concife, lively, and ftriking manner: There fhould be the fame difference between a mere hiftory and a difcourfe of this kind, as between a natural hiftory of an animal and a poetical defcription of it. The former defcribes minutely every particular regarding it; the latter choofes a few of the moft remarkable particulars, and, by combining them, exhibits a pleafing and ftriking picture of the object to the imagination. It is never allowable to exceed the bounds of truth; but the end of this difcourfe requires that the virtues of a perfon fhould be fet in the moft amiable and engaging light that truth will permit; and that the faults which were blended with thefe virtues fhould be either wholly omitted, or touched as flightly as poffible. This is evidently the way to excite admiration, and to promote imitation; and it is plainly allowable, becaufe the preacher's profeffed defign is, not to give a hiftory of the perfon, but to exhibit his example fo far as it is worthy of imitation. This fort of difcourfe fhould never be allowed to run into the florid; but it may approach nearer to it, and be more adorned with bold figures, than any other fort of fermon. A good deal of this is really neceffary for attaining its end.

Demonftrative difcourfes may be diftinguifhed into three kinds. The fubject of the firft is a perfon's whole life. Such a difcourfe as this will exhibit a lively picture of all the virtues which a

perfon

perfon has exercifed, in all the different periods, and in all the various fituations and emergencies of life. The fubject of the fecond kind is one period of a holy man's life; it may exhibit all the virtues which he exercifed, in all the different fituations in which he was placed during that period. Thus a difcourfe may be employed in exhibiting Jofeph's example before his advancement to the govern- ment of Egypt; or in difplaying his example after his advancement. The life of Paul after his con- verfion is another inftance of this kind of difcourfe. The third fpecies is that which has for its fubject a particular virtue, as difplayed in various circum- ftances through the whole of a man's life; as the patience of Job, the faith of Abraham. Thefe three kinds of demonftrative fermons differ only in the extent of their fubject; their end and general rules are almoft wholly the fame; they can fcarce differ in any other refpect, than the divifion of which they are fufceptible. The firft kind, which takes in a whole life, may be profe- cuted in two different methods. 1. The life may be divided into its different periods, and the virtues difplayed in each period exhibited to the view of the hearers. By this means, each member will become a difcourfe of the fecond fpecies. 2. It may be divided according to the different virtues which appear in it; and the difcourfe may fhow how each virtue feparately has been exercifed and difplayed through all the different periods and fituations in which the perfon has been placed.

In

In this way, the example of Chrift is represented in *The Life of God in the Soul of Man*, as reducible to piety, charity, purity, and humility; and the profecution of this fubject, in the firft part of that book, is not a bad example of a difcourfe of this kind. This fort of divifion has fome advantages, efpecially when a perfon's fituation has not undergone very great changes. The only inconvenience that attends it is, that fometimes different virtues are complicated in the fame action; but this is not of great confequence, for that action may be introduced under that virtue which is predominant in it; and all the other virtues which likewife appeared in it, may be at the fame time pointed out without any breach of method. And to compenfate this, one has an opportunity, by purfuing this method, to exhibit every virtue of the perfon's life entire; and in all the different points of light in which the perfon had, through his whole life, occafion to exert it. When this method is purfued, every part of the difcourfe becomes a demonftrative difcourfe of the laft fort. In this fpecies fometimes, but often in the two laft, no divifion is abfolutely neceffary; it is enough that the feveral actions of a perfon be reprefented in a natural order. In the fecond fpecies, where the fubject is fome period of a life, if the preacher choofe a divifion, it may moft naturally be made according to the different virtues which a perfon has had occafion to fhow in that period. In the third fpecies again, where one particular virtue is

the

the fubject, the divifion may be according to the different periods or fituations in which that virtue has been exercifed. There are many fermons extant, which are in fome meafure of the demonftrative kind; as all thofe on the example of Chrift. But few or none of them are profecuted according to the accurate rules of fuch compofitions.

In a word, it is the defign of a demonftrative or panegyrical fermon, at once to give a diftinct knowlege, and to excite high admiration of the virtues of a particular perfon, with a view to promote the imitation of them, by giving a lively view of thefe virtues as difplayed in a feries of actions.

ART. IV. *Of Suafory Difcourfes.*

The laft kind of pulpit difcourfe is addreffed to the paffions and the will; its end is perfuafion; we may therefore call it the fuafory. This is of all the moft complex kind; it includes all the reft, or at leaft it prefuppofes inftruction, conviction, and pleafing, and fuperadds fomething to them which is peculiar to itfelf, and conftitutes its diftinguifhing criterion. A fuafory difcourfe is intended to perfuade men to a certain courfe; and in order to anfwer its end, it muft difcover what that courfe is; it muft prove that it is fubfervient to fome end acknowleged to be of importance by the hearers; and that end muft be fo reprefented to the imagination, that it may excite a ftrong affection to it, by means of which the will may be determined to the courfe which leads to it.

In order to perfuade a man to any courfe, the underftanding muft be addreffed fo far, as to let him both know what the courfe is that you want him to purfue, and to convince him that his pur-fuing that courfe will anfwer fome good end. It is poffible indeed to move men, without enlighten-ing them; but this emotion is a mere temporary paffion, which neither has any fixed direction, nor can anfwer any purpofe. If you would move a man with any thing beyond fuch a tranfient emo-tion, if you would truly perfuade him, you muft enlighten as well as move. You muft not only let him know what is the courfe which you would have him to take, but alfo fhow the reafon why he fhould take it. In every fuafory difcourfe, there-fore, there muft be reafoning or argument ufed, in order to convince the hearers that they ought to do what you recommend to them; and till they be thus convinced, it is impoffible that they can do it. A reafonable being always propofes fome end, and it is for fome end that he does every action, and either indulges or curbs any difpofition. The reafoning, therefore, which can contribute to perfuade men to any action or any courfe, is of that particular kind which fhows that action or courfe to be conducive to a certain end or purpofe. To perfuade men to holinefs and virtue, one may,

for

for inſtance, prove that it is conducive to peace of mind, to preſent intereſt, or to future happineſs. This can be proved only by reaſoning or argument. If the arguments produced do not convince men that holineſs is neceſſary for theſe ends, they can have no tendency to perſuade them; however much they may deſire the ends, and however willing they may be to purſue them, yet they will not be prevailed on to purſue them in this way, except they be convinced that this way leads to the attainment of them, and is neceſſary for it. Thus the judgement muſt be convinced by proper arguments, before men can be excited to any action. Solid reaſoning is therefore one eſſential ingredient in that eloquence which tends to perſuaſion. But this is not alone ſufficient for perſuaſion.

It is likewiſe neceſſary to render the hearers fond of the end, to which the courſe recommended is repreſented as ſubſervient. Though a man be ever ſo much convinced that a certain action will redound to his honour, for inſtance, yet he will never think of doing that action, if he has no deſire of honour. To underſtand, therefore, what more than mere reaſoning is neceſſary to perſuaſion, we need only conſider, what principles of the mind they are that attach men to the ends which they purſue. They are, in general, the affections and practical principles of human nature. Conſcience renders the doing our duty, and obtaining the

appro-

approbation of our own minds, a defirable end to us. Self-love makes us fond of happinefs, and ready to do what is neceffary for obtaining it. Ambition attaches us to honour. Gratitude difpofes us to what will be agreeable to a benefactor; benevolence, to what will tend to the happinefs of others; and fo in other cafes. Now, to perfuade to a certain courfe, we muft excite thofe affections or principles, which attach men to thofe ends from which our topics of argument are deduced. Would we, for example, perfuade men to holinefs, from its neceffity in order to obtain the heavenly happinefs, we muft not only prove that it is neceffary for this, but alfo render them defirous of the heavenly happinefs. Would we excite them to virtue, from gratitude to God our benefactor, who requires it, we muft not only prove that it is the propereft expreffion of gratitude, but alfo we muft excite in them a difpofition to be grateful. But as it is thus neceffary to excite the paffions, as well as to convince the judgment, fo the former will not be fufficient alone without the latter. Let any paffion be ever fo ftrong in a man's mind, it will not lead him to any particular courfe, except he be convinced that that courfe tends to gratify it. You may raife in a man the ftrongeft defire of heaven; but this defire will not incline him to practife holinefs, till you have likewife convinced him that holinefs is the way to heaven. Thus neither argument alone, nor moving the paffions alone, is fufficient. The cool reafoner, who con-

fines

fines himself to the former, may convince men that certain actions are necessary to certain ends; but he does not excite their desire of these ends. The warm preacher, who has no solid argument, may raise a violent emotion, a present desire of a certain end; but he does not point out the means by which it may be attained; or, if he mention them, he does not sufficiently evince their necessity; and therefore, the emotion which he raised has no fixed direction, but evaporates without determining men to any settled course. The latter warms without enlightening; the former enlightens without warming. Both perform but half the business of persuasion. To complete it, the judgement must be convinced and the passions raised at one and the same time. When this is done, the will is immediately determined to resolve on the course, and to perform the action recommended. Affection makes us desirous of the end; reason shows us that we must do certain actions for obtaining it; and as soon as this is perceived, affection urges us to will the doing of that action; and when we are brought to will it, persuasion is accomplished, and we immediately do the action. A suasory discourse is, therefore, directly addressed to the will; its design is to seize and captivate the will, and lead it to exert itself in an effectual volition of the course recommended. And this is attained by convincing the hearers that that course is necessary for a certain end, and raising, at the same time, a strong affection to that end. The

preacher

preacher who can frame his difcourfe fo as to produce thefe two effects at once, will be a mafter of
perfuafion, · and attain that vehemence which is
the nobleft fpecies of eloquence, its very fummit
and perfection.

We have already obferved, how one of the parts
of perfuafion is to be performed; the judgement
is to be convinced by folid reafoning. It will now
be neceffary to fhow how the paffions may be
raifed; for in raifing them, the other part of perfuafion confifts. Now, there are only two ways
by which any paffion or affection can be produced;
either by giving an actual perception of the object
of that paffion, or by prefenting a lively idea of
that object. The actual prefence of the object of
a paffion never fails to excite the paffion; the
feeling of pain produces forrow; the fight of diftrefs raifes our fympathy. But it is feldom that a
preacher can prefent the objects themfelves to his
hearers; if their affections could be raifed only by
the actual prefence of their objects, it would be out
of his power to raife them in moft cafes. But God
has wifely conftituted us in fuch a way, that the
feveral paffions and affections of our nature may
be likewife raifed by ftrong and lively ideas of
their objects. Thus, the certainty of a very great
calamity will raife forrow, before we actually endure it; a defcription of deep diftrefs will excite
our compaffion to the perfon who fuffers it; merely
thinking of a favour will raife gratitude to the author

thor of it. It is by this way that the preacher has
accefs to the hearts of his hearers; he can raife
their paffions only by prefenting to them ftrong
and lively ideas of the objects of them. As it is
the imagination of the hearers that conceives thefe
lively ideas, fo it is by addreffing himfelf to their
imagination, that the preacher prefents thefe ideas
to them. All the paffions take their rife from the
imagination, and it is by firft touching the imagination, that we muft, by means of it, move the
paffions. In order therefore to explain how the
paffions are raifed, it will be neceffary to confider
how the imagination is addreffed, and what kind
of addrefs to it has an influence on the paffions.

Now, every defcription which tends to pleafe
any of our internal or reflex fenfes, is addreffed to
the imagination; whatever is new, beautiful, elegant, harmonious, or fublime, gratifies the imagination; and every defcription of fuch objects is
addreffed to it. Every fuch defcription is admitted
into poetry, which refts in gratifying the imagination, and whofe end is to pleafe. But there are
fome objects which, however much a lively defcription of them may gratify the imagination, have
no tendency to influence the paffions; becaufe they
are not the caufe or the object of any paffion.
Such defcriptions therefore cannot enter into fuafory difcourfes; they have no tendency to promote
the end of them; they would rather obftruct it, by
fixing the mind upon fomething elfe.

Again,

Again, fome defcriptions even of thofe things.
which are the natural objects and caufes of our
paffions, are unfit to excite them. If they be fo
florid and gaudy as to amufe or dazzle the mind,
it will reft in the amufement which they give,
without feeling any difpofition to be actuated by
the paffion which thefe objects might have raifed.
The defcription may be very beautiful in itfelf,
but it does not fuit its place, nor contribute to the
end to which it ought to have been fubordinate.
The defcriptions then which, in a fuafory difcourfe,
are addreffed to the imagination, muft be fo contrived as to fet thofe objects and caufes of our
paffions, of which they are defcriptions, in that
point of view in which they have the ftrongeft
tendency to excite the paffions. In order to this,
the paffions themfelves, with their objects and
effects, muft be well painted. The moft ftriking
circumftances of the objects and effects muft be
reprefented in fo lively a manner, that the hearer
may almoft fancy that he fees them. The workings of the paffion muft be reprefented fo naturally,
as to make them think that they fee one actuated
by it, and as may turn the lively idea of it which
they form, into the paffion itfelf. Metaphors,
fimilitudes, images, abrupt and ftrong expreffions,
rightly chofen and applied, and, in a word, many
of the figures of eloquence, are fubfervient to this.
Till a ftrong idea of the object, effects and workings of the paffion, be in this way imprinted on the
imagination, the preacher's difcourfe cannot excite
the

the paffions of the hearers. . But, if he can convey fuch a ftrong idea, the paffion will immediately
rife fpontaneoufly and without more ado.

Thus we have endeavoured to analyfe perfuafion,
to fhow all that it includes, and all that is neceffary
for accomplifhing it. Perfuafion always tends to
fome action or courfe of action; it operates ultimately on the will, which is the immediate caufe
of action; but in order to determine the will, it
muft previoufly convince the judgement, ftrike the
imagination, and move the paffions. A preacher
would perfuade men to a certain conduct; in order
to do this, he muft convince them by argument and
reafoning, that that conduct tends to fome valuable
end; he muft likewife bring them to perceive and
feel that that end is really valuable, by painting it
in lively colours: this picture will of courfe raife
the paffion or affection which attaches to this end;
and an affection for the end immediately determines
the will to purfue that courfe which was fhown by
reafoning to be neceffary for the attainment of the
end. All this is requifite; if any ftep of it be
wanting, perfuafion cannot be accomplifhed: the
difcourfe may anfwer other ends, but it cannot
anfwer this particular end, perfuafion. If it contain only argument, it will convince; if it contain
only gaudy painting of objects unconnected with
the paffions, it will pleafe; if it contain only proper
pictures of the objects, effects and workings of the
paffions, but without a mixture of reafoning, it
will

will be pathetic, it will move the paſſions. But in all theſe caſes it falls ſhort of perſuaſion. To accompliſh this, argument, painting, and the pathetic, muſt be combined.

It was neceſſary, for the ſake of diſtinctneſs, to conſider theſe parts of perſuaſion ſeparately. But we muſt not imagine that they are to be kept perfectly ſeparate in a ſuaſory diſcourſe. We are not firſt to prove by cool reaſoning, that a courſe tends to a certain end, and then with warmth to raiſe an affection to that end; nor are we firſt to raiſe a ſtrong paſſion for the end, and then when we have poſſeſſed the hearers with it, to convince them by cool reaſoning that, if they would gratify that paſſion and obtain the end, they muſt take the courſe which we recommend. If we were to keep the two parts of perſuaſion, argument, and the pathetic, in which laſt painting is evidently implied, thus entirely diſtinct and ſeparate, the effect of the one muſt be loſt and wear wholly off, before we came to the other; each would be weakened by their divorce; and the two parts of the diſcourſe would appear unlike and unſuitable to each other. The argument and the pathetic muſt be in ſome degree interwoven and incorporated together through the whole diſcourſe. It is not indeed neceſſary that they ſhould prevail equally in every part of it; ſometimes the one, ſometimes the other will preponderate; generally, argument ſhould prevail in the former part, and the pathetic in the

latter,

latter, though this does not hold without exception. But whichever prevails, there muft, through the whole, be a mixture of the other. The argument muft not be purfued in the fame unaffecting way, as if it were intended only for conviction, but muft be intermixed all along with fuch lively and pathetic defcriptions as may gently touch the paffions, and prepare them for rifing, when they come to be more profeffedly addreffed. The reafoning which evinces that the courfe recommended tends to a valuable end, muft be fo contrived as, at the fame time, to raife fome degree of affection to that end. In like manner, that part of the difcourfe which is intended chiefly to raife the paffions, muft be fo contrived as to preferve all along the conviction arifing from the argument. The colours by which the end is rendered affecting, muft be intermixed with fuch hints of the argument, as may keep in view that courfe by which the paffion raifed by the end may be gratified. A preacher who would perfuade, muft thus addrefs at one and the fame time all the powers of human nature, the underftanding, the imagination, and the paffions.

It is evident from what has been faid, that an addrefs to the paffions is neceffary in a difcourfe whofe end is perfuafion. But if a difcourfe contained only an addrefs to the paffions, its end would be properly, not perfuafion, but moving. And it was obferved before, that merely to move, is not a proper aim in a difcourfe from the pulpit, except

in fome very particular cafes. But as it is allowable in fome cafes, it will be proper juft to remark
what it is that forms the moving, as diftinguifhed
from the vehement or perfuafive. This latter refults from the union of reafoning with painting.
Now, if the former of thefe ingredients be re-
moved, if the difcourfe contain only moving pictures of the object of any paffion, without any
reafoning concerning the way of exerting that
paffion, it will produce the pure pathetic; a certain
paffion or affection will be raifed by it, but the
mind will not be determined by that difcourfe to
exert the paffion in any particular way. Again,
all our paffions do not lead equally to action;
fome of them lead to it very directly, as defire,
averfion, benevolence, anger; fome feem to lead
rather to inaction, or at leaft lead very faintly to
action, as joy, forrow, &c. If a difcourfe tend
chiefly to raife thofe of the latter kind, it will be
properly pathetic; accordingly, this term is very
commonly reftricted to fuch compofitions as tend
to produce forrow.

It is, I know, an opinion entertained by fome,
that a preacher ought not to addrefs himfelf at all
to the paffions of his hearers, but only to their
reafon. It is alleged, that to move their paffions,
is to put a bias upon their judgement, to miflead
them, and to raife an emotion which will be tranfient, and wear off without leaving any good effect.
But this opinion can proceed only from want of
attention,

attention, or from very fuperficial reflection. In matters of mere fpeculation, it is indeed wrong to work upon men's paffions; but wherever action is concerned, the cooleft fpeaker addreffes the paffions of men; and indeed, unlefs he fpeak to their paffions, he cannot fpeak to any purpofe at all. No argument can be propofed for any courfe of action, but what implies an addrefs to fome paffion or affection. If a man tell me, it is for my intereft, he addreffes my felf-love; if for my honour, he addreffes my ambition; if for the public good, he addreffes my benevolence; in a word, whatever motive can be propofed, it addreffes itfelf to fome one of thofe paffions or affections which are the only principles of our actions. Suppofe a perfon deftitute of thefe, and the ftrongeft reafoning will have no effect upon him. If I fhould prove clearly and convincingly, that a certain action tends to happinefs, this will have no influence on a perfon deftitute of felf-love. If I prove that an action tends to honour, a perfon void of ambition would tell me, I am convinced it does, but I have no defire of honour. Thefe principles cannot be difputed; and when they are admitted, to fay that a preacher fhould confine himfelf to cool reafoning, and not addrefs the paffions of his hearers, is to fay, that he fhould excite them to action, without applying to the only principles of their nature which can excite them to action; or rather it is to fay, that he fhould addrefs thefe principles, but that he muft be careful to addrefs them only in

fuch

such a way as has no tendency to engage them.
This is a plain abſurdity, though it be ſometimes
expreſſed in ſuch terms as to give it ſome ſhow of
plauſibility. Reaſoning which tends to ſhow that
a courſe is conducive to intereſt or honour, will
have ſome influence in determining thoſe to that
courſe, who have previouſly ſelf-love or ambition
in a conſiderable degree of ſtrength ; but if theſe
principles be weak, or be counteracted by other
principles, it will have no influence upon them.
But even when theſe principles are weak, or ſo
overborne by oppoſite principles as to be hindered
from exerting themſelves, they may be excited
and ſtrengthened by a proper addreſs to the
paſſions. The want of this muſt therefore be an
eſſential defect in a diſcourſe intended for perſuaſion.

.Having thus laid open the general principles of
ſuaſory diſcourſes, we ſhall now point out briefly
their different kinds. They are plainly diſtinguiſh-
able into two kinds. 1. Such as are deſigned to
diſſuade from vice. In order to do this, two
things are neceſſary ; to weaken the paſſions which
lead to vice, and to ſtir up and ſtrengthen ſuch
paſſions or affections as may oppoſe and check
theſe. To diſſuade from intemperance, for inſtance, one may give ſuch a view of ſenſual pleaſure as tends to check the deſire of it ; and he may
give ſuch a view of the pleaſure and reward of
abſtinence, or of the miſery and puniſhment of
                                        intem-

intemperance, as may raife defire of the former, and dread of the latter, for antagonifts to fenfual appetite. A paffion is weakened by methods contrary to thofe by which it is raifed. All that belongs to this fort of difcourfe is therefore eafily deducible from the principles which have been already laid down.—2. Such as are defigned to perfuade to virtue. In thefe too, it is neceffary both to ftrengthen virtuous affections, and thofe principles which co-operate with them, and to weaken fuch vicious paffions and principles as would draw off from the courfe recommended.

In fuafory as well as in probatory difcourfes, one may proceed either in the direct or indirect method of reafoning; either by urging direct arguments for any courfe of virtue, or againft any courfe of vice, or by removing the pretences by which men commonly prevail upon themfelves to neglect the virtue or indulge the vice, or excufe themfelves in doing fo. Thus a fuafory difcourfe intended to prevail on men not to delay repentance, might proceed either by proving directly the danger of delaying it, from the difficulty of religion, from the continual increafe of the ftrength of vicious habits, from the uncertainty of life, &c. or by removing the excufes which men plead for delaying it, from miftaken notions of grace, from want of leifure at prefent, &c.—Suafory difcourfes may be again divided in another view; into fuch as perfuade to virtue in general, or diffuade from vice

vice in general, and such as have for their object
some one particular virtue or vice. These kinds
differ only in the extent of their subject, not at all
in the rules of prosecuting them. It will be sufficient therefore to observe on this head, that,
because men are little affected with generals, it
will be often necessary to descend to particular
virtues and vices, and labour to inculcate a due
conduct with regard to them. If a minister
employ himself only in recommending religion and
holiness in general, men will have no distinct
conception of what is included in them, and every
person will find it very easy to satisfy himself that
he is not defective. But when particular branches
of conduct are made the frequent subjects of preaching, men will more readily discover their own
faults, and by this means be laid open to the full
force of all the arguments that are used. Whether
a general course of conduct, or a particular branch
of it, be the subject of a sermon, that sermon
may be employed in enforcing it, either from all
the topics that recommend it, or from some one
class of topics. These two differ likewise only in
the extent of the subject, and therefore admit the
very same rules. It is only necessary to observe,
that wherever different arguments, deduced either
from the same or different topics, are used in a
discourse, they should be placed in such an order,
that each may appear to spring naturally from the
foregoing, and that all may lend the greatest
strength to one another.—I shall mention but one
divison

divifion more of fuafory difcourfes. Some of them recommend one courfe from a variety of topics; others of them recommend a variety of courfes from one and the fame topic. The examples that we have already hinted at, are all inftances of the former kind. For an inftance of the latter, we may fuppofe the preacher, from this fingle topic, the confideration of death as our departure from this world, urging his hearers not to fet an immoderate value on prefent earthly things, not to entertain an immoderate fondnefs for them, not to employ endlefs labour about them, not to defpife thofe who are in lower worldly circumftances than themfelves, not to abufe their prefent poffeffions, not to commit fin in order to avoid the lofs of them, not to murmur for the want of them, not to be impatient under real and pofitive afflictions, not to envy others. There are many fubjects which naturally direct a preacher to follow this method in a fuafory difcourfe upon them.

We have not confidered the feveral branches of that divifion of pulpit difcourfes which we deduced from the ends of fpeaking; and this divifion has given us an opportunity of propofing the general rules of each kind of difcourfe, fo far as they arife from its peculiar end. There is nothing that can come within the province of a preacher, that is not reducible to one or other of the kinds which we have defcribed. And there is none of thefe kinds

x   which

which does not properly belong to his province. Indeed, all these aims are constantly considered as belonging to a preacher. There is but one respect in which the manner of their belonging to him is generally considered as different from that manner in which we have represented them. We have considered them as different kinds of sermons; and they are commonly considered as different parts of one sermon. Which of these two ways of considering them is most proper will appear afterwards, when we come to consider Preaching in another light. At present we shall only observe, that though they were to be regarded as different parts of one sermon, yet as the ends aimed at are different, and as the principles of composition suited to these ends are likewise different, it will still be necessary to consider them separately; and therefore all that has been said is equally applicable to Preaching on that supposition, as on the supposition which we have followed.

ART. V. *Of Invention.*

We have considered Preaching with respect to the various ends at which it aims, and the kinds of discourses which arise from that variety. This has led us to remark the most general rules belonging to each species of Preaching. The eloquence of the pulpit may be considered in another light; with respect to the different exertions of mind which it requires in the speaker. This is a light in which

writers

writers on the principles of rhetoric have always chosen to consider every kind of composition. There have been disputes among them concerning the number of mental exertions belonging properly to eloquence, which are too trivial to deserve our entering into them. They are generally reckoned five; invention, disposition, elocution, memory, and pronunciation; and according to this distinction, the parts of eloquence are commonly reckoned. By prosecuting this division, we shall have an opportunity of laying down the particular rules of pulpit discourses, regarding the subject, the method, the style, and composition, the mandating, and the delivering. As this is the division that is commonly followed, in explaining the principles of eloquence, by the writers of institutions, a number of their rules are applicable to Preaching; and as you can have recourse to them, we may treat more shortly of them.

The first exertion of mind necessary in every discourse is invention, which is therefore reckoned the first part of eloquence. Under this head we shall consider the helps of invention, the choice of subjects, the qualities of texts, the exordium, the explication of text and context, the laying down the design, the division, the prosecution, and the conclusion. These parts are common to all kinds of discourses.

The

The helps of invention are of two kinds, mediate or remote, and immediate. The former are of very great confequence; they in fome meafure remove the need of the latter; but without them, the latter cannot be fufficient. By the mediate or remote helps of invention, I mean previous application, and a fund of knowlege. This is fo neceffary for a public fpeaker, that all the ancient writers on rhetoric require almoft univerfal knowlege in an orator. Without a confiderable ftock of folid knowlege, a preacher's head will feem unfurnifhed; he will appear to labour for matter to fill up his difcourfe; he will not feem to fpeak from the abundance of his heart, but will talk as if he were at a lofs for the very next thing he is to fay. He lives, as it were, from hand to mouth, without laying up any ftock of provifion; and therefore, whatever pains he takes about his difcourfes, they appear always thin and half-ftarved. Though he could afford three months for ftudying a fermon, fuch particular preparations, however troublefome, muft needs be very imper-fect. Preachers ought to employ feveral years in laying up a plentiful ftock of folid knowlege; and then, after fuch a general preparation, their particular difcourfes will coft them the lefs pains. But if, without any preparatory ftudy, a man only apply to a particular fubject, as he has occafion to preach on it, he is forced to put off his hearers with common-place notions and fuperficial remarks.

If

If a man be only acquainted with controverſy, and have read ſermons, he may thus pick up a few thoughts; but either they will be merely ſpeculative, or by being borrowed at ſecond-hand, they will be indigeſted, dead, and pointleſs.

A ſermon is a diſcourſe founded on ſcripture, and addreſſed to men; a preacher muſt therefore have theſe three qualifications, the knowlege of ſcripture, of human nature, and of human life. Theſe ought to be the three great branches of his ſtudy.

The knowlege of ſcripture muſt be acquired by reading it much, and that in the original languages; and by reading it critically, that we may remember not only the words, the doctrines, the precepts, the hiſtories recorded in holy writ, but alſo thoroughly underſtand their meaning, and their application. The moſt beautiful and ſtriking parts of the beſt ſermons are the ſcriptures which are interwoven with them; and, if they were always entirely appoſite, and urged with their full force, they would be almoſt irreſiſtible.

Sermons ſhould alſo be deeply founded in human nature. I do not mean that ſermons ſhould be abſtract diſcourſes on the principles of human nature. But when men's feelings are truly delineated, when all maxims and directions that are given, are perfectly ſuitable to the principles of

X 3   the

the mind, then the fermon may be truly faid to be
founded in human nature; and no fpecies of argument will make a deeper impreffion, or produce
a more folid and thorough conviction. In order
to be able to give his difcourfes, in this manner,
a foundation in human nature, a preacher muft
ftudy carefully the philofophy of man, efpecially
of his moral and active powers. A perfon who is
unacquainted with this branch of knowlege muft
be often at a lofs and in danger of mifreprefenting
things, when he is to addrefs himfelf to mankind
on fubjects of practice. This part of philofophy
muft not be neglected when the ordinary time
of education in it is expired; it is rather to be
then begun, for it is generally only after this that
men's faculties are ripe for the ftudy of it.

The third requifite mentioned was the knowlege
of human life. Without this, our defcriptions
muft be falfe and unnatural, and can never ftrike.
It is to be acquired by obfervation, and by the
ftudy of hiftory. Biography is the moft proper
kind of biftory for this purpofe. It relates many
minute circumftances, actions, and fayings of a
perfon's life, which ferve very much to let us into
his real character. It is often proper in fermons,
to adduce profeffed examples, either of the nature,
influence, and deceit of vice, of the nature and
exertions of virtue in real life, or of their confequences, rewards, and punifhments. For moft
part, thefe fhould be taken from fcripture, and
more

more, sparingly at least from prophane history. But even when a preacher does not choose professedly to make use of examples, it will be extremely useful to have them in his eye, that he may frame his explication, description, or argument, according to what has really been. The perusal of history with a view to acquire a knowlege of real life, will, in a great measure, prepare men for using the other method of acquiring this knowlege; will train them to that acutenefs, attention, and thoughtfulnefs, which are necessary for their making observations themselves on mankind, and tracing out characters which they meet with in real life.

The immediate helps of invention are the works of other men, from which assistance may be derived. These may be reduced to two forts. First, models which are proper to be imitated. These are finished and regular discourses, either on the subjects which the preacher is to treat, or on other subjects. Those which are on different subjects are the most useful helps, as they give an impulse to genius, and a direction to judgement, without laying him under a temptation merely to transcribe. The ancient orations, particularly those of Demosthenes and Cicero; the most finished and elegant sermons, and even some of the poets, may be highly useful for directing genius, and forming the taste in Preaching. The second fort of helps are such sermons and compositions as are rude and

indigested

indigefted as to the manner, but contain plenty of materials. A preacher cannot copy after thefe as models, but he may dig in them as in a mine. ' They are like a piece of rich ore, in which he ' may find matter for the furniture of pulpit dif- ' courfes, and find, at the fame time, fuch a ' defect of refinement and polifhing, as to leave ' room for the exercife of his own genius and ' talents to finifh and rub them up. He may ' find a rich collection of noble fentiments, and ' ftrong and nervous expreffions, but delivered ' with fuch negligence of drefs, as to ftyle or me- ' thod, as leaves abundance of room for the ex- ' ercife of his own powers in altering and me- ' thodifing whatever materials he borrows from ' them. We may apply to fuch productions what ' Pope fays of the works of Shakfpeare; " One " may look upon them, in comparifon of thofe " that are more finifhed and regular, as upon an " ancient majeftic piece of Gothic architecture, " compared with a neat modern building : the " latter is more elegant and glaring, but the " former is more ftrong and more folemn."

In ufing the immediate helps of invention, a preacher may take two different ways. He may firft read and digeft all that he choofes to confult on the fubject, and then, laying afide the books, and meditating on his fubject, he may form his own plan, and difpofe the materials which he finds in his mind, in his own manner and ftyle. Or,

he

he may firſt form his own plan, and proſecute it
in the way which he thinks moſt proper, and
then-read over writers on the ſubject; and after
having read them, review his own compoſition,
and alter or add to it according to the new materials which he finds ſuggeſted to him by his reading. The latter method will give a ſermon moſt
the appearance of an original, and is, perhaps, for
the moſt part eligible; but the former may be
very properly uſed, either when one is not previouſly ſo well acquainted with a particular ſubject
on which he is to compoſe, or when he is obliged
to compoſe in haſte. Theſe are the only two ways
in which a preacher ought to uſe the works of
others. Merely to compile a ſermon by tacking
together paſſages which pleaſe him, from others
who have written on the ſubject, is always abſo-
lutely wrong; it gives the whole the appearance
of patchwork; there is no conſiſtence in the parts,
either as to the train of thought, or as to the ſtyle.
If one cannot compoſe ſermons in another way,
it were much better to borrow complete ſermons
from the works of others. But certainly, a man
who is under a neceſſity of doing either this, or
what is more improper, ought never to have attempted Preaching, or addicted himſelf to a profeſſion for which he is ſo ill qualified.

We proceed next to make ſome obſervations on
the choice of ſubjects. As to the nature of the
different ſubjects which may be properly choſen
for

for a difcourfe from the pulpit, it will be unneceffary to fay any thing, after what has been already faid concerning the kinds of difcourfes.
There have been unhappy differences about the
kind of fubjects on which a preacher ought to
infift.   An oppofition has been eftablifhed between
what is called Gofpel-preaching, and what is called
Legal-preaching.   I hope this ill-judged and ill-
defined diftinction is now pretty much out of doors,
at leaft with moft people; and therefore, it will
not be needful to enter fo deep into the fubject
as might, perhaps, have been proper when it was
more in vogue.   On this, as well as on moft fubjects, it appears to me that men have gone into
extremes. The patrons of what was called Gofpel-
preaching infifted chiefly on the doctrines of religion, or rather, on fome few of the peculiar doctrines of Chriftianity; on the righteoufnefs and
facrifice of Jefus Chrift, on faith in him, on the
great grace of the evangelical difpenfation, and on
the affiftances of the Divine Spirit.   They were
certainly in the right to infift much on thefe; but
they were, notwithftanding, blameable in feveral
refpects.   They confidered thefe doctrines, not in
the genuine ftrain of the New Teftament, which
explains them with the greateft fimplicity, and
always urges them as arguments for the practice
of holinefs; but in the ftrain of difputatious fyf-
tems, encumbered with technical terms and fubtle
diftinctions, and fo as wholly to draw off men's
attention from practice, inftead of contributing to

12   excite

excite them to good practice. They omitted many
other·parts of the gofpel, equally neceffary and,
important with thefe doctrines; while they enlarged on the bleffings of the gofpel and the means
by which they were procured, they were very
fparing in recommending the character which we
muft maintain, and the conduct we muft purfue,
if we would be partakers of them, though to·ani-
mate us to this is evidently the only end, for which
either the nature of the bleffings themfelves, or
the method of their conveyance, was revealed by
God. They indeed often defcribed faith in Chrift;
but they did not enough either defcribe or recommend that love and thofe works which will always
fpring from true faith; they rather feemed to de-
preciate them, as if they would have made mankind afraid of being holy, left they fhould truft in
it, and rob the Redeemer of his glory in faving
finners; thus directly oppofing the ftrain in which
both our Saviour and his apoftles fpoke, who always urge men to holinefs, and fet the righteous
in oppofition to the wicked. Inftead of reprefenting the affiftances of the Spirit as they are
always reprefented in holy writ, as encourage-
ments and incitements to diligence, they held them
forth in fuch a light as tended rather to make men
wait indolently till the Spirit fhould operate upon
them, than to exert their utmoft endeavours to
do their duty in a dependence on its aids. When
they either explained or recommended holinefs,
they were fo careful to reprefent it as arifing from
grace,

grace, that they fcarcely either exhorted to it, or fhowed the obligations men were under to culti-vate it. In fhort, their fermons were too little cal-culated to influence practice. On the other hand, the patrons of what was called Legal-preaching, reprefented religion as practical, explained and in-culcated the feveral duties of it, urged the argu-ments which reafon or revelation fupplied for the practice of virtue, infifted on the great doctrines of natural religion which the gofpel pre-fuppofes, as well as the doctrines of pure revelation which it fuperadds to them. So far they confidered Preach-ing in its proper light. But they were not wholly blamelefs. They often reprefented the virtues of the Chriftian life too much in the abftract manner of philofophy, and in the terms of art of modern fcholafticifm. They infifted, perhaps, too feldom on the peculiar doctrines of revelation, and on the duties which refult from the new relations of which it informs us. In oppofition to both extremes, a Chriftian preacher ought to infift both on the doc-trines and on the duties of religion; always repre-fenting the former as arguments for the latter, and the practice of the latter as abfolutely neceffary to render our knowlege of the former really ufeful to us; and always expreffing the whole, as much as poffible, in the ftrain of fcripture language. This is undoubtedly Gofpel-preaching; for it is to preach in the fame way that Chrift preached, and that his apoftles wrote.

What

What farther remains with regard to the choice of subjects is, the qualities of any particular subject which is chosen. The only quality that it will be necessary to take notice of is, that in every sermon there should be unity of design. This is a fundamental rule in every sort of composition; but in none is it more frequently neglected than in sermons. It is indeed so universally disregarded, that it may perhaps appear to many a singularity and affectation either to recommend it or to adhere to it in Preaching. But, however little it has been followed in practice, it has been recommended by some who have written on Preaching, particularly by Bishop Burnet and the Archbishop of Cambray. It is indeed a rule founded in the most essential principles of human nature. Man, being a reasonable being, thinks and speaks with some intention and design. He has always some end in view, however wrong and trifling the end itself, or however improper the means by which he endeavours the attainment of the end, may often be. It is therefore requisite that in all compositions the writer have some plan or object. A production without a design would resemble more the ravings of a madman, than the regular effects of thought and genius. Now, if there must be a design or plan, there ought likewise to be unity of design. When this is wanting, there is no bond of connection between the different subjects treated of, which may bring them under one plan or view, and which may easily convey the mind from one of

them

them to the other. The underſtanding finds it
difficult, when it has been filled with the concep⸗
tion of one object, to make a tranſition to another
wholly different, and cannot eaſily conceive that
other in a ſtrong and lively manner. Even the
underſtanding is perplexed and confounded and
diſtracted; but if the nature of the ſubject be
ſuch as tends to excite the paſſions, the inconvenience is ſtill greater. When the paſſions are
excited by one object, they will paſs eaſily to
another connected with it ; but they will paſs with
difficulty or not at all along different objects quite
unconnected with one another. By this means a
preacher, by introducing different ſubjects and
different deſigns into one ſermon, would loſe all
that communication of emotions by which alone he
can intereſt the heart, and raiſe the paſſions to a
proper pitch.

If unity of deſign be neceſſary in a ſermon, it
will be proper to conſider how it may be preſerved,
what is to be deemed a deviation from it, and
what degree of variety is conſiſtent with it. We
have already reckoned up ſeveral kinds of diſcourſes. It was with a view to the propriety of
unity of deſign, that we called them diſtinct
kinds ; for moſt commonly they are all united in
the ſame diſcourſe, and all ſeem to be equally
principal, and their ends equally ultimate in the
intention of the preacher. Now, by explaining
how far theſe kinds may allowably be combined,
and

and how far not, all will be done that is neceſſary on this ſubjeƈt of unity of deſign. There·is. one caſe, in which all or moſt of the kinds of diſcourſes that have been mentioned, may be joined together even profeſſedly in diſcourſing fiom one text. It is when that text is made the ſubjeƈt of ſeveral diſcourſes, and every ſeparate diſcourſe is the proſecution of one of the deſigns propoſed. ·For inſtance, if 2 Corinth. v. 14. be choſen for a text, " The love of Chriſt conſtraineth us, becauſe we " thus judge, that if one died for all, then were " all dead." To proſecute all the deſigns which are implied in this verſe, one might propoſe ſuch a method as this : 1. To ſhow that, previous to the interpoſition of Chriſt, all men were in a ſtate of death. 2. To ſhow that Chriſt died, that he might redeem us from this ſtate of death. 3. To ſhow that this interpoſition of Chriſt was a diſplay of the greateſt love. 4. To urge the death of Chriſt for us, and the love which it manifeſted, as an argument for Chriſtian obedience. If we conſider this as a method propoſed for one diſcourſe, it will have too little unity of deſign. But if. theſe four heads be made the ſubjeƈt of four diſcourſes, each diſcourſe will be properly one ; the three former of the probatory, the laſt of the ſuaſory kind. Each will be as really diſtinƈt from the other, as if it had been preached from a diſtinƈt text ; and each will have its own unity of deſign : the preacher only ſaves himſelf the trouble of finding out a new text for every ſermon, Sometimes it may be eligible to ufe this method; thus, if one choofe a text which is a general exhortation to any duty, as Ephef. v. 2. " walk " in love," he may with equal propriety propofe, in any fingle difcourfe, either to explain the nature of Chriftian love or charity, or to enforce the practice of it. If therefore he think it proper to infift on both thefe fubjects, he may certainly profecute the former in one difcourfe, and the latter in another difcourfe from the fame text, without tranfgreffing any of the rules of compofition. Sometimes again it will be more eligible to choofe different texts for the different points which one defigns to profecute; as when fome of them are but obfcurely implied in a text which treats of the others; when the fubjects which might be found implied in one text are very different and unconnected; when profecuting them all in fo many different difcourfes would occafion one's infifting too long on one text, fo that it might become tedious and difagreeable to the hearers, and wear off that expectation of novelty which a new text is apt to raife. But which of thefe methods he will choofe muft be left to the judgement of the preacher on particular occafions. Only it muft be remembered that the fubject of each feparate difcourfe fhould be ftrictly one.

In order to this, it is neceffary that in every difcourfe fome one of the ends of Preaching above taken notice of fhould be the leading and principal

design

defign of the preacher, and that every thing introduced into the fermon fhould be rendered fubordinate to that end. To propofe explication,
proof, perfuafion, as different ends all equally
principal in the fame difcourfe, is plainly to deviate
from unity. One of them diverts the attention
from the other, and tends to diftract the mind.
But though, to preferve unity, it be abfolutely
neceffary that fome one of the ends of Preaching
be the leading defign in a fermon, yet others of
the ends may be aimed at as fubordinate to that
end which is predominate. For inftance, if the
defign of a difcourfe be to explain any duty, what,
if it were alone, would form a demonftrative or
panegyrical difcourfe, may very properly be introduced as a means of explication. An illuftrious
example of that virtue exercifed by a perfon in
real life, will fhow the proper exertions of that
virtue more plainly than any abftract precepts that
could be given ; and, while it thus does not interfere with the end, explication, but promotes it, it
will very effectually, though without an appearance of defigning it, ftrike the confcience with a
fenfe of its obligation, and difpofe men to practife
what they are made to fee belongs to their duty.
Thus, in an explicatory difcourfe, the demonftrative may be incorporated, fo as to contribute to
the main end of the difcourfe.

Again, in a probatory difcourfe, it is neceffarily
fuppofed that the doctrine to be proved is previoufly
underftood.

understood. It would be a deviation from unity to
propose first the explication, and then the proof of
the doctrine, as two independent heads. But
though explication be not directly proposed, yet
the whole proof may be, and ought to be, conducted in such a way, as may of course carry
explication along with it, and really make the
doctrine understood, while it proposes only to
confirm it. Indeed, the eviction of a doctrine
includes explication so naturally, that an argument cannot be justly prosecuted, without its
showing, in every step of it, what is the nature of
the truth which it is brought to prove. In a probatory discourse, indeed in any discourse, it would
be wrong to make a digression to explain a difficult
text of scripture which is brought in incidentally ;
but yet some explication of scripture, viz. so far as
it is subservient to illustration or proof, may be
very properly introduced in any discourse. In a
suasory discourse, persuasion ought to be the only
professed design of the whole ; every thing that is
introduced should be regarded but as a mean of
promoting this end. But explication, proof, and
painting, are, from the very nature of this discourse,
necessarily introduced, not for their own sakes, or
as a part of the professed design of the preacher,
but as means of persuasion. Examples are very
proper motives to practice, and therefore may be
here displayed in all their beauty, and directly
urged as motives to good practice. In a word, all
that is necessary for preserving unity of design in a
sermon

fermon is, that one fimple defign be propofed;
that every thing introduced be fuch as tends to
promote that defign, and be fet in the particular light in which it will tend moft to promote it.

It will appear, from what has been faid, that the
ordinary way of dividing fermons into fo many
diftinct and independent heads, is fcarcely confiftent
with unity of defign. But it muft be remarked,
that every divifion is by no means inconfiftent with
it. A difcourfe is naturally divided into parts,
according to the branches of the fubject to be
explained, or the arguments which are urged.
But even a divifion, very little different from fuch
as are commonly propofed, and profecuted in a
manner very little different, may be eafily contrived
fo as to be rendered confiftent with unity of defign.
We may illuftrate this by fome examples. We
already mentioned a method which might be propofed, and would very probably be propofed in
the ordinary way of preaching, on 2 Corinth. v. 14.
and which is inconfiftent with unity of defign.
Yet if, in preaching on that text, it were propofed
as the defign of the fermon, to urge men to live
to Chrift by the practice of holinefs, from the confideration of his death, all the very fame heads
which we mentioned before might be introduced
very confiftently with unity of defign, with no
other variation but that of propofing and profe-

cuting

cuting them as motives or arguments to this con‑
duct. One might propose to pursue the design, by
showing that the death of Christ urges us to holiness
and the obedience of his gospel, by evincing,
1. That without being thus interested in his death,
we must be in a state of death and misery : 2. That
we are bound to it, because it was the very design
of Christ's death to deliver us from the bondage of
sin : 3. That we are bound by his death to obey
him, in gratitude for the love which his submitting
to death for us manifested. Thus again, in preach‑
ing from Matth. v. 8. " Blessed are the pure in
" heart, for they shall see God," the common
method is, 1. to explain purity of heart ; 2. to
explain the blessedness of seeing God ; 3. to show
the connection between them. Here, three differ‑
ent heads; though not unconnected, yet separate
and independent, are proposed as equally principal.
But if one would preserve unity of design on this
subject, it would be proper to propose, as the
design of the discourse, to enforce the practice of
holiness from the happiness in the enjoyment of
God which is connected with it ; and in prose‑
cuting this simple design, all that is necessary for
explaining either the nature of holiness or of its
reward might be introduced so as to be rendered
subservient to it. It is needless to multiply ex‑
amples. If men be once sensible that an adherence
to unity is proper, it will be easy to discourse on
every subject so as to preserve it.

I would

·I would not be underſtood to mean that an adherence to unity of deſign is ſo indiſpenſably neceſſary in every ſermon, that it ſhould never be departed from in a ſingle inſtance. But certainly it is a rule of compoſition ſo plainly founded in human nature, that it ought not to be departed from often, or without any reaſon at all. A ſtrict adherence to it will indeed render Preaching more difficult. It is not ſo eaſy to keep one deſign continually in view, and promote it through a whole diſcourſe, as, without forming any deſign, to ſpeak a little upon different views of a ſubject. But a Chriſtian miniſter ought to follow, not the method of Preaching which is eaſieſt, but what is moſt proper and uſeful.

In conſidering Preaching with reſpect to the different exertions of mind employed in it, which are commonly called the parts of eloquence, we naturally began with invention, and have already conſidered the helps of invention, and the qualities of the ſubject in general. We ſhall now conſider invention, as it regards the ſeveral parts of a pulpit diſcourſe.

The firſt of theſe is the text. It is a part of ſcripture which contains the ſubject of the diſcourſe, and by its being divinely inſpired, gives weight and authority to it. We already made all the obſervations that are neceſſary, with reſpect to thoſe paſſages of ſcripture which are the texts of ſuch

diſcourſes

difcourfes as we termed Lectures. The obfervations
which we are now to make, regard the difcourfes
which are properly termed Sermons. From the
nature and defign of a text, it will follow that the
principal qualities which fhould be fought for in
it, are fuch as thefe. 1. It fhould be a propofition containing the intention and fubftance of the
fermon, fo that the text may be the fermon in
epitome, and the fermon the text fpread out and
expanded. It is a fault to prefix a text as if it
were only a motto to a difcourfe which has fome
relation to it, but does not profecute its real intention and defign. It deprives the difcourfe of
the weight and authority which might arife from
its being evidently founded on the text. If the
fubject of the fermon be fuch that a text directly
expreffing it cannot be found in fcripture, it gives
a ftrong prefumption, that that is not a proper
fubject of Preaching; and if a text directly implying it can be found, it fhows want of judgement
in a preacher to choofe one that does not. It will
not be difficult to find texts which have this quality
for any fubject of true religion. A general af-
fertion of a doctrine will ferve either for a lermon
intended to explain that doctrine, or for one intended to prove it. For a fermon defigned to explain a duty, one may choofe either a general exhortation to that duty, or a place of fcripture
which enumerates the parts of the duty. In order
to perfuade to a duty, one may choofe a text
which either contains a general exhortation to it,

or

or expreffes its obligation, its neceffity, or advantages. 2. A text fhould be fimple; it fhould not only contain the whole fubject, but likewife it fhould contain nothing befides it. Without this, either there will be fome part of it which has nothing to anfwer to it in the fermon; or the fermon muft contain two or more fubjects inftead of one. At leaft, if the text be complex, one part of it fhould be made the fubject of each fingle difcourfe. 3. A text fhould be plain, that it may not require long time and great pains for clearing up the meaning of it, or making it underftood, and thus detain too long from the profecution of the fubject which it contains. 4. A text is the better if it be fhort, for it will be the more eafily remembered. All the qualities oppofite to thefe are faults in a text, though not all equally unpardonable. It may not be always eafy to find a text at once fimple, plain, and fhort, for every fubject which a preacher may think it ufeful to infift upon. And certainly he ought not to lay afide an ufeful fubject merely becaufe he cannot find a text in all refpects fuch as he would choofe. It is one of the moft unpardonable faults in a text, not to imply truly the fubject of the difcourfe. If it only refemble it in found, it is a mere playing upon words; it is in no proper fenfe a foundation for the difcourfe. All texts that, in relation to the fubject, have any appearance of wit, or humour, or conceit, are very improper, for they are unfuitable to the dignity and gravity of the pulpit. It has been difputed, whe-

ther

ther a text fhould be chofen for the fubject, or
the fubject chofen and the difcourfe made for the
text. In all difcourfes formed in the textual method, in all which we have comprehended under
the name of Lectures, the latter muft be the cafe.
And the opinion of thofe who have determined
that this latter fhould always be the cafe, feems to
have arifen from their admitting only the textual
method of Preaching. But in the feveral other
kinds of fermons of which we have taken notice,
there feems to be no impropriety in choofing a
text for the fubject. And any text expreffing the
fubject will obvioufly appear to fuit a difcourfe
properly made on that fubject. But a fubject may
often be diftorted or prevented from being reprefented in the moft natural and ftriking manner, by
being ftudioufly adapted to the phrafes and manner
of expreffion of a particular text. It is, perhaps,
the beft way in general to choofe the fubject and
form the defign of the difcourfe firft of all, then to
fix on a text which expreffes it, and with that text
in view to compofe the difcourfe.

The exordium naturally fucceeds the text. Its
end is to prepare the minds of the hearers for the
difcourfe. It is fometimes not neceffary to ufe an
exordium, becaufe their minds need no preparation; as when we are to difcourfe on a fubject
that is eafy and generally acceptable, and againft
which they entertain no prejudices. If one choofe
an exordium here, it may be employed in reprefenting

senting the subject-as generally acknowleged to be useful, and as, therefore, confessedly important and worthy of regard, though too little regarded in practice. Sometimes again, a preacher combats the prejudices of men, as when he defends a doctrine which they are disposed to reject, or inculcates a duty which is perhaps unfashionable. In this case an exordium seems to be necessary, or, at least, highly useful, and it should, with as much address as possible, expose the weakness of the prejudices against the subject, or insinuate the necessity of combating them, or give such an account of their origin as may dispose men to suspect them, or hint that it is the preacher's sense of their dangerous tendency that leads him to endeavour to remove them. The importance of the subject, and the near concern which the hearers have in it, is often a very proper topic for an exordium; but it should not spend itself in mere general assertions to this purpose, but suggest such sentiments as may convince the hearers. This will have a great tendency to engage them to attention, and to dispose them to give the discourse a favourable hearing. The exordium may sometimes be employed in laying open such principles as tend to make the subject better understood, and thus both dispose the hearers for attending to it, and prepare them for profiting by it. Sometimes, a piece of history, especially of sacred history, may be very properly turned into an exordium; particularly when the text is introduced by a history; in this case, the

exordium

exordium will coincide with the giving a view of
the context.   But it would be tedious to mention
all the topics from which introductions may be deduced, or to illuftrate them by examples.   From
whatever topics the exordium be deduced, it
fhould be fit for anfwering its end, for preparing
the minds of the hearers.   In order to prepare
their minds for profiting by the difcourfe, it is
neceffary to render them *attentive*, for without
this they cannot either underftand or apply it; to
render them *docile*, or fit to apprehend and receive
it; and *benevolent*, ready to give a fair hearing to
the preacher.   Thefe difpofitions fhould be kept
up through the whole difcourfe, but it is the bufinefs of the exordium or introduction to raife
them.   All the topics already mentioned, and all
the topics proper for introductions, muft be fubfervient to fome of thefe purpofes of the introduction.   An introduction is faulty if it be common, or fuch as may be applied with equal propriety to aimoft any fubject.   It ought to rife
naturally from the fubject, and to lead directly to
the next part of the difcourfe; it fhould appear to
be taken, as it were, from the very bowels of the
fubject, and be fit to give an opening to it; on
this account, it has been the opinion of fome rhetorical writers, that, though it comes fuft in
order, it ought generally to be thought of laft,
after the whole defign is thoroughly digefted; but
I imagine that, in this way, there would be great
danger of its being forced, and not cohering fufficiently

ciently with the fermon. The introduction fhould generally be cool, for it is natural to begin calmly, and to rife to warmth by degrees, in proportion as one is more engaged by his fubject. But when the fubject is obvioufly interefting, and when the text gives an affecting view of it, a warm and vehement exordium is allowable, and will have a great influence on the audience. That an introduction may be fit to produce the effects for which it is defigned, it is necefſary that the introduction itfelf both be underftood, and pleafe. In order to thefe, it muft be plain, the fentences fhort, every thing accurate, the expreffions proper, but without an appearance of labour and ftudy, yet fmooth and flowing; it fhould be fit to catch and entice the hearers all at once. Finally, an introduction fhould be fhort; immoderate length is a great fault; it makes it difproportioned to the difcourfe; it keeps the main defign too long out of view.

The introduction is fucceeded by the explication of the text and context. The defign of explaining the text is to make it underftood, and to fhow that it really contains that which is the fubject of the difcourfe. By fhowing this before-hand, the preacher is freed from the neceffity of diftorting his fubject during the profecution of it, to accommodate it to the precife words and form of expreffion in that particular text. Whenever, therefore, the text is perfectly plain of itfelf, and obvioufly contains the fubject of the difcourfe, it is

fuperfluous

superfluous to fpend time in explaining it. The
only defign of explaining the context is to fhow,
from the intention of the writer and the connection
of the text with what fgoes before, that the meaning which the preacher puts upon ft is its real and
genuine feufe, and that he, therefore, purfues in
his difcourfe what is its true import. On this account it is evident that when a context is plain,
no explication of it is neceffary for inveftigating
the true meaning of the text; and when there is
no dependence of the text on what precedes, any
notice of the context is fuperfluous. When an
explication of the text, or the context, or of both,
is neceffary, the rules of it may be deduced from
what has been already faid of lectures. We fhall
only obferve that the explication fhould be as fhort,
as poffible; for it is rather a preparation to the
defign, than a direct part of it.

The next part is the defign. It fhould coincide
with the import of the text, and fhould be propofed in a fingle propofition. By this means it
will appear clearly what is the point at which the
preacher is to drive; and the hearers will be prepared for perceiving the fubfervience of every
thing that he fays, to this point. It fhould be
propofed in as plain terms, and fet in as ftriking
a light as poffible. It will thus make the deeper
impreffion on the hearers, and throw greater light
on the whole difcourfe. An affectation of quaintnefs and ingenuity in propofing the defign is always

ways blameable, as it detracts from its solidity and weight, and renders it less apt to be under-stood or remembered.

From what has been said of the kinds of dif-courses, it will be easy to conceive how the design should be proposed; it will be to explain, to prove, or to persuade. It is sometimes very pro-per to join with the proposition of the design, an infinuation of the useful purpose which it anfwers; for example, when one propofes to explain any duty, he might add, that all may fee what it is that is incumbent on them, and may be enabled, on examining themfelves, to difcern how far they comply with their duty, and in what refpects they are negligent or defective in it. Or it may be proper to join with it a direction to fuch a difpo-fition in hearing, as may enable them to apply the difcourfe to its proper ufe, as to reflect on their own conduct, and examine their own confciences, while a duty is explained; to ponder the force of every argument produced, when a truth is confirmed; and fo in other cafes. It is very common with the French preachers to fubjoin an Ave Maria to the propofing of their defign. A Proteftant preacher may fubftitute, in place of this, a fhort prayer. If this were always ufed, it would degenerate into a mere unaffecting form. But fometimes, when the fubject is uncommonly ftriking or folemn, or when one has been raifed to a confiderable degree of warmth in the exordium, or when it has ended
with

with any mention of the aſſiſtances of the divine
ſpirit, a ſhort prayer for God's rendering the
deſign effectual may be very properly ſubjoined to
the propoſal of it, and will have great influence.
Sometimes the propoſition of the deſign may be very
properly implied in a prayer or invocation of this
kind. But the varieties which may be admitted,
and the occaſions that are proper for them, will
be naturally ſuggeſted to a preacher by his ſubject,
and the circumſtances in which he is to ſpeak.

The diviſion or method comes next in order.
It is the propoſing of the ſeveral parts or members
of the ſubject, before entering on the proſecution of
them. Diviſions were never uſed by the ancient
orators, and very ſeldom by the chriſtian fathers.
They were firſt introduced by the ſcholaſtics, and
have been ſince almoſt univerſally retained by
chriſtian preachers. The ancient orators, inſtead
of propoſing before-hand the diviſion which they
were to follow, often even ſtudied to conceal the
diſtinction of the parts during the proſecution.
Indeed, as their view in ſpeaking was to perſuade
their hearers to ſomething which was to be done
immediately, a formal diviſion might have had ſo
much the appearance of ſtudy, as to have prevented this effect. And as the effect muſt take
place immediately, it was not neceſſary to do any
thing which might aſſiſt them in retaining afterwards a diſtinct view of the tenor of the diſcourſe.
But a Chriſtian Preacher is to deliver diſcourſes on
important

important fubjects, which, it is taken for granted, he has carefully confidered before-hand, and therefore an appearance of ftudy will not fo directly obftruct any defign which he may propofe. His difcourfe is intended to influence them in a long courfe of conduct; and in order to influence them, it muft be remembered and recollected long after it is heard; in order to which it is neceffary that it be diftinctly apprehended when it is heard: the propofing a divifion contributes to this end, and is therefore no ways improper. In a word, a divifion is more neceffary to preachers, than it was to the ancient orators, on account of the different natures and defigns of their difcourfes; what were inconveniences to them will be none to preachers. There are doubtlefs fome cafes, in which a divifion will be inconvenient in a fermon. For inftance, it may fometimes happen that all the parts of a fermon rife naturally out of one another, and contribute directly to one defign; yet if they were all propofed in the beginning, their connection and dependence would not appear: in this cafe, it is better to omit any profeffed divifion, and to content onefelf with propofing the general defign. "When a divifion is given, it fhould be fuch as " arifes naturally from the fubject; fuch as gives " a light and a juft order to the feveral parts; " fuch a divifion as may be eafily remembered, " and, at the fame time, help to connect and " retain the whole; fuch a divifion as fhows at " once the extent of the fubject and of all its

6 " parts."

" parts." Thus the divifion of an explicatory fermon will be according to the different branches of the doctrine or duty to be explained; that of a probatory or fuafory difcourfe, according to the different arguments which are to be urged, for conviction or perfuafion. A divifion fhould not confift of too many members; if it does, moft fubjects will be, by this means, cut into pieces rather than properly diftributed into parts; befides, it will confound both the apprehenfions and the memories of the hearers, and will thus produce the very inconvenience which it is the only defign of it to prevent. This fault in divifion generally proceeds from an affectation of fubtlety in diftinguifhing wherever there is the minuteft difference, fometimes where there is no difference at all. The French preachers generally confine themfelves to three parts; but fome fubjects have more than three diftinct members; and, confidering the variety of fubjects, no certain number can be fixed on for every cafe. A divifion fhould be laid down as fhortly, and in as plain terms, as poffible, without either obfcure or fuperfluous expreffions. There fhould be no affectation of quaintnefs or conceit in a divifion. This is a fault very frequent in the French preachers. Where there is any degree of this, it renders the divifion worfe than it would be in the textual way of deducing the divifion, not from the members of the fubject, but from the expreffions and claufes of the text.

We

We come now to confider invention, as employed about the profecution or body of the difcourfe. This is in every difcourfe the principal part.
The way in which the ancient rhetoricians treated
of this part, was by pointing out the feveral forts
of topics, or common places, from which arguments
or illuftrations might be deduced. Thefe they
handled with great fubtlety. It is however found
by experience, that thefe are of little ufe in practice.
They fupply only fuperficial arguments at the heft;
they only give a hint to genius, and fometimes they
rather miflead than direct into the right way. They
may be an ingenious analyfis of the heads of argument; but they are of no ufe as a foundation for
fpeaking. We fhall not therefore fpend time in
accommodating them to fermons. A thorough
underftanding of the fubject will be a much better
means of inventing what is proper to be faid on it,
than any artificial topics. We have already prevented ourfelves in what might have been obferved
concerning the peculiarities of profecution, according to the different kinds of difcourfes. All therefore that remains is to confider what is common to
all the kinds.

The object of invention is the fentiment : it will
not therefore be improper to point out the feveral
qualities of fentiments or thoughts which a
chriftian preacher ought to feek after, and of the
faults which he ought to avoid. The firft and
fundamental quality of thoughts or fentiments on

z every

every fubject is; that they be true and juft. Frequently thofe thoughts or fentiments which appear
at firft fight the brighteft, are not juft and folid;
yet they are apt to dazzle and pleafe by their
glare, and on that account to be chofen. Such
falfe thoughts would not, however, pafs without
cenfure by a judicious critic, in a piece of wit, or a
poem. But they are, above all, unfuitable to the
gravity and folemnity of pulpit difcourfes, and
to the importance of the fubjects treated in them.
Truth is the firft quality, the very fubftance of
fentiment: if it want truth, the more bold and
fhining it is, the more faulty it muft be. Thoughts
are the images of things, and are true no farther
than they reprefent things faithfully. Again,
thoughts or fentiments ought to be natural: Natural thoughts are not far-fetched, but arife obvioufly from the fubject; fo that they feem to have
been found eafily and without any labour; and
one would think that they muft have occurred to
any perfon on the fubject. The oppofite of this
quality is affectation; when fentiments are ftudioufly ftretched and carried too far; when,
inftead of being fublime, they are extravagant;
when, inftead of being elegant, they are finical;
when, inftead of being delicate, they are fubtle
and refined. On the contrary, when thoughts are
natural, they bear no mark of ftudy or defign; if
an object be defcribed, it is by fuch appearances of
it as ftrike every perfon as foon as they are mentioned; the paffions are made to exprefs themfelves

felves properly in their own language. But in avoiding affected fentiments, we muft take care not to fall into fuch as are flat and languid.

Another quality of fentiment a-kin to the former is, that it be fuitable to the fubject. Thofe fentiments which fuit a familiar fubject, will not fuit a fublime or pathetic one; thofe which fuit explication would be cold in perfuafion; thofe which would be proper to perfuafion would be extravagant in explication. It is likewife neceffary that fentiments be perfpicuous or clear. Obfcurity fometimes belongs to the fentiment as well as to the expreffion. When it rifes to a great height, it becomes unintelligible and abfolute nonfenfe. Even when it is in a lefs degree, when a thought is fo abftrufe as to become dark and hard to be underftood, it is a fault. A thought ought to be fo clear, that perfons of tolerable underftanding may comprehend it, without being obliged to employ too great application of mind. Thefe qualities of fentiment are univerfally and indifpenfably neccffary. There are others which are not neceffary in every cafe, but ought to be attended to in cafes where they are proper; fuch as fublimity, beauty, delicacy, which are fo fully explained by critical writers that it will not be neceffary to enlarge on them.

The laft part of a difcourfe is the conclufion or peroration, which pretty much coincides with what

is

is commonly called the application. The conclufion fhould always be fuitable to the kind and end
of the difcourfe. We have formerly faid all that
is neceffary with refpect to the conclufion of all
forts of lectures and textual difcourfes, and likewife
of thofe which are explicatory of a particular
character. Thofe which are defigned to explain a
duty, may be concluded in different ways fuitable
to their defign. It is very proper, after having
explained fully the feveral parts of it, to recapi-
tulate the whole ; this will both affift the hearers
in remembering what has been advanced for the
direction of their conduct, and what can be of no
ufe for directing it except it be remembered ; and
will alfo tend to give them a ftronger impreffion of
the connection and dependence of the parts.
Sometimes a recapitulation is all that is neceffary
in concluding an explicatory difcourfe, but it ought
always to be at leaft a part of the conclufion.
Again, as the defign of explaining a duty is to
direct the practice of the hearers, and as they will
not think of altering their conduct except they fee
how far they are deficient, exhortations, or directions for examining themfelves how far they really
practife their duty, may very properly fucceed the
recapitulation. Whatever can contribute to their
forming a right judgement of their real character
and conduct in refpect of the virtue or vice that
has been illuftrated, may very properly be introduced here. Farther, any directions which may
conduce to their practifing the virtue or avoiding
the

the vice, will juftly find a place in the conclufion
of fuch an explicatory difcourfe. Sometimes arguments for the practice of a duty arife from the
very view of the nature of that duty. It is impoffible, for inftance, to explain refignation, without mentioning the freedom from inward anxiety
and folicitude which this temper implies. · In cafes
of this kind it will not be improper to mention
in the conclufion, that, in order to recommend
the duty, it is fufficient to underftand its nature,
and to hint at thofe arguments for it which are
fo properly internal, as to be implied in the very
conception of it. Sometimes too, in the conclufion, a preacher may addrefs exhortations or directions diftinctly to different claffes of his hearers,
according to the different ways in which the duty
explained refpects them; as to thofe who wholly
neglect it, and to thofe who already practife it in
fome degree; which will give an opportunity of
pointing out and rebuking fuch fins or practices as
are remarkably inconfiftent with it. Sometimes,
all thefe parts may be proper in the conclufion of
one difcourfe; fometimes one or a few of them
will be fufficient. It was already remarked, that a
difcourfe intended to prove a doctrine, fhould be
concluded by pointing out its influence on practice,
either in feveral inferences when it is equally connected with feveral duties, or in one deduction
when it is peculiarly fubfervient to fome one branch
of virtue. The fame holds of thofe difcourfes,
which are employed in explaining a doctrine. It

Z 3   remains

remains only therefore to point out briefly, what
ought to be the conclusion of a suasory discourse.
As the design of the whole discourse is to persuade
men to the practice of some duty, so the conclusion
should evidently be calculated for fixing and confirming this effect. What, therefore, ought to be
its nature, will easily appear by recollecting what
has been already observed on the means of persuasion. Argument is absolutely necessary to it;
the conclusion, therefore, ought to contain a sum-
mary or recapitulation of the several arguments
which have been urged in the discourse. It should
not merely mention the heads of them, but represent in brief their whole force, and their greatest
strength. It should, as it were, collect their whole
vigour into one point, that it may be more intense
and affect the more. But, as argument alone does
not persuade without an address to the passions,
so the conclusion must contain not only the substance of the whole arguments, but also something
fit to influence and interest the passions. Indeed,
though the pathetic should, in a greater or a less
degree, run through the whole of a suasory discourse, the conclusion is the principal seat of it, in
which it will naturally rise to the greatest degree
of warmth. It is not necessary here, any more
than in the other parts of the discourse, that the
argument and the painting, from which the pathetic results, should be kept distinct. It is much
better that they be incorporated together so perfectly as to be blended and undistinguishable; that

so

fo the conclufion may at once collect, as it were, into one point all the light and all the warmth of the difcourfe, and leave its full effect upon the hearts of the hearers.

So much for invention, the firft exertion of mind employed in the eloquence of the pulpit.

ART. VI. *Of Difpofition.*

The fecond exertion of the mind is difpofition, which is therefore reckoned the fecond part of eloquence. It is employed in reducing the whole train of the difcourfe, and all its parts, into their proper order. Order confifts in placing things to-gether which are naturally connected. Without a proper difpofition, the materials of a difcourfe would be a mere confufed chaos. In every art, the difpofition of the materials is as effentially ne-ceffary as the finding them out.

We are prevented in many obfervations regard-ing the particular difpofition proper for the dif-ferent kinds of difcourfes, by the account of each kind that was formerly given. Some of the moft general rules of difpofition are likewife fufficiently implied in the recital, that was made under the laft head, of the order in which the feveral parts of a difcourfe naturally fucceed each other. A few obfervations upon it will be all that is farther neceffary.

Difpofition

Difpofition regards both the whole plan and each part of it. In the whole plan that order fhould be obferved, by which every thing may prepare the way for what fucceeds, and preferve the force of what went before. "Every thing "fhould be introduced to the beft advantage, and "where it is fitteft to make a due impreffion. "Often, that which would feem nothing to the "purpofe, by being unfeafonably urged, has a "very great weight when it is referved for its "proper place, till the audience be prepared by "other things to feel all its force and confe-"quence." The heads of every doctrine, the parts of every duty, have a natural connection and dependence, fo that one is firft, and the others fucceed in a certain order; and this order ought to be obferved in explaining them. In proving or perfuading by arguments, there is greater latitude, as to the order. Sometimes, indeed, the arguments have a natural fucceffion, fo that one rifes and grows out of another, and one prepares the way for another. In this cafe, this natural order ought to be carefully obferved; the fimpleft fhould be placed firft, and all of them difpofed fo that one may prepare the way for our fully under-ftanding and feeling the force of thofe which fol-low, and every fucceeding argument may add to the weight of thofe which went before. But often, the arguments are more unconnected; fo that any of them may, with little impropriety, be placed firft or laft. Here, one is left at liberty to choofe

any

any order that he pleafes; but even in this cafe,
one order may be better than another. Thus,
fome have advifed to begin with the weakeft arguments, and to proceed gradually to the ftrongeft,
that fo the reafoning, by continually gathering
force, may complete its effect upon the hearers.
Some again have approved of beginning and end-
ing with the ftrongeft arguments, and throwing
the weaker reafons into the middle; becaufe we
are naturally attentive at the beginning, and if we
be pleafed with what is then faid, we hear the reft
with the more favourable difpofition, and what
comes laft fticks beft with us. But in the difpofition of the general parts of a difcourfe, a great
deal muft be left to the judgement of the preacher;
few univerfal or invariable rules can be eftablifhed.

Order is neceffary not only in this, but in the
arrangement of each particular part. In general,
it is proper on each head or argument, firft to propofe it briefly, and then to fpread it out in the
profecution, illuftrating or urging the whole of it.
But though it be eafy to difcern when a proper
order is obferved, or to difcover a particular fault
that is committed, it is not eafy to lay down rules
which would not be either too general to be underftood, or too particular to be ufeful in every
cafe. In paffing from one part of a difcourfe to
another, fome form of tranfition is neceffary.
Englifh preachers are generally very carelefs and
unartificial in this, contenting themfelves with
mentioning

mentioning one head when they have finished another, without being at any pains to run them, as
it were, into one another. Greater care, however,
in this respect, would often be attended with good
effects. A transition, for instance, may be made
from the explication of one part of a duty to that
of another, by hinting how the practice of the
former leads to the latter, or how insufficient the
former will be without the latter. In passing from
one argument to another, whether in a probatory
or a suasory discourse, especially in the latter, it
will be proper, not to seem to give up the former
arguments, or to allow their force to vanish when
we leave them and proceed to others. This will
be best done by recapitulating the former ones, at
least the one immediately preceding, and professedly superadding the next one to them. Various
ways of doing this will easily occur on trial.

Art. VII. Of Elocution.

The third exertion of the preacher is elocution,
which regards the language, style, and composition
of sermons. The language of sermons ought, first
of all, to be plain and perspicuous. In order to attain this, we must use words that are in common
use, words which are suitable to the subject, avoiding all technical terms of art, all terms borrowed
from the schools, and all such expressions as are
ambiguous or equivocal, or as are above the understanding of the people. "The figures must be
"easy

" eafy though not mean, fuch as tend to make the
" matter better underftood." Too frequent and
too diftant metaphors obftruct perfpicuity, and turn
the difcourfe in fome meafure into a dark allegory.
All confufion in the arrangement of words likewife
produces obfcurity. Long periods, fuch as contain
in them two or three different thoughts, are hard
to be followed or apprehended. Plainnefs ought
to be preferved in every kind of compofition, but
moft of all in explication; for the very defign of
this being to make things underftood, every degree
of obfcurity is perfectly unfuitable. The language
of a preacher ought likewife to be pure; we fhould
avoid all folecifms or faults in conftruction, all bar-
barifms, or words and terms that do not truly belong to the language. Mean and low expreffions
are unbecoming the dignity of the pulpit, and the
fublimity of the fubjects which are there treated,
and muft difguft every perfon of any degree of
underftanding. At the fame time very great
nicety and correctnefs of ftyle is loft in a difcourfe
that is to be but once heard by a common audience.
But a remarkable want of compofition, an obvious
roughnefs and afperity of ftyle, is difagreeable.
There muft be fome degree of harmony in order
to prevent difguft. The language ought likewife
to be nervous, animated, and affecting. A great
part of the force of a fentiment often depends on
the manner in which it is expreffed. What will
have great force if it be expreffed in one way, will
become perfectly languid and unaffecting by being

expreffed

expreſſed in another.　In general, ᵗthe language is
forcible and moving, when it is ſuch as ſhows that
the ſpeaker is touched with what he ſays; this
never fails to affect the hearers.　And moſt of the
figures of rhetoric are nothing elſe but different
ways of ſhowing this.　Theſe figures are fully
treated by the ancient rhetoricians, to whom we
ſhall refer you.　The ſtudying them, and having
all their variety in view, will give you an aptitude
and bent to light upon them, when it is proper to
introduce them.　In ſtudying them, it will be proper, firſt, to acquire a diſtinct idea of the nature
of each; and next, to conſider what is its real
effect; whether it conduces to perſpicuity, to ornament, or to vehemence.　Such a previous knowlege of them will prevent your introducing them
improperly, and enable you to uſe with a good
effect thoſe figures which ſuit the ſubject and the
occaſion.　It muſt be remarked that any appearance of deſign in introducing figures, or crowding
them together, muſt be carefully avoided.　If they
do not appear to riſe naturally from the ſubject
and occaſion, without being ſought for, they will
defeat their own deſign, and render the diſcourſe
florid, affected, and diſagreeable.

ART. VIII.　*Of Memory.*

The next exertion of mind neceſſary in a
preacher is memory; the next exerciſe incumbent
on him is to commit to memory the diſcourſe
which

which he has invented, compofed, and expreffed.
In moft places it would be unneceffary to attempt
proving that this exercife is incumbent on a public
fpeaker. . To fhow you, however, that reading is
not approved even by thofe among whom it is moft
ufed, I fhall give you the fentiments of Bifhop
Burnet upon it, in his own words. "Reading is
"peculiar to this nation, and is endured in no
"other. It has indeed made that our fermons
"are more exact, and fo it has produced us
"many volumes of the beft that are extant; but
"after all, though fome few read fo happily, pro-
"nounce fo truly, and enter fo entirely into thofe
"affections which they recommend, that in them
"we fee both the correctnefs of reading, and the
"ferioufnefs of fpeaking, fermons, yet every one
"is not fo happy. Some, by hanging their heads
"perpetually over their notes, by blundering as
"they read, and by a curfory running over them,
"do fo leffen the matter of their fermons, that as
"they are generally read with very little life o-
"affection, fo they are heard with as little regard
"or efteem. Thofe who read ought certainly
"to be at a little more pains than for the moft
"part they are, to read true, to pronounce with
"an emphafis, and to raife their heads, and
"direct their eyes to their hearers; and if they
"practifed more alone the juft way of reading,
"they might deliver their fermons with much
"more advantage. Man is a low fort of creature;
"he does not, nay, for the greater part he can-
"not,

" not, confider things in themfelves, without thofe
" little feafonings that muft recommend them to
" his affections. That a difcourfe be heard with
" any life, it muft be fpoken with fome; and the
" looks and motions of the eye do carry in them,
" fuch additions to what is faid, that where thefe
" do not at all concur, it has not all the force
" upon them that otherwife it might have; be-
" fides that the people, who are too apt to cenfure
" the clergy, are eafily carried into an obvious
" reflection on reading, that it is an effect of
" lazinefs[a]."

It is eafy to fee that this writer difapproved reading fermons much more highly than he thought
proper, on account of its univerfal prevalence in
England, to declare explicitly. Indeed, the
impropriety of reading fermons arifes from the
very principles of human nature, not from any
groundlefs prejudices. It is not the only defign of
language to communicate the ideas of the fpeaker,
by exciting them in the minds of the hearers; it is
its defign likewife to exprefs the fentiments and
affections of the fpeaker, and by this means to raife
them in the hearers. Reading may anfwer the firft
of thefe ends, but it is improper for anfwering the
latter. It is not a natural expreffion of the fpeaker's
being interefted in what he fays; it does not render
the

---

[a] Paftoral Care, ch. ix.

the hearers attentive, or contribute to touch or
strike them. It is neceffarily weaker, more languid, and more unaffecting than speaking.

Were we to inquire at length concerning memory, we might examine on what the remem-
brance of fingle thoughts, and on what the remem-
brance of their feries or connections, depends; and
we might deduce, from the general principles on
which both depend, the means of rendering both
eafier. But it will not be neceffary for our prefent
purpofe to enter fo deep into the matter; it will be
fufficient to make a few general remarks upon
mandating.

In order to perform this exercife eafily, it is
proper that the memory be fufceptible, fo as
quickly to receive what we would commit to it;
diftinct, fo as to retain not only the things themfelves, but likewife their due order or pofition;
and ready, fo as to fuggest them without difficulty,
when we have occafion for them. Thefe qualities
of memory are attained by pretty much the fame
means. A thorough underftanding of the fubject
is a great preparation for mandating eafily; for it
will enable every part to strike us with greater
force. In order to our remembering, it will likewife be proper that we fix clofe attention upon what
we would remember, without allowing our thoughts
to be diftracted or to run off to other fubjects,
when we are engaged in mandating. It is alfo

3   proper

proper that we dwell on every part till we have thoroughly acquired it, before we proceed to any other. If at firſt we ſhould be able to commit to memory but a few ſentences or periods in a day, we muſt take care to acquire them perfectly before we proceed to others. Order and diſtinctneſs in compoſition, and even writing a diſcourſe in ſeparate paragraphs, is of great help to memory; it makes it more eaſily ſuſceptible, by ſaving a great deal of labour that would be neceſſary for impreſſing every ſingle thought, if it were either diſpoſed or written confuſedly; it will make it lie diſtinctly in the mind, and give many handles for recollecting it. When we have looked over what we would commit to memory, we ſhould endeavour to repeat it to ourſelves; for this endeavour, and looking to it when we are at a loſs, will fix it more ſpeedily, than if we were to read it over much oftener, without any attempt to recite; and when we find ourſelves at a loſs at any particular place, and, by looking to it, endeavour to fix it, we ſhall ſcarcely be in any hazard of finding ourſelves again at a loſs at that particular place. It is found by ſome to be of great ſervice to look over what they want to remember, immediately before going to ſleep at night, becauſe then the mind is not afterwards buſied about any ideas which may drive it away; or to look it over in the morning on firſt getting up, becauſe the mind is not then pre-occupied with any ideas which may hinder its taking faſt hold of it. A perſon ought at firſt to commit every word

and

and fyllable to heart, whatever trouble it may coft him; for this will moft fpeedily perfect the habit of remembering, and make it more eafy for him to remember afterwards, though he only charge his memory with the principal things and the general order of the whole. It will be of great ufe frequently to recollect and endeavour to repeat what one has committed to memory, at certain intervals, before delivering it in public; for a man cannot at firft promife on what he has but lately-committed to memory; but the reviewing of it after a certain interval fixes it in the memory more deeply than it was before. Thefe are fome of the principal means of committing difcourfes to memory. The frequent ufe of thefe means will beget a habit of doing it eafily. No power of the mind is more improveable by ufe than memory: memory is in no way improveable to fo great a degree as in this exercife of mandating. Ufe makes it incredibly eafy to acquire what we want to remember; and it produces at the fame time fo ftrong a habit of recollecting readily, that though one had committed what he is to fay very imper-fectly to memory, he will run no rifk of miffing any part of it. The ufe you fhould make of this is to begin as early as poffible to mandate either fermons or any thing elfe, and to repeat them either by yourfelves or in the company of others. By this means the habit will be formed, and all the difficulties over, before you come to appear in public.

To many, however, mandating a fermon is a very difficult matter. Where the memory is naturally weak, it will take up fo much time as to leave little for any thing elfe; and even with the beft memory, diffidence and timidity may have fuch an effect upon one, as to make him forget, before a congregation, what he was perfect mafter of when alone in his clofet. Where it can be done with tolerable eafe, it is certainly moft natural; the preacher will feel it moft agreeable; and, in general, it will have greater influence on the audience. At the fame time one ought to have his notes before him, to which he may have recourfe in cafe of his being at a lofs; otherwife, if he happen any how to get difcompofed, he may find it difficult to recover himfelf.

But though mandating be not abfolutely neceffary to good preaching, good reading is indifpenfably fo. To read fervilely, with one's eyes conftantly fixed on his papers, is difgufting to an audience. It fhows fomething fo cold and lifelefs in a preacher, that what he fays, be it ever fo good in itfelf, can never affect his hearers. A preacher ought always to perufe his fermon till he enter thoroughly into the fpirit of it, and be able, with a glance at his notes now and then, to deliver it with facility and propriety. To read well, is an accomplifhment of much greater importance than many are apt to imagine. It admits of all that warmth and animation, of all that action which is

necelfary

neceffary or becoming in the pulpit, and will, in a great meafure, fuperfede the neceffity of mandating.

ART. IX. *Of Pronunciation or Action.*

The laft exertion employed by the preacher, and the laft part of eloquence, is Pronunciation or Action. You will find this topic treated largely by rhetorical writers, and even very minute rules for the modulation of the voice and the motion of the feveral parts of the body given by them, efpecially by Quinctilian. We fhall therefore ftudy the greater brevity. It is acknowleged by all, that the feveral languages which have prevailed in the world are merely artificial, and derive their fignification wholly from compact or tacit confent. But this neceffarily fuppofes that men had previoufly a natural language ; for without that, they could never have expreffed that confent, or entered into that compact, from which artificial language derives its origin. Now, this natural language could be nothing elfe but fuch inarticulate founds and motions as naturally expreffed the fentiments and paffions of men. The difficulty and fcantinefs of thefe made them inconvenient, and rendered artificial language neceffary. But they had in fome refpects greatly the advantage of this latter. This of itfelf expreffes only ideas ; they expreffed all the movements of the foul : this of itfelf is dead and unanimated ; they were animated and alive, as

it

it were. Each of them being thus imperfect by
itfelf, the perfection of fpeaking confifts in uniting
natural and artificial language as much as poffible.
In the union of them, all the rules of pronunciation
and action have their foundation. The natural
inarticulate founds which were in ufe before language was invented, cannot be mixed with the
articulate founds of which language confifts; but
their force is united to them when thefe articulate
founds are pronounced with the tone and modulation of voice which correfpond to the fentiment
or emotion which they fignify. The other part of
natural language, the motions by which men
expreffed their fentiments, may be joined with
language, and conftitute what is properly termed
Action. Whatever is inconfiftent with the union
of natural and artificial language, whatever implies
the mere ufe of the latter without any mixture of
the former, is a fault in pronunciation. The following obfervations may throw fome light on this
fubject.

Pronunciation includes two parts; the management of the voice, and the gefture of the body. In
general, a great compofure of both is abfolutely
neceffary; a gravity and compofure of look and
voice, equally diftant from a light carelefs behaviour on the one hand, and an affected tone and
wry faces on the other. Every thing muft be delivered in fuch a manner and with fuch an emphafis,
as may fhow that the preacher thoroughly under-

ſtands all that he ſays; is fully perſuaded of it, and has thoſe affections which he deſires to infuſe into others. The pronunciation muſt be always diſtinct, and the action lively, natural, and becoming, ſuch as may point out ſtrongly what his words alone would expreſs in a flat and languid manner. An orator muſt not always have his hands or his body in motion, for it is not natural to uſe many geſtures when we ſay common things, without any vehemence or emotion. Both the voice and the geſture may have a greater degree of vehemence in Preaching, than converſation could properly admit in ſaying the ſame things; for the ſight of a great audience, the importance of the ſubject, and the ſolemnity of the occaſion, will naturally give a greater degree of warmth than one could have in diſcourſing familiarly with his friends. It is ſometimes proper to expreſs ſome things with a leſs degree of force than their nature would ſeem to require, eſpecially when they are to be followed by things which require the utmoſt force of pronunciation and action; for men may waſte their ſpirits ſo much in ſaying plain things, as to be forced to utter thoſe things faintly which ought to be delivered with a vehement action; but when the preacher ſays things leſs warm with an eaſy and familiar manner, he will the more eaſily grow vehement, and attain energy of voice and action when the ſubject moſt requires it; and the audience will then be moſt affected. One of the moſt common faults both in voice and action is a monotony

or famenefs running through the whole, however
different the fentiments expreffed may be.   Many
things concur to lead men into this, as their not
having previoufly ftudied the varieties of pronun-
clation, the difficulty which they find at firft in
recollecting readily what they are to fay, the being
obliged to fpeak above the ordinary tone of their
voice in converfation. ·But it fhould be carefully
avoided; it appears tolerable when the cant or
tone is harmonious, but it is always improper and
unnatural.   When one's words are dictated by
his feelings, he always ufes many different geftures
and inflections of the voice, according to the different feelings by which he is actuated.   If one
would preach naturally, his voice muft affume a
variety of proper tones and inflections, and rife
and fall with a juft and eafy cadence according to
the nature of the things which he expreffes.   In
the fame way, the action fhould be varied fo as to
fuit both the fubject and the variations of the
voice.   The beft way of difcovering what is the
tone and gefture fuitable to any particular fubject,
is to obferve thofe which men have when they are,
undefignedly and without premeditation, engaged
on fuch a fubject.   By obferving how men fpeak
and move when they would explain any thing,
you may fee what is the tone of voice and gefture
which fits explication.   " Obferve what is the
" pofture, and what the voice of one, whofe
" heart is pierced with forrow, or furprifed at the
" fight of an aftonifhing object; remark the na-
                                    " tural

" tural action of the eyes, what the hands do, and
" what the whole body ;" and where thefe paffions
are concerned, let your manner be the fame. It
is neceffary that there be no appearance of affectation, either in the voice or action; and yet,
without endeavour and ftudy at firft, it will be
impoffible ever to attain a proper manner. The
only course, therefore, that can be taken, is to
employ onefelf much in whatever tends to form a
proper manner, before one has occafion to fpeak
in public, that he may not expofe himfelf to ridicule, or prevent the effect of the difcourfe, either
by improprieties, or by an appearance of art and
ftudy. You may begin with obferving the varieties of voice and action defcribed by rhetorical
writers; accuftom yourfelves to perform each of
them eafily and readily; remark which of them
fuits every particular fubject or paffion; frequently
repeat fomething which gives you an opportunity
of trying them, either by yourfelves, or rather,
when you can, in the company of others, who
may obferve any improprieties into which you fall.
By frequent exercife in this way, you may acquire,
before you appear in public, fuch a variety of
graceful pronunciation and action, that when you
are engaged in your fubject, you will naturally fall
into what fuits it, without any defign or thought.

Thus we have confidered fermons both with
refpect to their kinds and their parts. There are
many obfervations of great importance which might

be

be made concerning Preaching, confidered in a moral or practical, rather than a critical view; as, that fermons ought to convey the truths of religion pure and unmixed; in the language of fcripture as much as poffible; in a way fuited to the capacities of the hearers; in a way that is moft likely to promote their reformation; in a way which fhows that the preacher feels himfelf the whole force of the truths which he believes. But we fhall not enlarge on thefe; they are fully treated in many writings, particularly in fome fermons on this fubject, which are well known, and to which you can have eafy accefs.

When a perfon is fettled in a congregation, it is proper that in Preaching he fhould obferve fome regular feries or order, that all the parts of religion may be illuftrated in their real connection and dependence. For, in every fcience, order in teaching is abfolutely neceffary. The plan which a minifter lays down fhould not be either too fhort, elfe fubjects muft be treated fuperficially; or too long, elfe the very end of it will be fruftrated, becaufe many of the hearers will not live to fee it completed. There are many different plans into which a courfe of fermons may very properly be digefted, fome of which may be moft agreeable to one, and others to another, and which the fame man may, for the fake of variety, follow at different times. Thus, one may follow an hiftorical order, in which fubjects will fucceed one another

in

in fome fuch way as this. The being of God, his attributes, the creation, the fall and its confequences, the nature and ufe of the Jewifh difpenfation, the Chriftian difpenfation ; the life, death, and exaltation of our Saviour ; the effects of his mediation, the gofpel terms of acceptance, the various duties of Chriftianity, death, judgement, heaven, and hell. I mention this one only as a fpecimen, and I mention only the moft general heads. Whatever plan is chofen, the doctrines and the duties of religion ought to be intermixed with one another, that their real connection may appear.

Befides a minifter's ordinary courfe of fermons, there are occafional difcourfes which he muft fometimes ufe, as on fafts and thankfgivings, about the time of facraments, at fynods, and the like. Thefe are fubject to the very fame rules of compofition with other fermons. The matter of thefe fhould always be fuch as fuits the particular occafion of them, and excites to the practice of the particular duties which the occafion requires. And it muft be left to the preacher to judge what appears to him to have thefe characters. No doubt fome general directions may be given. Thus, on a public faft, it is proper to give fuch a view of the calamity which occafions it, as may excite the hearers to repentance: on a public thankf-giving, fuch a difplay of the bleffings acknowleged as may inflame their gratitude: on a faft

day

day before a facrament, what might either urge
them to repentance, or direct them in the exercife
of it: on a Saturday, or in an action fermon,
what is fit to excite thofe affections which fhould
be exerted in commemorating the death of Chrift:
in the afternoon or on Monday, what may confirm their good impreffions, and perfuade them to
the practice of holinefs.

There is one thing more that will deferve to be
taken notice of on the fubject of Preaching; whether writing difcourfes regularly, or Preaching on
mere premeditation, be the preferable way. This
latter way has been warmly recommended by two
writers on the fubject of Preaching, Bifhop Burnet
in his Paftoral Care, and the Archbifhop of Cambray in his Dialogues concerning eloquence. They
propofe that a man fhould be at great pains to
prepare himfelf for Preaching without writing, for
feveral years before he attempt it, by acquiring
great knowlege of the fcriptures, by comparing
together thofe paffages which belong to the fame
fubject; by often laying them together, and di-
gefting in his thoughts what arifes from them upon
any fubject; by acquiring a diftinct and connected
idea of the whole body of divinity, and by furnifh-
ing his mind with a large collection of fentiments
from practical writers upon all kinds of fubjects.
Being provided with thefe materials, in order to
qualify himfelf for this way of Preaching, he muft
accuftom himfelf to talk freely to himfelf, and let
his

his thoughts flow eafily from him; he muft frequently write on all forts of fubjects, that he may
bring himfelf to correctnefs both in thinking and
fpeaking; he muft for fome years accuftom himfelf
to preach as it were to himfelf on all forts of fubjects once or twice every day, that he may acquire
an eafinefs both of thought and of expreffion;
above all, he muft have in himfelf a deep fenfe of
the truth and power of religion, and muft, by
meditation and prayer, draw down divine influences, which are always to be expected when a
man puts himfelf in the way of them, and prepares
himfelf for them. This preparation will enable
him to pour out true thoughts in juft and eafy
expreffions. But even after all this preparation,
he muft at firft try fmaller excurfions from his
fixed thoughts; and as he fucceeds in thefe, he
may give himfelf farther fcope; and fo, by long
practice, he will at laft arrive at fo great an eafinefs both in thinking and fpeaking, that a very
little meditation will ferve him for preparing a
fermon. If one be to try Preaching in this way,
it is neceffary that he meditate fo carefully on his
fubject beforehand, as to have a diftinct and comprehenfive view of it, as to reduce his thoughts
into proper method, as to have thought of the
ftrongeft expreffions and figures. It is fuppofed
that in this way he muft have a great advantage
in the freedom and force of his pronunciation and
action; he will fpeak in an eafy, unaffected way,

and

and not like a formal declaimer; he can vary his difcourfe according to the occafions which caft up while he is delivering it.

In my opinion, thefe writers have carried the matter too far. It is very proper that a man fhould be able to preach in the way they recommend, when it is neceffary; but no man ought always to preach in this way. If he do, he will run into trite common-place topics; his compofitions will be loofe and unconnected; his language often coarfe or confufed; and diffidence, or care to recollect his fubject, will deftroy the management of his voice. At any rate, a perfon fhould accuftom himfelf to compofe regular difcourfes for many years after he begins to preach, before he attempt this method, except in fhort excurfions, or when abfolute neceffity requires it.

It is the defign of all the difcourfes that are prefcribed here, to prepare you for the bufinefs of Preaching. In order to their doing fo, it is beft that you compofe juft fuch lectures and fermons as fhould be delivered in public; that you imagine yourfelves preaching to a congregation, and make your fentiments, your method, your language, your pronunciation, and your action, precifely fuch as you would think proper for a popular audience.

Of presiding in the ordinary Public Worship of God, administering the Sacraments, and conducting Public Worship on extraordinary occasions.

WE have already considered the several private duties of the pastoral office, and we have largely explained Preaching, which is the first public duty of this office that we took notice of. The other public duties incumbent on a minister, which peculiarly regard the parish in which he is settled, may be reduced to these: Presiding in the ordinary public worship of God, administering the sacraments, and conducting public worship on extraordinary occasions. In explaining these as duties of the pastoral office, it would be superfluous to attempt a large explication of the nature of prayer or of the sacraments. In the view which we here take of them, it will be sufficient to make such observations as tend to show how a minister may perform with propriety his particular part in these sacred offices.

In the primitive church, the manner in which public worship was conducted seems to have been this. " When the congregation was assembled, " the first act of divine service which they per- " formed was reading the scriptures. When the " reading of the scriptures was ended, then fol- " lowed the singing of psalms, either such as
" were

" were taken out of the fcriptures, or fuch hymns
" as were compofed by any of themfelves; and
" thefe they were always careful to fing ἐμμελως καὶ
" συμφωνως, in good tune and concert: When the
" finging of pfalms was ended, then fucceeded
" the preaching of the word. As foon as the
" fermon was ended, then all the congregation rofe
" up to prefent their common and public prayers
" to God, ftretching out their hands, and lifting
" up their eyes to Heaven, and the minifter with
" a modeft and fupplicating voice prefented, in
" the name of the congregation, prayers fuited to
" their prefent circumftances." The manner of
public worfhip prefcribed by the directory of our
church coincides, in almoft every material circumftance, with this, which was obferved in the
church at leaft for three centuries. It appoints
that, the congregation being affembled, the minifter fhould begin with a fhort prayer, impreffing
them with a fenfe of the divine prefence, and
begging God's affiftance and acceptance. Next,
the fcriptures are to be read in their order. Then
pfalms are to be fung. After this, the minifter is
again to pray. Preaching fucceeds this prayer.
The fermon being ended, the minifter is again to
pray. After prayer, a pfalm is to be fung, and
then the minifter is to difmifs the congregation with
a folemn bleffing.

Of thefe parts, preaching has been already
confidered; reading the fcriptures has fomehow
gone into difufe; perhaps it has been infenfibly

joftled

joftled out by lecturing; fometimes a chapter which was read, would require fome obfervations for explaining it; and from making thefe after it had been read, men, at firft perhaps conceited of their own abilities, and fond of fpeaking, came by degrees to comment on every piece of fcripture which they read, till at laft the very notion of a lecture's being intended chiefly for reading a piece of fcripture is wholly loft. Reading the fcriptures feems to be fo neceffary and effential a part of Chriftian worfhip, that the omiffion of it is the moft faulty defect in the prefent practice of our church. Yet fo great is the perverfenefs and weak bigotry of many, that in fome places it would almoft create a fchifm to attempt to introduce it; and even the authority of our directory, framed in the revered ages of the church, would not be fufficient to fecure from blame the perfon who introduced it. I know nothing, however, which better deferves a man's running the rifk of giving offence, than reftoring the public reading of the fcriptures. In fome places it might perhaps be attempted without offence, and there it fhould be attempted. It might perhaps, in moft places, be introduced gradually, by lecturing on large portions of fcripture, firft making the explication fhorter than ordinary, then paffing over fome of the cafier verfes without any explication; then explaining only a few of the moft difficult verfes; and afterwards, reading a whole chapter, and only fubjoining fome practical obfervations upon it.

The

The only part that remains of ordinary public worſhip, on which it will be neceſſary to make any obſervations for directing the miniſter in the part he is to act in it, is prayer. In churches where compoſed liturgies are uſed, a miniſter has nothing to do but to read their prayers; he need only ſtudy to pronounce them with gravity and affection, and with a due ſlowneſs and emphaſis, which will be moſt effectually attained by bringing his mind to an inward and feeling ſenſe of thoſe things that are prayed for. But in our church, where no liturgy is impoſed, a great deal depends on the miniſter, and therefore he ought to be at the greateſt pains to fit himſelf for performing this important part of worſhip in a proper manner. It would be foreign to our preſent deſign to conſider the point of impoſed liturgies as a theological queſtion. But it may prepare the way for ſome of the obſervations which we are to make concerning public prayer, to begin with obſerving, that both eſtabliſhed forms of prayer and the total want of them have ſome advantages and ſome inconve- niences. When public forms are appointed, the people may be ſuppoſed to know more perfectly what are the devotions in which they are to join, to have a better opportunity of bringing them- ſelves beforehand to the temper which ſuits them, and may enable them to join with ſincerity in them. They may likewiſe be carefully drawn up by perſons of abilities, and may thus prevent many abſurdities into which weak and ignorant miniſters,

trufting

trufting wholly to their own gifts, may sometimes run. But it must be acknowleged, on the other hand, that when set forms are imposed, they cannot be so exactly suited to particular circumstances and emergencies as might be wished: they must be gone over so often that they become tiresome and disgusting, or at least unaffecting both to the minister and to the people, and, by thus degenerating into mere form, prevent all the good effect which might result from a previous acquaintance with them. Praying without set forms may, doubtless too, be productive of some inconveniences. Thus, when the audience know that the prayers are the performance of the preacher himself, they are too apt to consider them as a specimen of his abilities, to attend to them with a view to form a judgement of his talents, and thus to be diverted from expressing their devotion in the words that he uses, which ought to be their only employment. This appears to me to be the inconvenience which is most inseparable from public prayer without established forms. The best means of curing it will be, frequently to inculcate the necessity of joining heartily in prayer, and to contrive his prayers so that they may be fit to affect them with devotion, and to raise their minds in the exercise of it. It might however, without the imposition of forms, be effectually remedied by a proper directory (such as our own is in some measure), containing either a variety of forms, any of which might be used, or a large collection of materials

for

for prayer, out of which a choice may be made, put into the hands of the people, recommended to their ſtudy, and rendered by this means ſufficiently known to them. The other inconveniencies which are ſometimes imputed to prayer without ſet forms, really ariſe from faults in the manner of performing it, and will be avoided by miniſters taking care to perform it in a proper manner.

Thus it is ſaid that the people cannot join in prayer, of which they know nothing beforehand, and into which the preacher may perhaps throw peculiar ſentiments of his own, in which the congregation do not agree with him. But this objection can lie only againſt prayers which are very ill contrived. The proper matter of prayer all are acquainted with, and can join in, and none are wholly ignorant of the language in which it may be moſt fitly expreſſed. The miniſter, while he confines himſelf to the proper ſubject of prayer, can have no occaſion to throw in peculiar ſentiments of his own. In public prayers, he ſhould confine himſelf to thoſe expreſſions of adoration, thankſgiving, confeſſion, and petition, which are applicable to all, and might with propriety come from the mouth of any of the congregation. Peculiarities are proper for private devotions, not for public. Every part of public prayer ought, as much as poſſible, to be expreſſed in the language of ſcripture, which is both the moſt weighty in itſelf, and the moſt familiar to the congregation. When

other

other expreſſions are mixed with it, they ought to be as plain and ſimple as poſſible. Pompous, affected, and obſcure expreſſions are wholly improper for devotion. When the proper matter of prayer is thus kept to and expreſſed, all may bring themſelves to a fit temper for joining ſincerely in it as eaſily as if they knew the whole compoſition beforehand, and at the ſame time they are freed from the deadneſs and coldneſs which the conſtant uſe of eſtabliſhed forms is apt to produce.

If perſons not reſtrained to impoſed forms ever run into abſurdities for want of them, it is owing not to the uſe of extemporary prayer itſelf, but to a wrong manner in uſing it. Becauſe eſtabliſhed forms of prayer are not publicly impoſed, it does not therefore follow that arbitrary forms may not be uſed ; that a miniſter may not himſelf compoſe or collect forms proper for the different occaſions on which he is to uſe them. Becauſe a miniſter is not obliged to read a liturgy preſcribed by authority, it does not therefore follow that he is to pour out ſuch petitions or devotions as occur to him, without any method, choice, or premeditation. On the contrary, we ought to be as careful about what we ſay in prayer, as about what we ſay in preaching, as ſolicitous to ſpeak with propriety when we addreſs ourſelves to God, as when we addreſs the congregation. When a perſon firſt begins to appear in public, it will be very proper that he prepare his prayers with as great care and regularity as his fermons. It will likewife be generally proper, when any particular or public occafion demands a confiderable peculiarity in the fubject or manner of prayer, to compofe devotions fuited to it. By this means, a preacher of moderate underftanding will be able to avoid every thing unbecoming in prayer, and to perform it with greater propriety, and fo as to raife more fervent devotion both in himfelf and in others, than by going over public forms. If a perfon compofe a variety of prayers in this way, and become thoroughly mafter of them, he will foon be furnifhed with fuch abundance of materials for prayer, that he can eafily perform this part of public worfhip afterwards, without the neceffity of either compofing a diftinct form of prayer for every occafion, or recurring conftantly upon the fame form or the fame expreffions; but mixing together and difpofing in different manners, according to the prefent impulfe of his mind or the nature of the occafion, thofe petitions and devotions which he had formerly digefted into feveral diftinct prayers. There is another way which a preacher may take, and which he fhould fuperadd to the former, for forming himfelf to a readinefs, a copioufnefs and variety in public prayer. He fhould collect together, and write down, fuch proper adorations, expreffions of praife, petitions, and acknowlegements, as he meets with, particularly in reading the fcriptures; he fhould write them down in any order in which they occur. By this means he will

6   in

in a short time obtain a large stock, and by frequently looking it over and fixing it in his mind, the several things which he has written down will occur to him readily when he has occasion for them, without his needing to digest them into form before-hand; one thing will suggest another connected with it; and the disposition of his prayers, dictated in this manner by the present temper of his mind, will be more easy and natural, and will render them more striking and affecting, than if it had been contrived coolly in his closet.

Most other observations which might be made concerning public prayer, regard it rather as a Christian duty, than the peculiar part which a minister has in it by presiding in the public worship. There is one, however, that we may briefly touch upon, the order in which the parts of prayer may be most properly disposed. This may, no doubt, be different, and the proportion of time allowed to each will vary according to different occasions. In general, adoration is proper in the beginning, to strike us with a sense of the Divine Presence, and to excite, by the contemplation of God's perfections, those pious and devout affections which should prevail in the mind when it is engaged in prayer. From adoration, the transition to praise and thanksgiving is extremely easy and natural. Thanksgiving will be very properly succeeded by petitions for mercy, and, as connected with these, by confession of sin and expressions of repentance.

Petitions,

Petitions, not only for the direction and affiftance of God's fpirit, but likewife for all good things to ourfelves and others, will be very properly introduced by thefe. But, in fact, there is no neceffity for keeping thefe feveral parts diftinct. It is better to intermix them through the whole of prayer. This is the moft ordinary method in the devotional parts of fcripture, which are the beft models we can follow. It is the moft natural expreffion of a mind poffeffed by devotion, and actuated by piety. It gives fuller fcope for expreffing all the variety of affections which are combined in a pious temper. Indeed, though thofe which we have mentioned are commonly reckoned all the parts of devotion, yet there are fome affections which it is extremely proper to exert in devotion, that are not properly reducible to any of them. Such are expreffions of our truft in God, of our refignation to his will, of our good refolutions, of our regard to God's judgement of us, of our delight in him, of our fenfe of the beauty and excellence of holinefs; thefe are rather implied or fuppofed in fome of the parts of prayer, than explicitly contained in them. But, by confidering prayer, not as compofed of fo many parts which fhould fucceed each other in order, but as an exertion and expreffion of a pious and holy temper, we may very properly introduce the expreffions of all its branches, not confufedly, yet fo as not to be fcrupulous in keeping them feparate and diftinct.

The

The next public duty of the paſtoral office is the adminiſtration of the Chriſtian ſacraments. Theſe are two, Baptiſm and the Lord's Supper, which we ſhall conſider briefly, not in every view that might be taken of them, but ſimply in this one view of its being a part of a miniſter's funƈtion to diſpenſe them in ſuch a way as to render them moſt uſeful to Chriſtians.

To begin with Baptiſm. It is very neceſſary that a miniſter inſtruƈt his people frequently con-cerning the nature of baptiſm, that they may not go about it as a ceremony, as it is too viſible the greater part do, but that they may attend to its real deſign and importance. As it is very proper to inſtruƈt parents in this privately when they deſire to have their children baptiſed, ſo no time is more ſuitable for inſtruƈting the congregation publicly concerning it, than when it is to be diſ-penſed. As it is not convenient to make long diſcourſes on theſe occaſions, it will be proper to confine oneſelf to ſome one view of it at each time. And it may be conſidered in many differ-ent views, each of which will convey a ſtriking conception of its nature and uſe. It will be unne-ceſſary to go over all theſe views; every place of ſcripture almoſt in which it is mentioned, ſets it in a light ſomewhat peculiar. To give a few in-ſtances of the different lights in which it may be ſet. At one time it may be very proper to point out the foundation of ritual duties in our mixed

and

and compounded natures, their neceffity for exciting us to holinefs by fuch ceremonies as ftrike
the fenfes, the pronenefs of men in all ages to
abufe them, and to fubftitute them in the place of
true goodnefs, the care of our Saviour to prevent
this by the fimplicity and fignificance of his pofitive inftitutions, and particularly of baptifm. At
another time, one may enlarge on its being an inftitution of our Saviour, and therefore, its de-
ferving our clofeft attention to the real defign and
intention of it. Sometimes one may reprefent it
as the fign of our believing the truths of the gofpel
and receiving its precepts, from our Saviour commanding his difciples to baptife men in the name
of the Father, the Son, and the Holy Ghoft, and
to teach men at the fame time to obferve all things
whatfoever he had commanded them. At other
times it may be reprefented as, both by the declarations of fcripture and the original manner of
difpenfing it, an emblem of a fpiritual death and
refurrection. Sometimes it may be reprefented
as the feal of thofe religious privileges which God
has freely beftowed on the Chriftian church as
means of holinefs and improvement, as admitting
thofe who are baptifed, to them, and as a fign of
the obligation which the enjoyment of thefe privileges lays us under to the practice of holinefs.
At other times it may be reprefented as a ftipu-
lation to walk worthy of the Chriftian vocation;
which it is of great importance to fulfil fo as to
preferve a good confcience. Many different views
of

of it will occur by careful attention to its nature, and to the feveral places of fcripture relating to it. It will generally be fufficient to give one of thefe views of it at once. But whatever view of it be given, it fhould be made to iffue in urging all prefent to walk fuitably to their Chriftian profeffion, and inculcating on them the neceffity of holinefs.

As in the firft ages of the gofpel, when the perfons baptifed were adult, they were obliged at their baptifm to profefs that they believed the gofpel of Chrift, were willing to engage in the profeffion of it, and refolved to walk worthy of this profeffion; fo now, when infants are baptifed, it is proper that fome profeffions and ftipulations fhould be exacted from their parents or fponfors. It is proper that they fhould be obliged to make public profeffion of their own belief of the gofpel. This profeffion ought to be confined to the fundamental and uncontroverted truths of religion, and not extended to any of the diftinguifhing tenets of a party; for baptifm is an inftitution of Jefus, not of any leader of a fect; it is the fign of our admiffion into the Chriftian church, not of our admiffion into any particular divifion of Chriftians. It is likewife proper to exact an engagement from the parents or fponfors, to inftruct the child in the whole doctrine of the gofpel, in the import of its having been baptifed, and to fulfil their obligations to take care of its education.

Both

Both the propriety of the thing itfelf, and the conftant and univerfal practice of the Chriftian church requires that the exacting of thefe profeffions and engagements fhould be followed by prayer and invocation of God, which, on this occafion, may very properly confift in acknowlegements of God's goodnefs, particularly in the gofpel, in the continuance of it from one generation to another, in making us and our children partakers in his covenant, in his freely beftowing upon us our Chriftian privileges, in his appointing this fenfible action as a fign of our being invefted with them, and in petitions that he may blefs his own ordinance of baptifm at the time, that he may join the inward baptifm of his fpirit with the outward baptifm of water, that the wafhing with water may not be an empty ceremony to the child, but may be followed by that purity of heart and life, of which it is defigned to be only a type and reprefentation.

When the blefling of God is, in fome fuch way as this, implored on his inftitution, baptifm itfelf is performed by fprinkling, along with a repetition of the words of inftitution.

The difpenfing of baptifm is very properly followed by prayer, that it may be rendered effectual to the falvation of the child, that it may be followed by fanctification and remiffion of fins, that the child, now a member of the Chriftian church
and

and admitted to the outward privileges of the gofpel, may become a member of God's true invifible church, and be received into the enjoyment of the eternal bleffings of the gofpel, that the parents may be enabled to perform their duty to their child and family, and all the duties incumbent on them, and that all prefent may walk worthy of their holy vocation; and to thefe prayers fuited to the inftitution, any of the proper materials of devotion may be added as occafion requires.

The rules and practice regarding the circumftances in which any alteration is to be made in any of the ordinary methods of difpenfing baptifm, are fo well eftablifhed, that it will not be neceffary to enlarge upon them. Some cafes of difficulty may, no doubt, occur; but as thefe cannot be forefeen or enumerated, it muft be left to a man's own prudence and the beft advice he can obtain, to direct him in thefe cafes.

The other Chriftian facrament is the Lord's Supper. It is very neceffary to explain properly the nature of this inftitution, both in preaching and in private, that the people may be guarded againft the two extremes of irreverence and fuperftition. This is a part of teaching; but we are at prefent to confider this facrament only in the view of difpenfing it in fuch a way, that it may tend moft to the end for which it was defigned,

the

the promoting of true holiness and goodnefs. All
who profefs Chriftianity are not to be promifcu-
oufly admitted to it. They who are either grofsly
ignorant, or openly and cuftomarily vicious in any
particular way, act unfuitably to the common profeffion of Chriftianity; and nothing could tend
more to bring this folemn act of worfhip into contempt, than to admit thefe to it, who, it is plain,
could not perform it acceptably. At the fame
time, one fhould avoid the other extreme of too
great rigour and feverity in excluding perfons on
account of thofe faults, which may be refolved
into the weaknefs of the prefent ftate, and may be
confiftent with fincere goodnefs. The proper light
in which it fhould be confidered is, that it is a
means of improvement, but at the fame time a
means of improvement which cannot be ufed to
advantage, except by thofe who have already fome
degree of good difpofitions. In this view of it, it
is plainly abfurd to require fo great a degree of
perfection in thofe who are admitted to it, that, if
they were poffeffed of that degree, they could
fcarce need means of improvement. And, on the
other hand, it is wrong to receive thofe who can
evidently exert no good affections in it, and therefore cannot be improved by the ufe of it. A minifter, by confidering it in this light, and regulating his conduct by this view of it, may take
feveral advantages from this facrament for making
good impreffions on the people. Thus, about the
time of a communion, every minifter that knows
any

any one of his parifh guilty of eminent fins, may go to him, and admonifh him to change his courfe of life, or not to profane the table of the Lord. When a perfon defigns firft to partake in the Lord's Supper, a minifter may make good impreffions on the perfon himfelf and on others, by making him not only in private, but in as public a manner as he finds it convenient to ufe, to make folemn profeffion of his embracing the Chriftian faith for himfelf, and to vow that he will live fuitably to it, renouncing the fins which he has formerly indulged, and promifing to live henceforth as becomes a Chriftian. This is practifed by fome minifters with good fuccefs, and with a very great effect.

When the actual difpenfing of this facrament comes on, the firft part of the fervice is, what is called fencing the tables ; that is, defcribing thofe who are unfit for this part of worfhip, and thofe who are fit. In doing this, care fhould be taken to require no qualifications which are not abfolutely required by the fcriptures. All unbelievers and all wicked perfons fhould be declared unworthy ; but no minifter, except he can fhow a revelation from Heaven, declaring his explications of fcripture to be infallibly true, has a right to declare any perfon unworthy on account of fuch errors in judgement as are confiftent with a fincere belief of Chriftianity. This inftitution is the teft of Chriftians, not of any

one

one fect; it is the bond of Chriftian love, not of divifion and fchifm.

Again, a minifter fhould warn them who are unworthy, in fuch a manner as may fhow, in the moft obvious way, that his warnings are not arbitrary, tnat he does not merely fpeak from his own opinion or humour; in fuch a manner as may carry conviction with it, that the feveral characters which he defcribes do neceffarily, in their very nature, render perfons unfit for this act of worfhip. The eafieft and moft effectual way of anfwering this end feems to be, along with every character that is defcribed, to point the reafon why, or to exprefs in what manner, it renders thofe to whom it belongs unworthy. Thus, in general, the neceffity of fome preparation and previous good difpofition of heart arifes from this, that external acts of worfhip can improve the temper only by their being exertions of the good affections from which they proceed, and therefore cannot at all improve thofe who have not fome degree of thefe affections, and of confequence cannot exert them, or put them in exercife; and the matter may be reprefented in this light by the minifter. When atheifts are excluded, the obvious reafon may be hinted, that they cannot join in an act of religious worfhip; when deifts, that they cannot join in a chriftian inftitution. When the vices forbidden in the third commandment are mentioned, it may be hinted
that

that they are inconfiftent with that reverence of God which fuits fo folemn an approach to him. The vices forbidden in the fourth commandment fhow a want or a weaknefs of devout affections, and therefore unfit men for this inftitution, in which devout affections fhould be raifed to the higheft pitch of fervency ; and fo in other inftances. Proceeding in this way will give great weight to all that a minifter fays in this part of the fervice, will render it convincing, and keep it from being in any meafure regarded as a mere form.

In declaring who are fit for this act of worfhip, a minifter's view fhould be, not only to declare, in as plain terms as poffible, what are the characters that render one a good man and a true Chriftian, or at leaft, in fuch a difpofition of repentance as will render this act of worfhip acceptable, but alfo to remove the grounds of fear which weak or melancholy perfons are apt to dwell upon, from reflection on the prefent ftate of their minds, their want of warmth of devotion, their being diftracted with idle thoughts, or their not having found time for fuch particular preparation as they would have chofen.

As the whole office of a clergyman is properly minifterial, not lordly or dictatorial, fo in this fervice in particular, it feems to be more fuitable to this character of his office to exprefs his warnings as declarations of the neceffary qualifications of

commu-

communicants, by which they may examine and judge themfelves, than to affect the authority and folemnity which are fometimes ufed, of repeating continually, " I debar and exclude," or " I invite " in the name of Chrift."

After this part of the fervice is over, as this facrament is a pofitive inftitution, not of natural obligation, but deriving its obligation folely from its being appointed in fcripture, the inftitution fhould be read from fome of the places of fcripture where it is recorded. The reading of it fhould be followed by prayer, which will properly confift of two parts, thankfgiving for the bleffings of the gofpel, and petitions for God's bleffing on the inftitution, for his grace to excite and enliven all the devout affections which fhould be exerted in it, and for his affiftance to perform our vows, and practife all the duties of life to which they bind us. This prayer, which fhould be contrived, as much as poffible, to exprefs and excite fincere and fervent devotion, may be very properly followed by giving fuch a view of the nature of the inftitu- tion, as may difpofe both to a rational and to a devout obfervance of it.

After this is over, it would be extremely decent, that, except the minifter's diftributing the elements with the words ufed by our Saviour, all the reft were performed in folemn filence. And this is, in fact, the method prefcribed by our directory.
But

But cuſtom has introduced diſcourſes at every table. Theſe are attended with this inconvenience, that they employ the communicants too much in hearing, and divert them from what is their proper buſineſs, internal devotion. Since they are uſed, they ought therefore at leaſt to be contrived ſo as to produce this inconvenience as little as poſſible. Set diſcourſes, calculated for information, are always improper. The part of the diſcourſe which precedes the diſtribution of the elements ſhould be employed in giving ſome ſtriking view of the love of God in Chriſt, tending directly to inflame the affections which ought to be exerciſed. The diſcourſe ſhould not be continued after the elements are received; the miniſter ſhould either preſerve abſolute ſilence, or throw in only ſuch ſhort hints as may direct and animate the devotion of the communicants; any thing further interrupts entirely the exerciſe of devotion, which ſhould employ them. The remaining part of the diſcourſe will be properly employed in ſuch warm exhortations, ſtriking ſentiments, and practical maxims and directions, as may make an impreſſion on them, and influence their conduct.

After all have communicated, there generally is, and very properly may be, an addreſs or exhortation. For this, there are ſeveral very fit topics. The moſt common way is to give a deſcription of the different characters of communicants, by which they may know how far their temper has

been

been right or faulty, and exhortations fuited to the variety of their tempers. And if this be done with judgement, and with a fixed view to habitual practice, it may be very ufeful. Another proper topic may be, to rectify men's miftakes about the advantages to be expected from this facrament, in immediate and fenfible illuminations or confolations, to direct them to judge of their advantage by their after-conduct, and to improve their communication by a holy life. Or a minifter may urge upon them the obligations which Chriftianity, and particularly which this public profeffion of it, lays them under, to virtue and holinefs. In a word, whatever has a tendency either to perfuade or to direct them to a becoming conduct, is a very proper topic.

In general, great care is neceffary in every thing that is faid about this facrament, to avoid myftical and unmeaning expreffions, to ufe no word which does not convey a diftinct and rational conception, and to direct the whole to practice. Moft men's minds are, at this time, peculiarly fufceptible of good impreffions ; and a minifter fhould feize this favourable opportunity of fixing in them fomething practical, fomething moral, fomething fit to enter into their temper, and regulate their life.

As to the worfhip of God on extraordinary occafions, we have already taken fome notice of the peculiarities of fermons fuited to them. . And, with

with regard to conducting public devotion on them, it will be sufficient to observe, that the subject of the devotion should be suited to the particular occasion; that for this end, the greatest proportion of time should be allowed to that part of devotion which most suits the occasion; as to confession on fasts, to praise on thankfgivings; and that, in general, it may be proper to spend more time in devotion than on ordinary occasions.

CHAP. IV.

Ecclefiaſtical Duties reſpecting the Church in general.

THE public duties of the paſtoral office, which have been hitherto conſidered, are incumbent on a miniſter as paſtor of a particular pariſh, and regard all the congregation under his care. But, beſides theſe, there are other duties of a ſtill more public nature, which are incumbent on him as a member of the church in general, and which do not immediately or neceſſarily reſpect the pariſh committed to his care. Theſe we ſhall briefly conſider.

We ſhall begin with a part of the paſtoral office, which is indeed often exerciſed by a miniſter in his own pariſh, but which we have choſen to conſider under this head, becauſe it is often alſo exerciſed by him in a more public capacity, and without any immediate reference to his own pariſh, and becauſe it bears ſome relation to the other duties which regard the government of the church; I mean the exerciſe of public diſcipline.

We have already conſidered the ſeveral private ways of checking or rebuking wickedneſs, which

a miniſter

a minifter may, and ought to ufe. But private
rebukes are not fufficient in all cafes; the apoftle
Paul exprefsly commands Timothy, in fome cafes,
to " rebuke them that fin before all, that others
" alfo may fear [b]." And our Saviour directs our
conduct in this matter : " If thy brother fhall
" trefpafs againft thee, go and tell him his fault
" between thee and him alone : if he fhall hear
" thee, thou haft gained thy brother. But if he
" will not hear thee, then take with thee one or
" two more, that in the mouth of two or three
" witneffes every word may be eftablifhed. And
" if he fhall neglect to hear them, tell it unto the
" church : but if he neglect to hear the church,
" let him be unto thee as a heathen man and a
" publican [c]."

In the firft ages of the church, the difcipline
was extremely ftrict, much ftricter than the temper
of the prefent age will permit. And though the
greateft care fhould be taken not to flacken difcipline more than abfolute neceffity requires, yet
prudence forbids to ftretch it farther than the
fituation of things will bear ; for attempts to do fo,
by proving ineffectual, will difappoint their own
defign, and make the fpiritual arms of the church
even more defpifed than they were before.

Every

---

[b] 1 Tim. v. 20.   [c] Matt. xviii. 15, &c.

Every thing effential to the manner of exercifing difcipline is prefcribed in the form of procefs
eftablifhed by authority, which is compofed with a
fpirit of moderation and good fenfe perfectly inconfiftent with that inquifitorial fpirit which fome are
difpofed to exert in difcipline. An acquaintance
with the rules which are there prefcribed is abfolutely neceffary for every minifter, in order to
fecure him from blunders in appointing cenfures.
And the rules of procedure being there fully laid
down, renders it only neceffary here to make a
few general obfervations, which may be of ufe for
directing you to apply the rules with prudence and
judgement.

All fins require repentance, and repentance will
always fhow itfelf by obvious and open effects;
but all fins are not the proper objects of church
difcipline. Chriftian charity will not allow us to
pry into the fecret faults of others; it is only their
open and public fins that give fcandal, and deferve
public animadverfions. All open and public fins
are in themfelves proper objects of difcipline; yet
all of them cannot be eafily brought under difcipline. Some of them do not fhow themfelves by
overt and determinate acts; they do not admit of
definite meafures. It is not eafy to fix the limits
where the lawful ends and the unlawful begins.
On this account they cannot eafily be cenfured
publicly, for it is not eafy to prove that perfons
are guilty of them; and to inflict cenfures in cafes
which

which do not admit determinate and fatisfactory proof, would open a door to tyranny and oppreffion. For the fame reafon, many vices which difplay themfelves in determinate and overt acts, cannot, in all cafes, be eafily fubjected to public cenfure, becaufe they cannot be fully proved. Thefe caufes have reduced the vices which are now publicly cenfured to a very narrow compafs, to fuch as difcover themfelves by effects-perfectly unqueftionable and free from all ambiguity. Yet even thefe are more than are generally fubjected to the exercife of difcipline, as fwearing, fome inftances of drunkennefs, many cafes of lying, difhonefty, and calumny, and many overt acts of impiety. All fuch fins, which are both open and capable of legal proof, ought, doubtlefs, to be much more fubjected to difcipline than they are, for they are properly fcandalous. But it will not be prudent to attempt the exercife of difcipline againft fins, to which thefe characters do not agree. In ages when a fenfe of religion prevails, they who have fallen into fin may, from a true difpofition of penitence, be ready to acknowlege it when they are accufed, and to make all the reparation in their power for the fcandal they have given. But that is not the temper of the prefent age; men will acknowlege nothing which cannot be proved againft them. In this fituatinn, all that can be done is to extend the exercife of church difcipline uniformly againft thofe fins which can be clearly

proved,

proved, and to attempt only private admonitions or reproofs againſt other ſins.

The abuſes of the Popiſh church have intro-duced an inveterate and deep-rooted miſtake, which it will not be eaſy to eradicate, that ſub-miſſion to church cenſures is a ſort of penance which expiates the guilt of the ſin. All methods ſhould be taken to remove this error, and to in-culcate that they are only ſpiritual chaſtiſements deſigned to increaſe true repentance, and to ex-preſs it, and that no farther than they do ſo, can they be of any avail for obtaining pardon. In inflicting cenſures, a miniſter ſhould carefully re-member that he is a judge, and ſhould therefore preſerve perfect impartiality and ſtrict juſtice. It is particularly baſe to make the power entruſted to him in any degree an inſtrument of his own re-ſentment. If he bear any grudge at a perſon whoſe conduct expoſes him to public cenſure, it would be much better to decline, as much as poſſi-ble, any ſhare in judging of it, in order to avoid even the ſuſpicion of partiality. All diſcipline ought to be managed in ſuch a way as may tend moſt to promote true virtue; and in order to this, it ſhould always be directed by prudence, joined with a ſpirit of meekneſs.

In almoſt all the public duties which are incum-bent on a clergyman as a member of the church in

in general, he acts the part of a judge, and therefore ought to be careful to maintain the character
of a judge, the peculiar decorum of which is strict
and inflexible integrity. Here indeed, all extremes
are to be avoided. We must not, by studying to
be impartial, become rigid or severe; nor, in
avoiding rigour, ought we to swerve from integrity. We must be strict, yet not captious; un-
biassed, yet not rigorous; meek, yet not remiss.

The subjects of judgement which principally
come before ministers as members of judicatories,
(besides cases of discipline,) are two; the decision
of settlements, and the qualifications of candidates
for the ministry. It will not be improper to
make a few observations on these separately,
because there are some circumstances peculiar to
each.

In questions concerning settlements, the property
and rights of men are as truly concerned, as in any
questions that are brought before a civil judge.
An honest man can have no more scope for favour
in cases of this sort, than a civil judge can have in
trials for life and property. It cannot fail to be a
great reproach to a clergyman to be thought more
open to solicitations than any other judge. Yet it
has somehow happened, that they who would never
think of soliciting a civil judge in a cause depending
before him, make no scruple to solicit clergymen
with regard to causes depending before church
judicatories,

judicatories, and imagine they have a right to be offended with a perſon, and to reſent it, if he refuſe to give his voice as they require. Clergymen have given too great countenance to this ſhameful practice, by liſtening to ſolicitations, by yielding to them, by not expreſſing ſufficient indignation againſt them, by not remembering that it is incumbent on them to ſuſtain the integrity and inflexibility of the judge. One circumſtance has greatly contributed to this; the laws of the church regarding ſettlements have ſcarcely ever been fixed and determinate; and this has led not only clergymen, but all others concerned in church judicatories, to aſſume a liberty, and to think that they might allow themſelves a great latitude in determining according to circumſtances in any particular caſe; and partiality or attachment eaſily made them conceive circumſtances in the moſt favourable light for that ſide which they were diſpoſed to eſpouſe. This cannot excuſe the conduct; for the aſſuming this liberty evidently tended to make every thing looſe and uncertain; and it is reproachful to any court to be guided by no fixed principles. In this ſituation, it was plainly incumbent on every clergyman to lay down a ſettled rule of judgement for himſelf, and to adhere to it uniformly till he found a better, for which he might exchange it in all caſes. He ought not to hearken to ſolicitations; if they are made by perſons to whom he lies under obligations, he may profeſs his readineſs to oblige them in every way in his
power,

power,. but at the fame time tell them refolutely, that in queftions before a judicatory he confiders himfelf as a judge, and muft be determined folely by the merits of the caufe. By whomfoever he be folicited, he may declare his readinefs to receive information of any facts on which the caufe depends, but exprefs a firm refolution to liften to nothing elfe, and an honeft indignation at the fuf- picion of his being capable of partiality or corrup- tion. This is the conduct which integrity dictates, and which is neceffary for keeping a good con- fcience. This is the conduct which will redound to the honour of the whole order; it is indeed neceffary for preferving it from reproach or con- tempt. And this conduct will moft effectually fecure a man's own eafe and independence; for if it be once known that this is a man's fixed deter- mination, he will meet with no importunities; and if he adhere to it uniformly and facredly, no per- fon will think that he has a title to be offended, on whichever fide he gives his judgement; he will not only preferve more general efteem, but will run lefs rifk of incurring the difpleafure of individuals, than they who are more open to influence, who therefore offend in every inftance where they do not hearken to it, and who are often reduced to fituations in which they muft incur the difpleafure of fome one of the contending parties.

The other great fubject of judging, about which a clergyman has occafion to be converfant, is the qualifications

qualifications of candidates for the miniftry. This is evidently a duty of great importance. Nothing can have a nearer connection with the prevalence or the decline of religion and virtue, than the abilities and manners of the clergy. The greateft care is therefore incumbent on thofe on whom the choice of them depends. A minifter ought to take all the pains he can, to learn the true character of thofe who are propofed for this office ; and if he be not fully fatisfied, either by his perfonal knowlege, or by the information of thofe who have perfonal knowlege, that they are, in refpect both of underftanding and morals, really qualified for this office, he fhould not be prevailed on, by friendfhip, or attachment, or compaffion, or any fort of influence, to concur in bringing them into this important office. It is an exhortation of the apoftle Paul, " Lay hands fuddenly on no man, neither be partaker of other men's fins [d]." To do it fuddenly, is to do it without a ftrict and accurate inquiry into a man's real character ; and by doing it thus fuddenly, men in fome meafure incur a fhare in the guilt of the unworthy perfon to whofe promotion they contribute. This is, in general, very little attended to ; but every clergyman ought to charge his confcience, in a deep and particular manner, not to contribute to bring any perfon into the miniftry, if he have any reafon to think that his abilities

---

[d] 1 Tim. v. 22.

abilities are not fuch as may raife him above contempt, and render him really ufeful, or that his
life is not fo regular, and his temper fo virtuous,
as to make him fit to be put in holy orders. This
will be particularly incumbent on a clergyman in
prefbyteries, where motions for licenfing take their
firft rife; for there one has the beft opportunities
for information; and fuperior judicatories are often
obliged to take things for granted on the information of thofe leffer courts, to whom it is fuppofed
a perfon propofed is fully known. Both intellectual and moral qualifications ought to be regarded; but the latter are of much greater confequence than the former. In fome fituations, a
moderate degree of the former will be fufficient;
but in any poffible fituation a fenfible defect of the
latter cannot fail to produce the worft confequences,
with refpect both to the ufefulnefs of the minifter,
and the general interefts of religion. Were clergymen as careful in this part of their duty as they
ought to be, it would in a great meafure prevent
all the inconveniencies which could be apprehended from any particular method of fettling
parifhes.

Minifters, as members of church courts, have
not only a power of judging, but likewife a fort of
legiflative authority. All the fundamental laws of
religion are contained in the fcriptures; thofe of
particular eftablifhments or forms of religion are
fixed by the original conftitution of particular
churches;

churches: but there is a neceffity for additional laws on account of particular emergencies and changes of circumftances. Thefe ought always to be confiftent with fcripture; they ought to pre-fcribe the beft means of anfwering the ends of re-ligion, in the prefent fituation, and according to the particular circumftances which take place. In ecclefiaftical, as well as in all other matters, the true fpirit of a legiflator is the fpirit of moderation, difpofing to avoid all extremes. Care fhould be taken that laws which are made really tend to anfwer the end for which they are made; for it is no un-common thing for legiflators to underftand fo little the nature of fome laws, that by fome of their confequences they obftruct the very ends for which they were defigned, and which, confidered in one light, they appeared fit to promote. All ambiguity, obfcurity, and confufion, ought to be avoided in making laws; for it will prove a fource of endlefs queftions and cavil, and an occafion of arbitrary fentences, when the laws come to be executed. No ufelefs laws fhould be made, for they always weaken fuch as are neceffary. A law fhould al-ways be framed fo that it may not be eafily eluded, for when it can, it never fails to detract from the authority by which it was enacted. Penal laws in matters of religion and fpeculative opinions are always pernicious; as the clergy cannot enact them by their own authority, they fhould never wifh to fee them enacted by the civil power. If they be executed, they only deftroy mankind; if
they

they be not executed, they fhow the impotence of thofe by whom they were enacted.

There feems to me to be more of a moral obligation on clergymen to attend judicatories of which they are members, than is commonly apprehended. Many things may be done by a few, reflecting difhonour on the whole body, which the prefence and influence of others might have prevented. In this cafe, it is not eafy to fee how one whofe bufinefs it was to have been prefent, can excufe himfelf to his own confcience, if he neglected attendance without good reafon.

I fhall conclude the confideration of the duties of the paftoral office, with a few obfervations concerning the behaviour of a clergyman to his brethren of the fame profeffion. God has wifely conftituted human nature in fuch a way, that relation of any kind excites a peculiar degree of love and benevolence. This conftitution of nature leads men to love thofe of their own profeffion, and to be concerned for the intereft of the fociety to which they belong. It is acknowleged that the profeffion of clergymen unites them by as clofe ties, as any other profeffion does thofe who exercife it. By this means, it demands a great degree of benevolence from clergymen to one another. This benevolence fhould exert itfelf in urging clergymen to be peculiarly ready to do thofe good offices to one another which they owe to men in general.

general. They fhould be warmly interefted in the concerns, and folicitous for the profperity of each other. Notwithftanding the great degree of equality which is eftablifhed among minifters by the conftitution of our church, there muft neceffarily arife fome difference in the circumftances of clergymen, from their fituation, their demands, and their advantages or difadvantages; and from the very nature of man, and the greater or lefs opportunities of men, there will be differences with regard to prudence, learning, and abilities. That benevolence which men of the fame profeffion owe to one another, obliges thofe clergymen who have, in any refpects, the advantage of their brethren, to be fo far from defpifing them becaufe they are not fo happily fituated, as, on the contrary, to do all they can to affift and encourage them. Benevolence to the clergy as belonging to our own profeffion will very naturally exert itfelf in a love of their company, which will produce not only the feveral exercifes of hofpitality towards them, when they fall in the way, but likewife a defire to contrive being in their company, and maintaining a friendly correfpondence with them. Nothing can be more improving than clergymen's being frequently together, efpecially if, either when they are accidentally in company, or in meetings concerted on purpofe, they would promote the knowlege, and give advice in the affairs of one another, and contrive the propereft means of promoting the interefts of religion and virtue. " Hereby they

" would

" would be cemented into one body; they might
" underſtand what were amiſs in each other's con-
" duct, and try to correct it by prudent advices. It
" is a falſe pity in any of the clergy, to ſee their
" brethren running into ill courſes without giving
" them warning; it is a real cruelty to the church,
" and may prove a cruelty to the perſon himſelf;
" for things may be more eaſily corrected at firſt,
" before they have grown to be public, or are
" hardened by habit and cuſtom." A due degree
of that benevolence which clergymen owe to one
another as members of the ſame body, eſpecially
if it be joined with a ſincere regard to the intereſts
of religion, the good cauſe in which all are engaged will effectually extinguiſh thoſe little rival-
ſhips about popularity or the like, which create
grudges, animoſities, and diviſions, and turn off
men's attention from what is eſſential in religion,
to things which are at moſt but appendages of it.
Benevolence will likewiſe produce moderation towards one another on account of difference of ſentiments and opinions, which cannot fail to ariſe
among fallible men. The clergy will naturally
have peculiar occaſion to exerciſe this virtue towards one another, becauſe their ſtudies are, more
than thoſe of other men, confined to matters of
religion, and ſo will moſt readily give riſe to a variety of opinions; and likewiſe, becauſe they have
peculiar opportunities of knowing each other's
ſentiments. " Now, it is by conſidering our
" brethren in the ſeveral endearing views in which

D D " benevo-

" benevolence will reprefent them, that we fhall
" feel ourfelves," to ufe the words of an excellent
writer, " infpired with the principles of true
" Chriftian moderation. When we obferve others
" differing from us in opinion about leffer points,
" or even, as it appears to us, erring from the
" truth in more important matters, it will imme-
" diately occur to us, that we are all in a ftate of
" much darknefs, and equally liable to miftakes
" and errors. Real love, and affectionate fym-
" pathy, and juft views of human nature, will lead
" us to reflect on all that vaft variety of circum-
" ftances which may prevail on honeft and worthy
" minds to embrace opinions widely different from
" thofe which we reckon true." Thefe are fome
of the principal duties which clergymen owe to
one another, which are all natural exertions and
effects of the peculiar degree of benevolence which
their being of the fame profeffion tends to produce.

All the duties which we have enumerated are
incumbent on every clergyman; and all thefe
together are certainly fufficient to occupy the
whole man, to engage all his attention, and to
employ all his time. Yet he cannot, with a good
confcience, neglect any of them: he muft devote
himfelf to them: he muft not fatisfy himfelf with
performing them in any way, but muft be always
folicitous to perform them in the beft way, and
muft perfift in performing them with greater and
greater

greater care and prudence, till they really anfwer their defign in a thorough reformation of the people. This difplay of the duties of the paftoral office fully juftifies the view of its importance and difficulty with which we fet out, and even fhews that the higheft picture of its importance and difficulty which can be drawn in general terms, falls far fhort of the truth. Every fingle duty almoft belonging to this office requires the exertion of all the powers of human nature; but all its duties together feem to require more than human abilities. A minifter is engaged to pro-mote the moft important of all ends, the im-provement and falvation of mankind; the failure of which is neceffarily attended with everlafting confequences of dread and horror; and nothing but unwearied affiduity in the difcharge of nume-rous duties, which will occupy every part of his time, and which it is not eafy to difcharge aright, can prevent a clergyman's being account-able for thefe confequences. A juft conception of the duties of the paftoral office muft produce a vigorous fenfe of its moment and difficulty; and this fenfe muft excite all who aim at the office to the greateft care in fitting themfelves for it, and poffefs them with the deepeft folicitude that they may not be unworthy. The firft ftep to their being fit is to know what are the qualifi-cations requifite, and by what preparation they may be obtained. Some obfervations on this fub-ject will complete our view of the paftoral care.

PART III

The Requifites for performing the Duties of the Paftoral Office.

FOR every profeffion fome qualifications are requifite, fuitable to its nature, and deducible from its functions, which every one that makes choice of it fhould labour to acquire. For acquiring thefe, fome means adapted to them are neceffary, and fhould be carefully employed; and with fome plain thoughts on the qualifications neceffary for your profeffion, and the means of acquiring them, I fhall conclude this fubject.

CHAP. I.

The Qualifications for the Paftoral Office.

THE qualifications which are neceffary for the paftoral office may be eafily deduced from the confideration of the duties which belong to that office; for they will include every thing that is neceffary for the proper performance of thefe feveral duties. In deducing them we fhall ftudy brevity, becaufe they have been very fully illuftrated

trated and set in different striking lights by many who have treated of the ministerial character.

The qualifications which are of importance to a clergyman are partly natural, and partly acquired. It is not unneceffary to take notice of the former, becaufe, though they are not in our power, yet the want of them fhows that a man was never defigned for this difficult profeffion, and fhould determine him, or thofe at whofe difpofal he is, to make choice of fome other occupation, for which fo great talents are not requifite, and in which he may fucceed better.

A clear and found underftanding and good fenfe are gifts of nature abfolutely neceffary for a perfon who intends to be a clergyman. They are neceffary for acquiring the knowlege which his profeffion demands. They are neceffary for applying this knowlege in the feveral ways of inftruction, as occafion requires. They are neceffary for enabling him to avoid thofe errors and imprudences both in teaching and in living, which would obftruct the end of his function and the fuccefs of his labours.

A ftrong and firm memory is likewife a talent of great advantage to a clergyman. Memory is neceffary for acquiring the knowlege which fuits his profeffion. If it be remarkably defective, the greateft application to thought or reading will be

infuffi-

infufficient to furnifh him with the neceffary ftock of knowlege.

A warm, lively, and ftrong imagination is highly ufeful to a clergyman. It gives him a readinefs in applying what he knows, with propriety, to particular occafions which occur. It gives a great advantage for the compofition of public difcourfes, and enables him to fet every fentiment in a ftriking light. It adds an ornament to all the knowlege which he poffeffes, and enables him to apply it to ufe with the greateft luftre.

Thefe are intellectual talents derived from Nature, which the occupation of a clergyman demands. When Nature has denied thefe, it points out that a man was not defigned for this profeffion, as much as its denying a man the bodily ftrength which is requifite for any fevere employment fhows that he was not defigned for that employment and that he ought not to make choice of it.

There are other intellectual qualifications neceffary for the minifterial office, which may be acquired by thofe who are not defective in the natural talents already mentioned, and which all who make choice of this profeffion ought to be careful to acquire. Knowlege is abfolutely neceffary for a teacher. If it be afked, what kind of knowlege? we may anfwer, that no part of real knowlege is ufelefs or fuperfluous. It is proper, however, not to to reprefent the neceffary knowlege as too extenfive, left the view of its extent fhould difcourage the diffident from attempting this profeffion; or left folicitude to acquire all parts of it fhould confound our ftudies, and render us fuperficial in every part. But all the knowlege which is ftrictly connected with the fubject of a minifter's teaching is certainly indifpenfably neceffary; fo that no perfon who has not a competent meafure of it can be qualified for the minifterial office.

A competent knowlege of the original languages in which the infpired writers deliver themfelves, and of the biftory, antiquities, and cuftoms of the ages and nations in which they lived, or to which they allude, is neceffary for enabling us to find out the true fenfe of the fcriptures, and to illuftrate them in a juft and clear manner; and this is the bufinefs of every clergyman.

An acquaintance with the rules of right reafoning is neceffary for enabling us to argue conclufively and with ftrength, both in private and in public; for qualifying us for detecting the fophifms, and anfwering the cavils of the enemies of our holy religion; and for defending either the whole or particular parts of it againft their attacks.

A clergyman muft poffefs that knowlege of human nature which may fhow him the beft and

moft

moſt ſuccefsful methods of addreffing men, of informing their minds, or influencing their hearts.

Without ſuch a knowlege of human life and of the world as may make him in ſome meaſure a judge of the charaċters of men, he cannot advife or reprove them in a proper way, nor execute any of the duties of his office prudently, with a due regard to place, time, perſons, and other circumſtances.

The knowlege of natural religion and morality is ſtill more nearly conneċted with the paſtoral office. Natural religion is the foundation of revealed ; its principles and the duties of morality are all adapted, illuſtrated, and improved in the Chriſtian ſyſtem. Acquaintance with theſe will furniſh him with materials for all the funċtions of his office.

. The knowlege of the evidences of revealed religion is neceffary, both for eſtabliſhing his own faith on a rational foundation, and for enabling

lievers.

The ſcriptures are the proper ſtudy of a clergy-man ; they are the fountains from which his inſtruc-tions are chiefly to be drawn ; the knowlege of them is requiſite for the diſcharge of every part of
his

his duty. He fhould underftand not only the meaning of them critically, fo as to be able to perceive it on confulting them ; but he fhould have fuch an acquaintance with them, as to be able to recollect and apply many paffages of them as occafion requires.

A knowlege of the feveral doctrines and duties contained in the fcriptures, in their proper order and dependence ; a knowlege of the different opinions which have been entertained by different fects of Chriftians ; and a knowlege of the hiftory of the feveral revolutions of religion and the Chriftian church, will be highly ferviceable to a clergyman on many different occafions.

A collection of juft and ftriking fentiments on religious and moral fubjects, and of examples from facred and profane hiftory, treafured in the memory, and rendered familiar by frequent thought and meditation, will enable a minifter to perform all the kinds of teaching incumbent on him with readinefs and eafe.

A knowlege of the principles and rules of compofition, and good tafte, formed by the ftudy of thefe, and by an intimate acquaintance with the beft writers of every kind, is neceffary for enabling a clergyman to acquit himfelf properly in his public performances.

We

We may add, though it will perhaps appear trivial, that a propriety, juftnefs, and force of pronunciation, will give great advantage to all that a clergyman fays, and ought by no means to be neglected. The want of it often prevents the belt things from having their full effect upon the bulk of mankind.

But the moft important qualifications of a clergyman are thofe of the heart, fincere and uniform, virtue and goodnefs. A good heart, with a moderate degree of underftanding and knowlege, will enable a man to do much greater fervice in the church, than the higheft abilities joined with a vicious character. All virtues are neceffary to a clergyman; all vices are unallowable in him; but not all precifely in the fame way. Some virtues are fo indifpenfably neceffary, that the leaft appearance of the want of them is fcandalous, and renders him abfolutely ufelefs and contemptible. Other virtues may not perhaps be fo readily or fo generally miffed, but to poffefs them will greatly adorn his character. Some may properly be confidered in both thefe lights.

Some things, which are fcarcely regarded as virtues, at leaft are not rigoroufly infifted on in other men, are abfolutely indifpenfable in a clergyman. Of this kind is what is commonly termed Decency. Levity in converfation or in behaviour, which

which would fcarcely be at all cenfured in others,
will be fufficient to render a clergyman ridiculous
and defpicable. Decency obliges him to ferioufnefs
in thefe refpects, to moderation in the ufe of diverfions and amufements, to ftrict abftinence from
every appearance of evil. In every thing he fhould
keep himfelf, to the conviction of all, at a great
diftance from what is unlawful. He muft rather
abftain from things indifferent, than run a rifk of
offending fuch weak perfons as are truly honeft,
and do not pretend fcruples as a cloke for pride, or
a pretence for cenfuring. .

. Particular care is neceffary in abftaining from all
thofe vices which are regarded not merely as
defects of good difpofitions, but as indications of
difpofitions pofitively bad. Acts of thefe vices are
determinate; every fingle act throws an infallible
and lafting ftain upon the character of a clergyman. Thus every plain act of covetoutnefs, every
undue attempt to gain or to fave money, as it is
always mean and gives a contemptible idea of a
man, fo it brings a great ftain upon a clergyman.
Every attempt in him to carry on a lucrative employment, or to involve himfelf in bufinefs, even
fuch as is lawful in itfelf, will be regarded as a
mark of avarice.

· . Any act of injuftice, whether dictated by avarice
or by any other principle, will appear to all to be
deteftable in a clergyman.

All

All lying, falfehood, or perfidy, are likewife regarded as pofitive vices, rendering the character of a clergyman either odious or defpicable.

Every degree or kind of intemperance is eminently of the fame nature. A fingle overt-act of it is fufficient, in the opinion of the world, to eclipfe and overbalance many virtues. It muft therefore be guarded againft with the greateft care. A freedom from every habit, and even from the fufpicion of this vice, is a qualification abfolutely neceffary in a clergyman.

Pofitive acts of impiety, or expreffions of irreligion, of whatever kind they be, whether fwearing, neglect of the feveral duties of outward devotion, expreffions of indifference about the principles of natural or revealed religion, fcoffing or talking lightly of religious and important fubjects, will always be perfectly fhocking in a clergyman, and will render his character perfectly deteftable.

A freedom from all thefe vices is indifpenfably neceffary in a clergyman; and in order to keep free from them, he muft poffefs a confiderable degree of the virtues oppofite to them: an affectation of them, or an hypocritical pretence to them, will not look natural, but will betray itfelf by its appearance of force to the more difcerning; it it will not always hold out; the mafk will fall off

in

in some unlucky moment; all will see that it was
only pretence from the beginning; the detestation
which is due to hypocrisy will be added to that
which the vices attempted to be concealed excite;
and both together will be thrown on the detested
criminal. There are some of the virtues opposite
to the vices which we have mentioned, that though
they be possessed in the highest degree by a clergyman, will only be sufficient to preserve him from
blame, but will not be considered as giving any
considerable positive worth or beauty to his character. Such particularly are temperance and
justice. Temperance implies an absolute command
over all the sensual appetites, so as to be able to
restrain them at all times from leading us into what
is unlawful. A minister must cultivate this virtue
in the highest degree, else he will more or less
expose himself to contempt; but to cultivate it to
the highest pitch will not be considered as doing
any more than preserving him from contempt.
He must adhere to strict justice. All his dealings
with others must be strongly marked even with
justice improved into equity: but the highest
improvement of it will only keep him blameless.
There are some other of the virtues already hinted
at, which, though some degree of them be absolutely necessary for rendering the character inoffensive, yet when they are cultivated in an eminent
degree, bestow great dignity upon it, and are
highly ornamental to the profession. These, considered in this view, we shall have occasion to men-

6

tion

tion again, along with fome others, which likewife adorn the character of a minifter, and qualify him greatly for the feveral functions of his office.

We fhall begin with Piety. Piety in all its branches, as founded in juft fentiments of the divine nature, including love, reverence, gratitude, refignation, truft, imitation, and fear of God, and leading to the fervent and conftant exercife of devotion, is a temper of the greateft importance to a minifter. It was remarked already, that expreffions or acts of impiety are perfectly fcandalous. Such a degree of piety as may preferve from thefe is abfolutely neceffary to hinder his becoming odious: but fuch a low degree of it is not fufficient to qualify him for his office. The higheft pitch of it is neceffary to render him an example of godlinefs, to give him that conftant regard to God which will be the only fettled principle of diligence in the difcharge of the feveral functions of his office, to enable him in teaching to give a ftriking view of the obligations of piety, or to give amiable difplays of the feveral acts of devotion, or an inviting view of the pleafures of religion. The higheft pitch of piety is neceffary to animate us in leading the devotions of Chriftians, and to prevent our whole application to them from degenerating into a train of hypocrify or formality.

A great

A great degree of benevolence to mankind is another neceffary ingredient in the character of a clergyman. We might have mentioned properly enough expreffions of refentment, malice, envy, and the like malevolent paffions, among thofe vices which difgrace the character of a clergyman. Such a high degree of benevolence as may not only pre-ferve a minifter from thefe, but alfo produce a warm concern for the good of others, a concern efpecially for the falvation of their fouls and their eternal interefts, as may lead him to forgive injuries, and exert itfelf notwithftanding the im-pulfes of refentment, is neceffary for adorning the character of a clergyman, for enabling him to exert himfelf without grudge or wearinefs in the feveral duties by which he may benefit his people, to give him fpirit and earneftnefs in his feveral miniftrations, to give him a conftant motive to do all the good he can.

Benevolence will contribute greatly to form another virtue of great importance in the character of a clergyman, true Chriftian moderation. This is a virtue which will have many occafions of fhowing itfelf, and is neceffary for many purpofes in the paftoral office. It is neceffary for his living peaceably with others, in a world where all men cannot be of the fame opinion. It is neceffary for convincing thofe who are in error. It is neceffary for his treating controverted points, either in public or in private, with decency; and for preferving

serving him from that rancour, fury, and intemperate zeal, which, being indulged, has expofed the clergy to the higheft cenfure among their more difcerning adverfaries. It is nearly connected with that meeknefs and gentlenefs which is fo often recommended in fcripture, and fets off the character of a minifter to fo great advantage.

Humility will be of great ufe for enabling a minifter to fubmit eafily to all the little offices of beneficence which may contribute to the advantage of men, or to his own ufefulnefs. A vain, felf-conceited perfon can have no true relifh of divine truths.

It was already obferved that plain expreffions of avarice and worldly-mindednefs expofe a minifter to abfolute contempt: but it is; neceffary that he have a much greater degree of elevation above the world, than to preferve him merely from contempt. A fettled view of the vanity of the enjoyments of this earth, and a fuperiority to them, would banifh all the workings of avarice and ambition, party-fpirit and faction, and would add the greateft force and life to all a man's fentiments and difcourfes on fpiritual things.

I fhall mention one other qualification of great moment. It is to be poffeffed with the true fpirit of his office. A fenfe of the importance of this office, an ardent defire to combat and overcome
-the

the difficulties of it, a zeal for promoting its end, a pleaſure in being employed in its duties, are ingredients in this ſpirit. And this ſpirit raiſed to a high pitch is neceſſary for keeping a clergyman's buſineſs from being a drudgery, and for enabling him to perform it with true force and reliſh.

Theſe ſeveral qualifications it is the buſineſs of a miniſter to cultivate as long as he lives. It cannot therefore be expected that he ſhould be perfect in them when he enters into this office. But every man who has not in him the principles and begin‑ nings of all theſe qualifications, and a ſettled reſo‑ lution and eager deſire to improve and become perfect in them, is unfit for this office, and inca‑ pable of diſcharging its duties properly.

Theſe are only hints on the principal qualifica‑ tions for this office, and the way in which each is conducive to it.

C H A P. II.

Of Preparation for the Pastoral Office.

AS the qualifications necessary for the pastoral
office are easily deducible from the several
duties of that office, so the necessary preparation
may be deduced from the consideration of these
qualifications. Whatever study or exercise is proper for forming or improving any of these qualifications, is very proper for preparing those who
design to enter into the pastoral office.

Good sense and understanding are improved by
employing reason and judgement often upon all
kinds of subjects both of science and life, and by
imbibing just and solid principles from reflection,
reading, and conversation.

Memory will be cultivated by frequently accustoming ourselves to recollect what we know, and
by frequently committing things to memory and
repeating them.

There is no faculty of the mind, on improving
which so little care is commonly bestowed in education, as the imagination: yet it is certainly improveable to a very considerable degree. It is
improved

improved by reading works in which real genius and invention are difplayed. Thefe not only fupply hints to a perfon's thoughts, but at the fame time give an impulfe to his fancy, and prompt him to purfue thefe hints. Works of poetry are particularly proper for improving fancy, in what regards figures, images, and ornament; but too much ftudy may hurt fancy, inftead of improving it. The exertion of memory is always eafier than that of invention. On this account, if a perfon's memory be ftored with many things faid by others on a fubject, his thoughts will fall moft naturally into that track which they have followed; whereas, if he had been ignorant of their fentiments, he might have perhaps purfued a new and original track. If one be acquainted with the images which others have ufed, fancy will be apt, from the repofitories of memory, to fuggeft fuch as have been nfed already; but if it had not been fo much cramped by memory, and more accuftomed to invention, it might have difcovered new and original ones. Compofition on different forts of fubjects is the proper method of improving Invention. It would not perhaps be improper likewife, fometimes to fet the mind a fearching for all the images or illuftrations which can be applied to a particular fubject: this exercife might fharpen the inventive faculty, and give it a habit of ranging eafily and freely.

With

With refpect to the acquired intellectual qualifications before mentioned, or the different forts of
knowlege neceffary for a clergyman, it is only
needful to obferve, that each branch of knowlege
is to be acquired by ftndying it with care and
application. All then that is proper on this head
is either to give general directions concerning the
beft method of ftudy, or to fhow the order and
manner in which the feveral branches of knowlege
already mentioned may be acquired. The former
is fo extenfive a fubject, that it would require too
much time to enter into it particularly; and it is a
fubject to which it is prefumed none of you are
abfolutely ftrangers. The latter we fhall now
touch upon.

It is fuppofed that every perfon who aims at the
paftoral office has been educated in the Greek and
Latin languages; and that, during the time of his
application to the fciences, he has improved in the
knowlege of both, and acquired an acquaintance
with, and tafte in, claffical learning. It is likewife
taken for granted, that he has ftudied the feveral
parts of philofophy, particularly the abftract fci-
enees, which lay open the principles of human
nature, which teach the rules of reafoning, and
the truths of natural religion and morality. But,
in improving himfelf in thefe parts of knowlege,
by applying profeffedly and ftatedly to the ftudy of
them, he may very properly fpend the firft year

after

after he devotes himfelf to the ftudy of divinity.
By clofe application for that fpace of time, he
may make confiderable progrefs in all thefe, fo as
to be able not only to retain, but to carry himfelf
forward in them afterwards, by making them a
bye-ftudy or an amufement, while he is carrying
on others profeffedly and as his ftated bufinefs.
The fecond year he may make himfelf mafter of
all that regards the truth and evidences of revealed
religion, and make fome progrefs in the ftudy of
the fcriptures. It may juftly be fuppofed, that
from the very beginning of his application to the
ftudy of divinity, and even before, he has, by
frequently reading the fcriptures as a Chriftian,
acquired confiderable knowlege of the plain and
practical parts of them, and has a great deal of
thefe parts digefted in his memory, and in readinefs to be recollected, when occafion requires.
But what we affign to this period of his ftudies is
a more profeffed and critical application to them.
In ftudying the truth of revealed religion, he ought
firft of all to attain a thorough knowlege, and to
form a comprehenfive idea of the pofitive evidences
of religion, whether external or internal, and
afterwards to examine the particular objections
that are raifed againft them, and the anfwers to
thefe objections. In ftudying the fcriptures, he
fhould read them in the original languages, beginning with the New Teftament, taking the affiftance
of the beft commentators, and, at the fame time,
carrying on the ftudy of fuch things as tend to
illuftrate

illuſtrate the ſcriptures; as the rules of genuine criticiſm, and the hiſtories of antiquities, cuſtoms, ſects, &c. which are alluded to in them. If one be a diligent ſtudent, the ſecond year will be ſuffi- cient to give him the knowlege of the evidences of revelation, and to carry him through the ſtudy of the New Teſtament. The preparatory ſtudies already mentioned are uſually attended with the ſtudy of ancient and modern hiſtory; and if this ſtudy be carried on as a relaxation through all the period we have hitherto conſidered, the ſtudent will have made conſiderable progreſs in it, and may eaſily, as he certainly ought, carry it on ever after in the ſame way. In the third and fourth years one may make conſiderable progreſs in ſtudy- ing the Old Teſtament, and in acquiring the knowlege of the hiſtory of the church, the ſyſtem of religion, and the ſeveral controverſies that have ariſen in it. The ſyſtem and the hiſtory of the church ought always to be ſtudied together; they will throw mutual light on each other, and they are in fact little elſe than different ways of conſider- ing the ſame thing. A fifth year may be very properly employed in ſuch ſtudies (not dropping thoſe entirely which have been already mentioned) as have a more immediate connection with Preach- ing, and the ſeveral methods of inſtruction neceſ- ſary in the paſtoral office. A perſon may be employed in ſtoring his mind with a variety of religious and moral ſentiments, by the ſtudy of the beſt writers both ancient and modern, on practical ſubjects, fubjects. He may likewife apply to ftudy carefully the rules of compofition, and the beft models of eloquence, particularly the orations of Cicero and Demofthenes, and accuftom himfelf, more frequently than before, to compofition and to juft pronunciation. We do not fuppofe thefe things to be wholly delayed till now; on the contrary, the ftudies already mentioned cannot be carried on without a man's having dipped into them; we only affign this as the proper time for applying to them more profeffedly, and making them one's leading ftudy.

The time we have thus parcelled out will be fufficient for a man's acquiring the elements of all the parts of knowlege neceffary to a clergyman: and by ftudying them in this regular order, he will preferve diftinct all the knowlege he acquires, and fix fuch a regular plan in his mind, that whatever acquifitions he makes afterwards in any of the parts, will fall naturally into their proper places. But it is only the elements that he will acquire. Every time that he reviews any of the parts, he will difcover fomething new, and make farther progrefs. He may afterwards, through the whole of his life, be employed in profecuting any of thefe branches to which his inclination or opportunities determine him at a particular time. And if he has acquired a true fpirit of ftudy in youth, he will find enough in thefe feveral

branches

branchès to make his whole life pafs both agrèeably and with continual improvement.

I would recommend it to thofe who are juft beginning to ftudy divinity, to fet out on the plan we have delineated ; and if any of greater ftanding have not hitherto obferved it or fome other regular order of ftudy, they will perhaps find their account in beginning it immediately. They will be able to complete it in a fhorter time ; and in purfuing it, all the knowlege they have acquired by more defultory ftudies, will eafily fall into its proper place, and be rendered more clear and ftrong.

But though a competent degree of knowlege in thefe feveral fubjects be neceffary, before one's entering into the miniftry, and may be acquired in the manner now pointed out, yet every perfon ought to fet himfelf to make farther progrefs and improvement after that time. " What is a very " good beginning, is by no means a fufficient " ftock to go on with ; and even that will leffen, if " no pains be taken to increafe it. Perfons of lower " abilities and attainments are in danger, without " this, of becoming ufelefs and defpifed ; and they " who fet out with greater advantages are bound to " endeavour at doing, in proportion, greater " fervices to the church of God,e."

It

---

e Secker's ıft Charge.

It is abfolutely neceffary, as a preparation for carrying on thefe ftudies, indeed for acquiring any real knowlege, and therefore a neceffary preparation for the paftoral office, to lay afide all prejudices, and to cultivate a fair, unbiaffed temper of mind, difpofing to the impartial examination of every fubject.

The feveral moral qualifications mentioned can be acquired only by practifing the virtues which they imply. It is of importance for the divine to begin from the earlieft youth to practife them. As foon as he refolves on his profeffion, he fhould immediately begin with firm refolution to practife that blameleffnefs of behaviour, and to cultivate that true worth of heart, which are neceffary in his calling. The virtues which are effentially requifite to keep the character of a clergyman blamelefs and free from contempt, he fhould be mafter of from the very firft, fo as to be never chargeable with any acts of intemperance, injuftice, falfehood, impiety, nor even of levity in converfation or behaviour : and his whole conduct fhould fhow, even in the earlieft life, that he has the feeds of the fublimer virtues which adorn the minifterial character, and that he is cultivating them with diligence and fpeed. This early practice of univerfal virtue is neceffary on many accounts. Any defect of virtue which a man has fhown, any indecency in which he has allowed himfelf, though long before, will be remembered

to his difadvantage after he has. entered into the
paftoral office, and will throw a reflection on his
character. It will expofe his after-virtue to the
fufpicion, or perhaps the accufation of hypocrify,
which will greatly diminifh his ufefulnefs. Befides,
a confiderable change of manners on one's entering
on this office, or a little before, is always ungrace-
ful, and has the difagreeable appearance of force
and conftraint. Farther, one's indulging himfelf
while young, in manners which he muft break off
when he becomes a clergyman, fofters habits which
it will be difficult for him to overcome, and which
may perhaps make him a flave to vice or levity
through his whole life. Many things which are
regarded as indecencies in a minifter, may be
efteemed mere trifles, and perhaps they are fo in
their own nature. But trifles have often very important confequences. A minifter can execute his
functions only by the authority which the opinions
of men give him ; and therefore muft regard the
opinions of men, while he endeavours to rectify
them. As vice is wholly inconfiftent with the
minifterial character, fo it is of importance that
one who is preparing himfelf for this office have as
many reftraints from it as poffible; and it will be a
confiderable reftraint that he be known, wherever
he appears, as a perfon who has the facred function
in his view. In a word, one who would prepare
himfelf for the paftoral office, fhould always act,
in every refpect, in fuch a way that he may have
no occafion, when he enters into this office, to

make

make the leaft alteration in his manners or behaviour.

All that has been faid on the paftoral office has
no tendency to gratify idle curiofity, or to give
fcope to a difputatious humour. It tends wholly
to practice; and the knowlege of it is of no ufe,
except it be reduced to practice. It will deferve to
be remembered by you, that it is very poffible for
a perfon to have a fublime idea of morals, either in
general or as regarding a particular profeffion, and
yet be very defective in practice.

THE END.

NEW EDITIONS *of the following valuable* WORKS *have been lately publifhed by* T. CADELL *jun.* and W. DAVIES, Strand,

---

1. ISAIAH ; a new Tranflation, with a preliminary Differtation, and Notes critical, philological, and explanatory. By the late *Robert Lowth*, D.D. F, R. S. Lond. and Gœtting. Lord Bifhop of London. Third Edition. 2 Vols. 8vo. 14s.

2. JEREMIAH and LAMENTATIONS ; a new Tranflation, with Notes critical, philological, and explanatory. By *Benjamin Blayney*, B. D. Rector of Polfhot in Wilts, and formerly Fellow of Hertford College, Oxford. 1l. 5s.

3. The FOUR GOSPELS, tranflated from the Greek ; with preliminary Differtations, and Notes critical and explanatory. By *George Campbell*, D.D. F.R.S. Edinburgh, Principal of Marifchal College, Aberdeen. 2 Vols. 4to. 2l. 10s.

4. A DISSERTATION on MIRACLES ; containing an Examination of the Principles advanced by David Hume, Efq. in an Effay on Miracles ; with a Correfpondence on the Subject, by Mr. Hume, Dr. Campbell, and Dr. Blair, now firft publifhed. To which are now firft added, SERMONS and TRACTS. By the Same. 2 Vols. 8vo. 12s.

5. An EXPOSITION of the NEW TESTAMENT ; intended as an Introduction to the Study of the Scriptures, by pointing out the leading Senfe and Connection of the Sacred Writers. By *William Gilpin*, A. M. Prebendary of Sarum, and Vicar of Boldre in New Foreft. 2 Vols. 8vo. 14s.

6. LECTURES on the Catechifm of the Church of England. By the Same. 12mo. Fourth Edition. 3s.

7. EXPOSITORY NOTES, with practical Obfervations on the New Teftament. By *William Burkitt*, M.A. late Vicar and Lecturer of Dedham in Effex. 4to. 1l. 8s.

8. An

8. An EXPOSITION of the Thirty-nine Articles of the Church of England. By *Gilbert Burnet*, Lord Bishop of Sarum. 8vo. 6s. 6d.

9. An EXPOSITION of the CREED. By *John Pearson*, D.D. late Lord Bishop of Chester. 2 Vols. 8vo. 14s.

10. PHYSICO-THEOLOGY, or a Demonstration of the Being and Attributes of God, from his Works of Creation : being the Substance of Sixteen Discourses delivered in St. Mary-le-Bow Church, London, at the Hon. Mr. Boyle's Lectures, in the Years 1711 and 1712. By the Rev. *W. Derham*, Canon of Windsor, Rector of Upminster in Essex, and F.R S. A new Edition ; with additional Notes, a Translation of the Latin and Greek Quotations, and a Life of the Author. 2 Vols. 8vo. with a newly-engraved Set of Plates. 16s.

11. Dr. LELAND's VIEW of the DEISTICAL WRITERS ; with an Appendix, containing a View of the present Times, with regard to Religion and Morals, and other important Subjects. By *W. L. Brown*, D.D. Principal of Marischal College, Professor of Divinity, and Minister of Grey-Friars Church, Aberdeen. 2 Vols. 8vo. 14s.

12. The ANALOGY of RELIGION, natural and revealed, to the Constitution and Course of Nature, by *Joseph Butler*, LL. D. late Lord Bishop of Durham. With a Preface, giving some Account of the Character and Writings of the Author, by *Samuel Halifax*, D. D. Lord Bishop of Gloucester. 7s. 6d.

13. A Collection of THEOLOGICAL TRACTS, in 6 Vols. 8vo. By *R. Watson*, D. D. F. R. S. Lord Bishop of Llandaff. Second Edition. 2l. 2s. On large Paper 3l. 3s.

14. A complete CONCORDANCE to the HOLY SCRIPTURES of the Old and New Testament. By *Alexander Cruden*, M. A. Fourth Edition. 1l. 7s.

15. An ECCLESIASTICAL HISTORY, ancient and modern, from the Birth of Christ to the Beginning of the present Century ; in which the Rise, Progress, and Variations of Church Power are considered, in their Connection

with

with the State of Learning and Philofophy, and the Political History of Europe during that Period. By the late learned *John Lawrence Mofheim,* D. D. Tranflated and accompanied with Notes and Chronological Tables, by *Archibald Maclaine,* D. D. To the Whole is added an accurate Index. Fourth Edition, corrected and improved by additional Notes and feveral Appendixes. 6 Vols. 2l. 2s.

16. SERMONS on feveral Subjects, by the Right Rev. *Beilby Porteus,* D. D. Bifhop of London. Sixth Edition. 2 Vols. 14s.

17. SERMONS by *Hugh Blair,* D. D. one of the Minifters of the High Church, and Profeffor of Rhetoric and Belles Lettres in the Univerfity of Edinburgh. Sixteenth Edition. 4 Vols. 1l. 8s.

18. SERMONS on various Subjects, and preached on feveral Occafions. By the late Rev. *Thomas Francklin,* D. D. Chaplain in Ordinary to his Majefty, and Rector o Brafted in Kent. 3 Vols. Third Edition. 1l. 4s.

19. SERMONS on the Relative Duties. Preached a Queen-Street Chapel, and St. Paul's, Covent-Garden. By the fame Author. Third Edition. 6s.

20. A Third Volume of SERMONS on important Subjects. By *David Lamont,* D. D. Minifter of Kirkpatrick Durham, and one of the Chaplains to his Royal Highnef the Prince of Wales for Scotland. 8vo. 7s. in Boards.

21. DISCOURSES on various Subjects, delivered i the Englifh Church at the Hague. By *Archibald Maclaine* D. D. Member of fome Foreign Academies. 8vo. 8s.

22. SERMONS on various Subjects, more particularly on Chriftian Faith and Hope, and the Confolations of Re ligion. By *George Henry Glaffe,* A. M. Rector of Han well, Middlefex. 8vo. 8s.

23. SERMONS, chiefly upon practical Subjects. By the Rev. *Samuel Bifhop,* A. M late Chaplain to the Bifho of Bangor, Rector of Ditton in Kent, and St. Martin Out wich, London, and Head-Mafter of Merchant Taylors School. Publifhed by Thomas Clare, A. M. 8vo. 7s.

24. DISCOURSES on different Subjects. By *Georg Ifaac Huntingford,* D. D. Warden of St. Mary's College Winchefter. 2 Vols. 13s.

25. SER

25. SERMONS, by *William Leechman*, D. D. late Principal of the College of Glafgow. To which is prefixed, fome Account of the Author's Life, and his Lectures, by *James Wodrow*, D. D. Minifter at Stevenfton. 2 Vols. 14s.

26. SERMONS, by the late Rev. *John Dryfdale*, D. D. F. R. S. Ed. one of the Minifters of Edinburgh, &c. &c. With an Account of the Author's Life and Character, by *Andrew Daizel*, M. A. F. R. S. Ed. Profeffor of Greek, &c. &c. &c. in the Univerfity of Edinburgh. 2 Vols. 14s.

27. SERMONS, by *George Hill*, D. D. F. R. S. Ed. Principal of St. Mary's College in the Univerfity of St. Andrew, one of the Minifters of that City, and one of his Majefty's Chaplains in Ordinary for Scotland. 8vo. 7s.

28. SERMONS on ufeful and important Subjects. By the late Rev. *John Cofens*, D. D. Minifter of Teddington. 2 Vols. 14s.

29. SERMONS on different Subjects, left for Publication by *John Taylor*, LL. D. late Prebendary of Weftminfter, Rector of Bofworth, Leicefterfhire, and Minifter of St. Margaret's, Weftminfter. Publifhed by the Rev. *Samuel Hayes*, A. M. Ufher of Weftminfter-School. 2 Vols. 12s.

30. EVIDENCES of the CHRISTIAN RELIGION, briefly and plainly ftated. By *James Beattie*, LL. D. F. R. S. Second Edition. 2 Vols. 6s.

31. A VIEW of the EVIDENCES of CHRISTIANITY, in Three Parts. By *William Paley*, M. A. Archdeacon of Carlifle. 2 Vols. 8vo. Fourth Edition. 14s.

32. A COMMENTARY on the BOOK OF PSALMS, in which their literal or hiftorical Senfe, as they relate to King David and the People of Ifrael, is illuftrated; and their Application to Meffiah, to the Church, and to Individuals as Members thereof, is pointed out; with a View to render the Ufe of the Pfalter pleafing and profitable to all Orders and Degrees of Chriftians. By *George Horne*, D. D. Lord Bifhop of Norwich. 2 Vols. Fourth Edition. 14s,